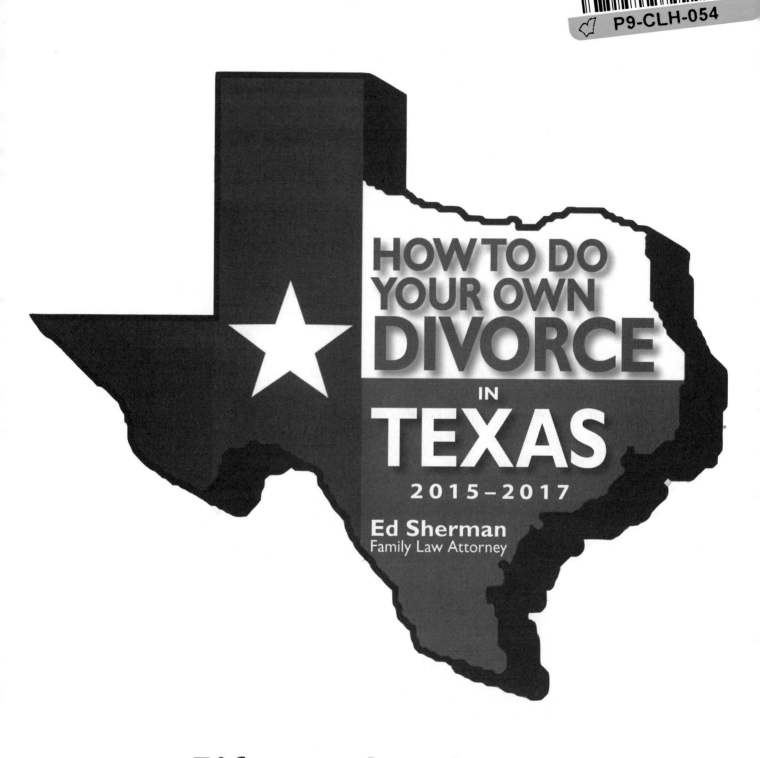

HOW TO DO YOUR OWN DIVORCE IN TEXAS

2015–2017

Ed Sherman
Family Law Attorney

Fifteenth Edition
Sept. 2015 THRU Aug. 2017

Nolo Press Occidental
2604 El Camino Real, Suite 353B
Carlsbad, CA 92008
(831) 466-9922

DATED MATERIAL

THIS BOOK WAS PRINTED IN
SEPTEMBER 2015

Check with your local bookstore to be sure this is the
most recent printing of the book before you start!

DO NOT USE AN OLD EDITION OF THIS BOOK!
Out-of-date forms and information can cause trouble

30% OFF ON LATEST EDITION
If you have an older edition of this book and want to update, tear off
the cover and send it to us with $20.97 plus $5 shipping = $25.97 total.

FREE UPDATE NOTICES ONLINE
Look for new laws, forms, and fixes at
www.nolodivorce.com/alerts

ISBN13/EAN: 978-0-944508-99-2
ISSN: 2326-2079

Contents

Part One: All About Divorce

Contents

Part Two: How to Do Your Own Divorce

CD with forms, codes, MSA and more!   **Inside back cover**

Part One:

All About Divorce

This book is dedicated to all of my clients
and to my ex-wife
from whom I have learned so much
about the subject in these pages

And to Sandra Borland
for her invaluable contributions

A. Doing Your Own Divorce

You might not know it, but you are going through two divorces at the same time—your Real Divorce and your Legal Divorce.

This book is about getting through the legal divorce with minimum involvement with courts and lawyers. It explains Texas divorce laws, with practical advice to help you make decisions, and shows you exactly how to do the paperwork to get your divorce or find someone to do it for you inexpensively.

The real divorce is your life, your relationships with your Ex, family, friends, children, and—most of all—yourself. It's what you go through in practical, emotional, and spiritual terms. The real divorce is about breaking old patterns, finding a new center for your life and doing your best with the hand you've been dealt. These matters are not assisted or addressed in any way by the legal divorce.

The legal divorce cares only about how you will divide marital property and debts, whether there will be spousal support, and how you will arrange parenting and child support if you have minor children. If you can settle these matters out of court, there's nothing left but paperwork and red tape to get your Decree of Divorce.

If you have trouble agreeing on terms, the problem is almost never legal, but almost always about personalities and emotional upset, for which there is absolutely no help and no solutions—zip, zero, nothing—in court or in a lawyer's office. In fact, getting involved with lawyers and courts almost always makes things worse—much worse. If you follow my advice, you'll avoid the traps and pitfalls of the legal system, and things will get much better much sooner.

1. Can you do your own divorce? Should you?

Yes! You can! Since this book was first published in 1980, hundreds of thousands of Texans just like you have used it to do their divorces without retaining lawyers, so you can almost certainly do it, too. This book can save you thousands of dollars!

Yes! You should do your own divorce! Taking charge of your own case leads to a smoother, faster, less painful, and less expensive experience. Most people would be better off if they reduced or eliminated their use of attorneys, because the legal process—and the way attorneys work in it—tends to cause trouble, raise the level of conflict, and greatly increase the cost. While you might decide to get advice from a family law attorney who primarily practices mediation or collaborative law, you should not *retain* an attorney to "take your case" unless you have an unavoidable need for doing so. In section 7 below I explain when you should get help and, in section 8, how to get the right kind of help from an attorney without *retaining* him/her to take over your case.

What if things don't go smoothly—easy and difficult cases. If your spouse will not oppose you in court because he/she is gone, doesn't care, or you expect no trouble agreeing on terms, then you only need some paperwork to get your divorce done, and this is the only book you'll need. However, if you have trouble agreeing on divorce terms (or think you will), or if you prefer to have a professional stand with you and take an active role in negotiating for you, or if your case seems headed for court, you can still do your own divorce, and this book is an important place to start, but you will need more help. Solving divorce problems is discussed below in section 6 and getting the right help is discussed in section 8.

2. What "do your own divorce" means

Doing your own paperwork is not the important thing—the essence of it is thinking things through and making informed decisions. It means that you take responsibility for your case, your decisions, your life. You find out what the rules are and how they apply to your case. You explore all options, then decide what you want and how you want to go about it. If you use an attorney, *you* make all the decisions and control how your case is run. If your spouse is in the picture and cares what happens, doing your own divorce means having detailed discussions—perhaps with help—to reach a thoroughly negotiated agreement.

Above all, doing your own divorce means that you do not *retain* an attorney (more on this below). No one should *retain* an attorney unless they have an emergency situation like those discussed below in section 7, but that doesn't mean you can't get advice and help from an attorney if you feel the need (section 8).

Many people find it difficult to think things through carefully and make decisions about their divorce, and they are *extremely* nervous about discussing divorce details with their Ex. This is completely understandable, but it is something you need to do if you don't want to become a victim of divorce. If you want it, you can get help from an attorney-mediator or a collaborative law attorney (section 8) to help you think things through, talk to your spouse, and work out an agreement.

a) What it means to "retain" an attorney (and why you don't want to)

It's okay to use an attorney, but most people should not *retain* one in their divorce unless there is a clear reason for doing so (see section 7 below). Here's why. When you *retain* an attorney, you sign a "retainer agreement" where the attorney takes responsibility for acting in your behalf—to represent you. You are *literally* handing over your power and authority to act. Standards of professional conduct require any attorney who represents you—even one with good intentions—to act in ways that will complicate your case and make it worse instead of better. Attorneys typically start cases in court quickly, even when that is likely to cause upset and make settlement more difficult.

An attorney who represents you must go to great lengths to protect himself against later malpractice claims by his own client—you. This means doing things for the attorney's benefit instead of yours. Doing the maximum may or may not help you, but it will certainly raise the level of conflict, and it will cost plenty.

Never forget that when you *retain* an attorney, the more trouble you have, the more money the attorney makes. That's hardly an incentive to keep things simple.

Our legal system is known as "the adversary system," which means that attorneys work as combatants who fight to "win" in court. This is not the best way to go about solving family and personal problems, and what an attorney thinks of as winning is probably not the best thing for you, your family or your future. There are no winners in a nasty legal battle except for the attorneys.

b) Making decisions

Part of the service you are supposed to get from a lawyer is help with making decisions. Lawyers know what has to be decided and the general standards and rules by which things are done in courts in your community. This is what the first part of this book is all about. It tells you what needs to be decided and how things are done in cases where there is no fight. It gives you information and help with making your own decisions.

If, after reading this book, you can make your own decisions based on your own knowledge, then you probably do not need a lawyer. If you read this book and still have doubts or questions, then you probably should have professional advice. It may be that you can find an attorney who will help you settle your mind, then you can go on to do the rest on your own. Section 8 below tells you how to find such a person.

Things that must be decided

- that the marriage should be ended forever, and
- how to divide any property and bills that you may have accumulated during the marriage, and
- whether there will be alimony and, if so, how much.

If you have no minor children, that's all there is to it. If you do have minor children, you must also decide:

- who is to have custody of the children,
- how care time (visitation) will be arranged, and
- how much is to be paid for support.

As far as the law is concerned, this is what a divorce is all about—settling the practical affairs of the couple and watching out for the well-being of the children. These are the things you must decide about in order to get a divorce. If your spouse is in the picture and cares about what happens in the divorce, then either you must be able to talk things over and agree on these things, or you must be sure that your spouse will not get a lawyer and oppose you legally.

c) Advantages to doing your own divorce

Getting a good divorce

Studies show that active participation in your divorce is the single most important factor in getting a good divorce. "Good divorce" means such things as better compliance with agreements and orders after the divorce, less post-divorce conflict, less post-divorce litigation, more good will, and better co-parenting.

People who take an active role generally do much better emotionally and legally than those who try to avoid the responsibility for solving their divorce problems. This doesn't mean you shouldn't get help from an attorney or mediator—it means you should be actively involved, become informed about the rules, and make your own decisions. Be in charge of your case and your life. Don't be a victim; be a participant in your divorce.

It's much cheaper

A huge advantage to doing your own divorce is the savings in cost. When an attorney takes your case, the initial retainer could be anywhere from $750 to $5,000, but the retainer is only the beginning. The average cost of a divorce is about $20,000 *for each party*, but that's only because the average couple has no more than that to spend. If you have more, it will cost more—much more. Depending on the size of your estate, a contested case can cost many tens or hundreds of thousands of dollars *on each side!*

Keeping it simple

Most people start off with a case that is either fairly simple or that could probably become simple if handled right. Such cases don't usually stay simple after an attorney is retained. Divorces are sensitive, so it doesn't take much to stir them up, but lawyers and the legal system tend to make things more complicated, stirred up, worse instead of better. This is because of the way the system works and the way lawyers work in it.

When one spouse or partner gets an attorney, the other is likely to get one too, and then the fun really begins. Two attorneys start off costing just double, but pretty soon they are writing unpleasant letters, filing motions, and doing attorney-type things as a matter of routine that may not be helpful. Now we have a contested case, more fees and charges, and a couple of very upset and broke spouses.

In the end, you will still have to negotiate a settlement with your Ex. Over 90% of all cases settle without trial, but when attorneys are retained, settlement usually comes after the parties are emotionally depleted and their bank accounts exhausted. Why go through all that?

The moral of this story is this: don't *retain* an attorney unless you absolutely must (section 7 below). If you do it entirely yourself, or with a little help from an attorney *who you have not retained*, you have a much better chance of keeping a simple case simple and of reaching a settlement much earlier.

3. Divorce basics

a) Grounds for divorce

To get a divorce, you have to have a legally approved reason, known as *grounds*, for your divorce. Uncontested divorces are almost always based on the grounds that the marriage is *insupportable*—that is, it is no one's fault, but the marriage has broken down so badly that it can't be saved. This is called a no-fault divorce and is the most civilized way to go. Unfortunately, Texas law makes it possible for a spouse to get a larger share of the community property by proving that the other spouse was at fault, typically by alleging adultery or cruelty. Attempting a case based on fault will likely lead to lawyers and a long, nasty, and very expensive divorce with an unpredictable outcome. In this book, we assume you will be getting a no-fault divorce.

The grounds of insupportability. You can be divorced if your marriage ". . . has become insupportable because of discord or conflict of personalities that destroys the legitimate ends of the marriage relationship and prevents any reasonable expectation of reconciliation." This probably means that you don't get along in a way that seems both important and permanent. But you can't just say it this way—that would be too easy. Instead, when you go into court you must tell the judge exactly those words quoted above. If you had an attorney, he or she would say the words for you, then ask you, "Isn't that true?" while nodding "Yes." You would then say "Yes," and that would be that. If you can bear the burden of saying these words on your own, then you don't need the attorney. It is, by the way, almost unheard of for a divorce not to be granted because of insufficient grounds.

There are six other grounds for divorce, two of which also involve no fault (living apart for more than three years and confinement in a mental hospital), and four of which involve fault (cruelty, adultery, conviction of a felony, and abandonment). Way over 99% of all cases are run on the grounds of "insupportability." Even if your case falls under one of the other categories, you still call it "insupportability." It's easier and it's the expected thing.

b) Jurisdiction (power of the court)

"Jurisdiction" means the legal right and power to make and enforce orders. In a divorce case, you are asking the court to make orders about your marriage, your property, your kids, and your spouse. The court has power to make orders about matters within the borders of Texas, so if you, your spouse, the kids, and the property are all in Texas, everything is fine. Just show that you satisfy the residency requirement, and you're on your way. But where would a Texas judge get off making orders about a spouse or kids or property if they were in some other state?

If your spouse resides permanently outside of Texas, then the court cannot have personal jurisdiction over your spouse unless your case satisfies the requirements of the "long-arm jurisdiction" rules. As a matter of fact, in many cases, you can get along just fine without having personal jurisdiction over your spouse. This is where there are no children, no property outside of Texas that you want to have, and no need to order your spouse to pay debts. But where there is a child, or important property outside of Texas that you want, or a need to order your spouse to pay debts, then you cannot do your own divorce in Texas unless you satisfy the long-arm rules.

"Long-arm jurisdiction" is, just as it sounds, when the court gets the right to make orders that reach out beyond the borders of Texas. There are actually two long-arm rules—the "marital long-arm" and the "parent/child long-arm."

1) **The marital long-arm.** If your spouse permanently resides outside of Texas, then the court can have personal jurisdiction over your spouse only if Texas is the last state in which you and your spouse had marital cohabitation (lived together as man and wife) and if your divorce suit is started within two years of the last time you cohabited. Even if you cannot satisfy this rule, you can still do your divorce if you do not need an order for the transfer of out-of-state property or for the payment of debts.

2) **The parent/child long-arm.** If there is a child, then you must satisfy this rule. The court can have jurisdiction over your case only if:

   i)   your spouse is personally served with Citation while in Texas; *or*

   ii) your spouse consents to jurisdiction in Texas, by appearing in court or filing a document such as the Waiver (chapter 6A); *or*

   iii) the child resides in Texas because of some act of your spouse, or with your spouse's approval; *or*

   iv) your spouse resided in Texas and provided prenatal expenses or support for the child (this is presumed if you and your spouse were living together during the pregnancy); *or*

   v)   the child was conceived in Texas.

There may be other ways for the court to get power to act in your case, but you will need an attorney to explore them and to plead them to the court properly.

c) Residency requirements

Residency in Texas is what gives the court power to dissolve your marriage. No matter where you were married—some other state or some other country—if you meet the residency requirement, you can be divorced in Texas.

The residency requirement. In the period immediately before filing your divorce, either you or your spouse must have been a domiciliary (resident) of Texas for at least six months and a resident of the county where you file it for at least 90 days. "Domiciliary" means you have your residence in Texas with the intention to live here permanently. It is okay to be absent on a temporary trip so long as you always intend to return. Also, a person does not lose domiciliary status if absent from the state for military or public service for the state or nation. You are a "resident" of a county simply by living there, no matter what your intentions. Finally, you don't have to stay in Texas or in your county after the divorce is filed; it is okay to move anywhere you like once those papers are stamped by the clerk.

d) Notice to your spouse

A lawsuit is regarded as a struggle between two contestants, conducted before an impartial authority (judge) who decides the matter. It seems obvious (doesn't it?) that you can't have a proper contest if the other side doesn't even know one is going on.

The court cannot act in your case unless you can properly notify your spouse of the lawsuit. Chapter 6A shows how this is done, but in general terms, either your spouse must sign a Waiver before a notary stating that court papers have been received, or else the papers must be served properly by a Sheriff. If your spouse is on active military duty, then the only way you can do your own divorce is if your spouse will sign the Waiver. If your spouse successfully avoids service, or if your spouse is on active military duty and refuses to sign a Waiver, you will need the help of an attorney to proceed with your case.

If your spouse is long gone and all attempts to locate him/her have failed, you are in for a little more work and expense. The law still requires that the missing spouse be given proper notice, but says you can do it by publishing your Citation in a newspaper. You can find forms and instructions for "Citation by Publication" or "Citation by Posting" on the CD that comes with this book. You can also download them for $15.00 at **www. nolodivorce.com/TX,** or call Nolo at **(800) 464-5502,** or order by mail using the order form in the back of this book.

Proper notice means, among other things, that your spouse gets a copy of your Petition, and so can be presumed to know what the suit is about and more or less what you want. After proper notice, a lawsuit can go one of three ways:
- by agreement—parties agree in writing on property, debts, support, parenting.
- by default—the Respondent does nothing; Petitioner completes the case alone.
- by contest—the parties take the case to court and fight for a judicial decision.

The best and easiest way is if you work it out by written agreement, of course. The hardest way is where your spouse gets an attorney and files an Answer on time and you end up in a legal battle. The most common way is by default.

e) Waiting periods

Waiting period before the hearing. The hearing is the time when you finally get your divorce, but you can't rush right into it. It's okay to wait longer for your hearing, but the earliest you can have your hearing is governed by more than one waiting period. The short answer is that you can't have your hearing sooner than at least 61 days after you filed your Petition. There are also some shorter waiting periods following the date your spouse was served that vary depending on how service was accomplished. The details are discussed in chapter 11A, the Prehearing Checklist.

Wife pregnant? Not exactly a waiting period, but if the wife is pregnant, few judges would finalize a divorce until the baby is born and child related orders are included in the Decree.

Waiting to remarry. You are not free to marry anyone (except the person you just divorced) for 30 days after the judge signs your Final Decree and it is filed with the Clerk.

f) Change of name

In a divorce case, if it is requested by either party, the judge will change the name of either spouse. In actual practice, this rule is almost always used to restore a former name to the wife, but the way the law reads, you can change the name of either spouse to any name they used before. The court *must* grant your name change request unless they state in the Decree a reason for denying the change. They may no longer deny a change of name just to keep the last names of the parents and children the same.

4. How to start a divorce—Petitioners and Respondents

The Petitioner and the Respondent. Every divorce starts with a Petition. The Petitioner is the person who first files papers and gets the case started. The Respondent is the other party. A Response need not be filed, but it is a good idea, otherwise the inactive person has little say about when or how the divorce is completed, unless there is already a written agreement. In general, the more both parties participate, the better. After a Response is filed, the divorce can be completed only by written agreement or court trial. Agreement is better.

Equality. Once a Response is filed, Respondent has equal standing and there is no legal difference between the parties or their rights, and either party can take any available legal step. Where instructions in this book indicate "Petitioner," Respondent can substitute "Respondent" and take the same action.

The Petition. To get your case started, you file a Petition and serve it on your spouse. The only thing you need to know before you do this is that you want to start a divorce. The issues can all be sorted out and resolved later. On the other hand, it wouldn't hurt to read through Part One before you start.

Advantages to serving the Petition:
- Starts the clock ticking on waiting periods.
- If standing orders are in effect in your county, filing the Petition causes very useful automatic restraining orders to take effect (see page 100).
- Helps establish the date of separation.
- Has psychological value for Petitioner and tells Respondent a divorce is really going to happen.

Possible downside. Serving papers can upset the Respondent and stir up conflict if you don't properly prepare the Respondent ahead of time.

Getting a smooth start. Unless your Ex is an abuser/controller, you will probably want to start things off as nicely as possible. An abrupt start will probably increase conflict, as an upset spouse is more likely to run to an attorney who will probably make your case more complicated. So take some time to prepare your Ex and let him/her get used to the idea that a divorce is about to start. If you aren't comfortable discussing things in person, write a nice letter. Let your spouse know you are committed to working out a settlement that you can both agree to and live with. Unless you are under time pressure, don't serve your Petition until your partner seems ready to receive the papers calmly.

5. Three ways to get it done (see map on next page)

After you file your Petition, there are only three ways you can get your Divorce Decree: (1) by default, (2) by contest, or (3) by written agreement.

The default divorce

In a default case, Respondent is served with the Petition but does nothing. No Response is filed, so the case is completed by default, without participation by Respondent. Default should be used only if you have little property or debts, no children, and no need for spousal support, or where Respondent is long gone or doesn't care to participate. If Respondent is around and cares, you'll need to work out an agreement, otherwise you'll have a complicated contested case to resolve all issues in court.

MAP – How to get there from here
(Discussion in section 5)

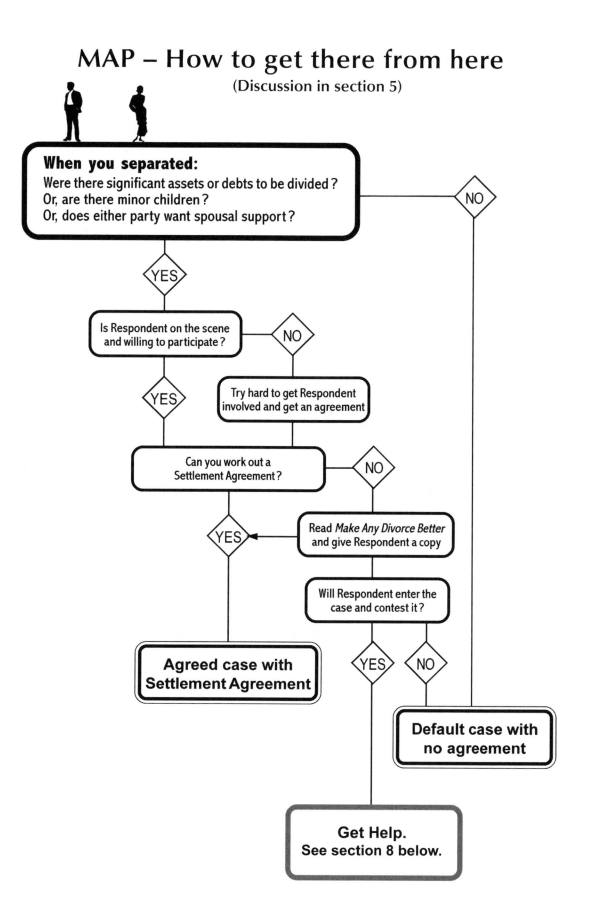

The contested divorce

If a Response is filed, you can complete your divorce only by written agreement or by taking the case to court and having a judge decide issues that you can't settle. Until there is an agreement, your case is *technically* considered to be contested. Whether or not there is a battle and a lot of legal activity depends on how you go about solving problems and reaching agreement. If you have problems reaching agreement, read *How to Make Any Divorce Better.* If you find yourself headed into a court battle, get help. See section 8 below.

Divorce by settlement agreement

When the problems are all solved and you finally reach an agreement, one of the parties files a Waiver (chapter 6A) and steps out. The case is now uncontested and sails through. If your spouse is in the picture and you have children, significant property or debts, or you need to arrange spousal support, then you should make *every* effort to reach a written agreement on all issues. Look what you gain:

- You can be certain exactly what the orders in the Decree of Divorce will be;
- You can complete your case by mail and almost certainly won't have to go to court;
- Both parties participate, so the Respondent can feel confident about letting the divorce go through without contest or representation because the terms of the Decree of Divorce are all settled;
- It invariably leads to better relations with your ex-spouse or partner. Where there are children, this is extremely important; and
- You are far more likely to get compliance with terms of the divorce after the Decree of Divorce.

These advantages are so important that you should struggle long and hard to work out an agreement, with or without the help of a mediator or collaborative law attorney (section 8). Chapter E discusses written agreements in detail.

6. Solving divorce problems

The steps you take to make your case go more smoothly depend on what your situation is right at this moment. Five divorce profiles are described below with steps you should take in each situation. See which profile best fits you.

Early cases

You haven't broken up yet, or broke up only recently. This is good, because the earlier you start, the easier it is to heal wounds and lay a foundation for a smoother trip. The way you go about doing things now will have a powerful influence on how things work out in your future—for better or worse.

Your goal is to solve problems and settle issues without taking problems to court or spending much (if any) time in a lawyer's office. Your goal is to end up with an Easy Case (below).

Here are steps you can take to achieve these goals. The articles can be found in the Reading Room at my web site at **www.nolodivorce.com**.

- Get my free *Divorce Checklist* and start working on those items. It calls your attention to practical things you should know and things you should do. It will help make sure you don't overlook anything important.

- Read my article, "The Good Divorce," so you will have a model to keep in mind and an idea of things you can try to accomplish to keep your divorce peaceful.

- Read Part One of this book to learn about divorce laws and skim Part Two to get a sense of how divorce paperwork is done.

- Get my book, *How to Make Any Divorce Better*, and learn specific things you can do to smooth things out and keep easy cases easy. Get a copy for your Ex, too, so you can discuss ideas in it.

- **Do not talk to your spouse about divorce** until you learn how to reduce conflict, create a foundation for negotiation, and negotiate effectively.

- **Do not go to an attorney** until you are better informed and prepared—unless, that is, you face an emergency as described in section 7 below.

Before you visit an attorney, you should gather and organize all the facts and documents in your case as described in the Easy case profile below. Also read section 8 below to learn what you can and cannot expect from various types of attorneys and other professional services.

Easy cases

If your spouse won't come to court to oppose you, you've got an easy case. It could be because he/she is gone, doesn't care, or because you are able to sit down and agree on terms. All that's left is to file papers and go through some red tape to get a Decree of Divorce. You can do the paperwork yourself with this book or get it done inexpensively by negotiating a low price with an attorney.

Spouse on board? It's very difficult to divide major assets or arrange parenting without your spouse's participation, so your goal is to settle things in a written settlement agreement. Here are steps you can take to complete an easy case and make sure it stays easy. The articles are in the Reading Room at my web site at **www.nolodivorce.com**.

- Get my free *Divorce Checklist* and start working on those items. It calls your attention to practical things you should know and things you should do. It will help make sure you don't overlook anything important.

- Read Part One of this book carefully to learn about divorce laws and skim Part Two to get a sense of how divorce paperwork is done. If you have major assets (real estate, retirement funds), it would make sense to have expert advice and an agreement drafted by a family law attorney, or at least reviewed by one. See section 8 below. If you're thinking of using online divorce forms, go to the Reading Room at **www. nolodivorce.com** and read my article that explains why online forms services are *not* a good idea.

- **Keeping easy cases easy.** Most divorces are delicate and easily stirred up. To learn how to keep an easy case from blowing up into a difficult one, I recommend that each spouse have a copy of *How to Make Any Divorce Better* and follow specific steps to calm conflict and negotiate effectively. Discuss ideas in it.

- **Get organized.** As soon as you can, organize your facts, gather documents, and start thinking about how to divide community property, how much spousal support will be paid (if any), and how children will be supported and parented. You'll find a set of Divorce Worksheets on the CD that comes with this book. These will help you organize, think about, and discuss the facts and finances in your case. They will definitely save you time and money.

- **A written settlement agreement** is very important in most cases. The simple sample agreement that comes with this book is not ideal for dealing with major assets, but **DealMaker** software is (see inside front cover). **DealMaker** clarifies the many possible options for real estate or retirement funds and also guides you in the creation of a parenting plan if you have minor children. **DealMaker** guides you to enter information and make some decisions, then it writes a sophisticated, professional settlement agreement that you can sign as is or edit with any word processor.

Difficult cases—when things don't go smoothly (or might not)

This profile fits most divorces. Your spouse is in the picture and cares about how things will end up, but you're having some trouble (or you expect to) with discussing and settling terms.

The reason divorce agreements are difficult is almost always personal—bad communication, bad history, bad habits, etc.—and almost never about the law. Neither the law nor lawyers have any tools to help you settle problems that originate in your personal relationship. In fact, the things you can do yourself are far superior to anything a lawyer can do for you.

Your goal is to take specific steps that will make your case smoother and easier, to turn it into an Easy Divorce (above), so you can make a written agreement and do the paperwork yourself or get it done inexpensively. There are a lot of things you can do for yourself to make things better, steps that have helped tens of thousands of couples, so they can help you, too.

Here are the steps you should take. The articles are in the Reading Room at my web site at **www.nolodivorce.com**.

- Get my free *Divorce Checklist* and start working on those items. It calls your attention to practical things you should know and things you should do. It will help make sure you don't overlook anything important.

- Read my article "The Good Divorce," so you will have a model to keep in mind and an idea of things you can try to accomplish to keep your divorce peaceful.

- Start working on the Property Checklist on the CD in the Forms folder.

- Get *How to Make Any Divorce Better* and learn about the specific things you can do to smooth things out. Get a copy for your Ex, too, so you can discuss ideas in it. Section 7 below discusses strategies for difficult cases.

- **Do not talk to your spouse** about divorce until you learn how to reduce conflict, create a foundation for negotiation, and negotiate effectively.

- **Do not talk to an attorney** until you are informed and prepared—unless, that is, you face an emergency like those described in section 7 below.

- **Organize your facts.** Start now to organize your documents and facts. I created a set of Divorce Worksheets to help you organize, think about, and discuss the facts and finances in your case. They will definitely save you time and money. These worksheets can be found on the CD that comes with this book or can be purchased separately.

- **DealMaker.** Your highest goal is to get a written settlement agreement of all issues in your case. The sample agreement in this book is not ideal for dealing with major or complex assets, but **DealMaker** software is. You'll find a trial version on the CD in the back of this book. **DealMaker** is especially useful for dealing with the many possible options for real estate and retirement funds, and it helps you create a custom parenting plan. DealMaker guides you to enter information and make some decisions, then it writes a sophisticated, professional settlement agreement that you can sign as is or edit with any word processor.

- **Mediation.** If you have trouble working out terms, you don't need an attorney, you need a mediator. See section 8, below.

- **Collaborative law.** If you want to be represented by an attorney, try to get a collaborative lawyer on both sides. Read more about this in section 8, below.

- **Arbitration.** If you can't resolve issues in mediation, consider taking your case to arbitration rather than court. It is similar, in that the arbitrator imposes a decision, but the setting is less formal and an arbitrator is paid by the hour, so will take all the time you need to understand the facts about your family and situation. A judge has to move cases along quickly, so will tend to hurry through divorce motions or trials.

Domestic abuse and violence (DV)

DV includes physical attacks, threats, intimidation, verbal attacks (put-downs, insults, undermining your self-confidence) and other efforts to control you. It can be difficult to distinguish between high levels of divorce conflict and forms of domestic abuse and violence. The DV profile is about cases where your spouse is an habitual controller/abuser, someone who has abused repeatedly. These people are not responsive to reason because their need to control or abuse is too strong, so when dealing with an habitual controller/abuser, your only choice is to go somewhere safe and get specialized help.

Safety first. If you fear for the safety of yourself or a child, go somewhere safe where you can't be found. Ask the local police for domestic abuse support groups near you. What you need most now is personal advice and counseling from someone who specializes in domestic abuse.

Legal battle

If you follow my advice, you probably won't end up in a legal battle, but sometimes you simply can't avoid one or you might be in one already. If you're already in a legal battle, or if you can't avoid a battle even after following the steps in *How to Make Any Divorce Better*, then you have to do what you have to do—get an attorney and fight. If you must fight, you might as well learn how to do it effectively, so welcome to the Battle Group. Keep in mind that this is a legal battle, which is all about business. You do not want to battle on a personal or emotional level. In fact, you will be more effective and healthier if you don't. But you do need to learn:

- How to deal with extreme conflict
- Damage control
- How to protect children
- Winning strategies—hardball or softball?
- How to fight effectively at less expense
- How to choose and use your attorney
- How to fire your attorney (if you want to)

My book, *How to Make Any Divorce Better* discusses this information in detail. Order it at **www.nolodivorce.com/TX** or by mail using the coupon in the back of the book.

If you're in a legal battle, you should make persistent efforts to move your case toward negotiated or mediated agreement, using all the steps discussed in *How to Make Any Divorce Better*. Discourage legal action or activity that you think is not necessary and instruct your attorney that you want to mediate as soon as possible and be kept informed of every effort to make that happen. Also talk about this directly with your spouse, if possible, either in person or by mail.

7. When you should get some help

Emergencies—when retaining an attorney makes sense

If your situation is described below, read the recommended articles to decide if you need to retain an attorney. If your situation is not described below, you should read Part One of this book and also look through *How to Make Any Divorce Better*, then take some time to think things over and take the steps I recommend for your type of case.

a) Personal emergencies

- **Fear for the safety of yourself or your child.** If your spouse is an habitual controller/abuser and you fear it will happen again, you need advice from a domestic violence counselor. Ask your local police or Superior Court Clerk's office for a list of local DV support groups and call them to ask for names of people who can advise you and, if necessary, help you find a safe place to stay.

- **Fear of sneak attack.** If you think your spouse might do a sneak attack by filing for court orders for custody and support without discussion or warning, or maybe just take the kids and the money and run, or both, read about strategies in Chapter 5D of *How to Make Any Divorce Better* and decide if you are going to be defensive or take the offense first.

- **Desperately broke.** If your financial situation is truly desperate—or if your spouse feels this way—go to the Reading Room at **www.nolodivorce.com** and read my article "Funding Your Separation."

- **Parenting children.** Many people run to an attorney because they are afraid they won't get to see their children often enough. If this describes you, go to the Reading Room at **www.nolodivorce.com** and read "Parenting in the Early Stages."

b) Legal emergencies

- **Divorce papers served on you.** This may not be an emergency. If you've only been served with the Petition and you want to have some say in the outcome, you need to file a Response—see section 8 to read about who can help you do this—before the deadline stated on your papers. If the deadline has passed, call the clerk of the court named on the Petition and ask if you are still able to file a Response even though the deadline has passed. If so, quickly file a Response. If not, you'll need an attorney to help you make a motion to allow you to enter the case late. In either situation, read section 8 below about how to find the right kind of help.

However, if a motion has been filed and a hearing scheduled in the near future to determine support or child custody issues, you need to get an attorney right away to either represent you at the hearing or seek a continuance so you can prepare. Read section 8 about what kind of attorney you want. If you don't have time to get an attorney, show up in court at the time and place indicated on your papers and ask the judge for a continuance so you can get an attorney. Even if you are in litigation, you should read *How to Make Any Divorce Better* and look for ways to move the action out of court and into mediation.

- **You are already in litigation.** If you are already in a legal struggle with attorneys on both sides, read *How to Make Any Divorce Better* to learn how the law works and how to guide your case toward negotiation, mediation, or collaborative divorce. If all else fails, arbitration is better than going to court. What you do not want is to end up stuck in a court battle where everyone loses but the attorneys.

c) Legal advice—when to get it and from whom

In some situations, you can get a lot of good from a little advice. In *any* case, you can get peace of mind from knowing you are doing things right. A few hundred dollars for advice may not seem unreasonable when weighed against the value of your property, debts, possible tax savings, all future support payments, and the importance of a good parenting plan. You can often save more than you spend.

If you have any of the situations listed below in your case, you have good reason to get some legal advice. Section 8 suggests who to go to.

Property
- The division of assets and debts is not equal.
- A major asset is being divided or sold—avoiding capital gains problems.
- You aren't sure how to value some assets, such as a business or a professional practice, etc.
- You have stock options—valuation, division, relationship to child and spousal (partner) support.
- Separate and community money was mixed together in a major asset.
- Pension or retirement funds accumulated at least in part during marriage—how to value and how to divide without penalty.

Debts
- You have lots of debts and/or you want to protect yourself from your spouse's debts.
- Either party might declare bankruptcy.
- Joint credit card or other accounts have not been not closed.

Your spouse (solutions are discussed at length in *How to Make Any Divorce Better*)
- You can't agree about important issues.
- You can't get information from your spouse about income, assets, debts.
- You suspect your spouse might be hiding assets.

Children

- There is disagreement over parenting arrangements.
- One parent doesn't want the other to move.
- One parent earns much more than the other—consider saving on taxes by arranging for family support instead of child support.
- There are special needs or health problems.

Spousal maintenance (support)

- You have been married five years or more.
- There is more than 20% difference in incomes.
- One spouse is not self-supporting.
- One spouse put the other through school or training.
- You have preschool children.
- There are special needs or health problems.

Personal

- With a good income and busy schedule, you would be better off if someone else did the paperwork.
- You want to be sure you're doing the right thing and know things are being done correctly.
- You don't understand your situation or what to do about it.
- You want help and suggestions for how to negotiate with your spouse.

8. Who can help?

Friends and relatives are the least reliable sources of advice. Accept all the moral support you can get, but when they give you advice, just smile and say, "Thank you," but do not take it to heart. Also be wary of "common knowledge." If you didn't get it from this book or a family law attorney in Texas, *don't trust it!* Just because you like or trust someone doesn't make them right.

Online divorce services

There are services on the Internet where you can fill out divorce forms for anywhere from zero to $250 or more. What's wrong with that? Well, if it was a good idea, we would have done it long ago, but it is not a good idea. What you really want is someone you can meet with face to face and discuss the options for your case. Here's what online services don't tell you:

Not enough information. Divorce is not about filling out forms—it is about understanding your situation and making decisions. To fill out forms, you need to know what it means to check one box rather than another or file one form rather than another. You need to know where you are in the paperwork, what's going on, where you are going. At all online services we have reviewed, this information is either totally inadequate or completely missing. Not good.

Limited and incomplete. These services have one fixed way to do cases that does not cover a wide variety of situations. You can easily discover partway through that your case does not fit their pattern. Some services get you started but do not complete the case or do not provide important options.

Inflexible. Once you start to fill out the forms, you are stuck on a very long path that you can't get off. It is not easy, maybe not possible, to jump about from one form or page to another. What's worse, you can't step back and get a long view, so you are forced to work without a good understanding of what's going on, where you are in the process, where you are trying to go, or why you are doing things their way.

The better option. If you and your Ex can agree on how to divide property, whether or not there will be alimony and, if you have minor children, how they will be supported and parented after your separation, then you can use this book to complete your forms, or find someone in a city near you who will complete your paperwork for relatively little, a few hundred dollars. Get a copy of our **DealMaker** software (inside front cover) and make a settlement agreement. Then go on the Internet and search for "Divorce Assistance" plus the name of a city near you, or call lots of attorneys and explain that you have a settlement agreement and only need paperwork completed and ask how much this will cost. Keep calling until you get a price that seems reasonable.

Mediators

If you can't work out an agreement on your own, unless there is an emergency, you should try mediation before taking any legal action beyond simply filing a Petition. A mediator can help you communicate, balance the negotiating power, develop options you haven't thought of, solve problems, break through any impasse and help you reach a fair agreement. If your problems are primarily personal or about parenting, you can use a non-attorney mediator, but if property or legal issues are in dispute, it might be better to select a family law attorney-mediator.

Mediation is not just for friendly divorces. Angry, conflicted couples can benefit the most from mediation, particularly if they have children, as litigation will only fan the flame, escalate conflict, and likely do permanent harm to the parties, their finances, and their children. Mediation can be very effective, even in cases with high conflict, when conducted by a good family law attorney-mediator.

Lawyers

Advice. Unless you expect (or want) a legal battle, the best place to get advice is from a family law attorney who mostly does mediation rather than litigation. This way, you are more likely to get practical advice designed to solve problems rather than contentious advice that can lead you to court.

Traditional lawyers who *specialize* in divorce and work in the court system know a lot that could help you, but, because of the way the system works and the way lawyers work, they will almost certainly create unnecessary conflict and expense if you retain one. Unfortunately, getting information and advice from traditional attorneys without retaining them can be tricky, because they don't really want to help you help yourself; they want to be retained to do it all.

Attorneys will frequently do the first interview for a fairly small fee, but too often they spend that time convincing you that you need them to handle your case. Hourly rates can run from $150 to $450, but $175–$350 per hour is normal. Most attorneys require a retainer—$1,200 to $5,000 is typical—but the amount doesn't matter because the final bill will be *much* higher. Few attorneys will give you a definite maximum figure for the whole job. You are doing *very* well if you end up spending less than $5,000 *per spouse* on the *simplest* case. The average in urban areas when both spouses are represented is *well* over $18,000 *per spouse*, but couples with larger estates can expect costs to run into tens or hundreds of thousands of dollars—*per spouse!*

Limited representation. A small but growing number of lawyers are offering representation limited to specific tasks or portions of your case while you keep overall responsibility. For example, they will represent you only to draft your agreement, or only to appear in court if you are asked to show up there for some reason, or only to file and appear on one motion. If you need a bit of service from a family law attorney, call around and ask if they offer "limited representation" or "unbundling," the two names by which this service is known.

Attorney-mediators. See "Mediators" above. When you're looking for advice, it would be best to get it from an attorney who does mostly mediation, as the advice you get is more likely to be practical and about solving problems rather than going to court.

Collaborative divorce. Increasingly popular, spouses and their attorneys pledge in writing not go to court or threaten to go to court as a way to solve problems. Instead, they will use advice, negotiation, and mediation to reach a settlement. If there's no settlement, the spouses will have to get different attorneys to take the case into litigation. In some cases, the collaborative team might include other professionals, such as a divorce coach, family counselor, child specialist, accountant, or financial planner. Collaborative divorce has a good track record and, even with all the professional services you get, it will still cost less than a court battle.

9. Some Common Questions and Answers

- **How much will it cost to do your own divorce?** The filing fees are set from time to time by law, and costs vary slightly from one county to another. These days, it costs at least $200 to file papers in a case where your spouse signs a Waiver of the Citation, and as much as $50 more if the Citation must be issued, plus the Sheriff's fee (about $60) for serving the Citation on your spouse. Add to this a few dollars for photocopies and postage, and that's it. If you were to hire an attorney or a typist or buy a kit, you would still have to pay these fees in addition to the base cost. You'll be hard pressed to find a better bargain than this book.

- **How long will it take?** The shortest possible time to complete a divorce is 61 days from the filing of the Petition, but plan on a bit longer, say three months. It is okay to take longer if you are in no hurry.

- **What if we reconcile?** If you file a divorce Petition and later reconcile and change your mind, just let it lie there. Within a few months, it will be dismissed for lack of prosecution, after a written notice from the clerk.

- **When can I remarry?** After your final Decree of divorce is ordered, you must wait at least 30 days before marrying anyone other than the spouse you just divorced.

- **What about alimony?** In 1995, Texas finally joined the other 49 states in granting alimony (called spousal maintenance) upon divorce. It was a stingy little law at the time, and even though it has been expanding bit-by-bit ever since, there are still significant limitations on amount and duration that are described in chapter D. But whatever the law allows judges to do, the spouses are free to reach almost any kind of agreement about alimony in a written marital settlement agreement and the courts will almost certainly go along with it.

• **What if the wife is pregnant?** You should wait until the child is born to get your divorce. Judges do not like to see a child born out of wedlock, and enforcing child support could be a problem. If you can't wait, see an attorney.

• **Am I liable for my spouse's bills?** During the marriage (even if you are separated), both spouses are liable for the bills of the other. After the divorce, the parties are responsible only for their own bills.

• **What if I am common-law married?** Three elements must exist to form a common-law marriage: 1) an agreement to be married (whether explicit or implied); 2) after the agreement, you lived together as husband and wife; and 3) you represented to others that you were husband and wife. If your marriage is common-law, the same rules for divorce apply to you as to couples married in a ceremony. However, if you believe you are common-law married, you have only two years from the date you separate to file for divorce. If neither party files within that time, it is presumed that no common-law marriage existed, and you won't be able to use this book to get a divorce.

• **Does divorce have tax consequences?** Yes. Almost every aspect of divorce could possibly have important tax consequences. Depending upon what property and income you have, you could possibly save a lot of money by seeing a tax expert, especially before making a marital settlement agreement. There are also rules you should know about if you have children. The tax rules are numerous and they change frequently, but fortunately there is an excellent little booklet that tells you everything you should know, and it is absolutely free. Simply call your local Internal Revenue Service office and ask for IRS publication 504, "Divorced or Separated Individuals."

10. Looking ahead

As mentioned in section 4 above, you can file your Petition and serve it at any time, assuming you have arranged for a smooth start by preparing your spouse or partner to receive it. You can then take some time to make decisions and work out the details about your property, support, and children. We discuss the basic rules of these subjects in chapters B, C, and D. Chapter E shows you how everything can be wrapped up in a settlement agreement once you get things worked out. If you have a more complex estate, real estate, or retirement funds, you should get **DealMaker** software (inside front cover), which uses the power of software to make it easy for you to deal with the many options available for major assets. You just enter requested information, make requested decisions, and **DealMaker** drafts a comprehensive settlement agreement that you can sign as is or edit in any full-featured word processor.

Preparation. Eventually, to complete your divorce you will have to create a complete list of all of your assets and debts, and it will be extremely useful if you start doing that now. Start filling out the worksheets that come on the CD with this book and gather all documents and records related to your assets, debts, and family. Getting prepared in this manner will help organize your facts, your documents, and your thinking. It will suggest other information or questions you might have.

If you have trouble getting information you need, read "Getting the Information You Need," which is in the appendix in *How to Make Any Divorce Better.*

Go to my web site, **www.nolodivorce.com**, look in the Reading Room, get my free "Divorce Checklist," and start working on those items right away.

Study the Decree of Divorce. While you are reading through the next few chapters, at some point you should jump ahead to chapter 7 and take a look at the Decree. Read the language in the various orders that are used in the Decree so you can understand where all this information you are reading about will end up. Then you'll have a better idea of where you are going while reading about how to get there.

B. Dividing Property and Debts

One of the most important parts of a divorce action is dividing the property and debts (the estate) of the marriage. One of the most important services of an attorney is going over your estate with you to see what you own, what you owe, and how it can all be divided. The attorney will have an eye to getting you, the client, the best deal possible. Unless you have a large or complicated estate, this book will tell you how to understand your own estate and decide for yourself how to divide it.

1. Cases where there is no property

Do not conclude that you have no property without going over the checklist in section 3 to make sure that you have thought of everything.

Cases without property are very easy to do, because you merely tell the court that there is no significant property to be divided, and the court does nothing. There will be but little inquiry into your property and no orders about it.

Several types of cases can be handled this way. Perhaps there's not enough property to worry about, or maybe your spouse is long gone or doesn't care, so has abandoned what little property there is to you. Or maybe you have already divided things between you, so at the time you file there is nothing left to be divided by the court. In cases like these, you may decide that you do not need or want the court to make orders about the division of your property.

Do not use this approach if there is any chance of future argument about property of any significant value, or where there is real estate that has not yet been divided correctly, or where there is a community interest in a pension plan.

2. Cases where there is some property

Make sure you understand your marital estate and know all that it contains. Read section 3 and go over the checklist very carefully to make sure you have thought of everything. Be sure to include property acquired anywhere else that would have been community property had it been acquired in Texas. If you think it likely that your spouse has hidden assets that you don't know and can't find out about, then you might benefit from the services of an attorney who can get the spouse in court and under order to reveal everything.

If at the time of your divorce your estate contains property or bills of any significant value, then you will want to have things divided properly as part of the divorce.

Property can be divided by the parties or by a judge. Spouses can agree to divide their property any way they see fit. If this is completed before the Petition is filed, then there is no community property to divide and the case will be very easy to process. If there is some community property but no agreement at the time of filing, then that property must be listed in the Petition. If by the time of the court hearing there is still no agreement, the property will be divided by the judge. In this case, neither spouse will be entirely in control of how the property gets divided, although the judge will be strongly influenced by the suggestions of the Petition or the spouse in court.

When thinking about dividing your property, keep in mind that getting the last cent may not be your best or highest goal. Consider the children, if any, the relative earning ability of each of you, your general situation, fairness, and other such things. Try to consider what will be best for everyone, both now and in the future.

If you have a lot of property, you might want to think about getting professional advice from an accountant or lawyer. A professional can tell you how to locate it, value it, divide it, transfer it, and generally protect your interests.

3. Understanding your estate

a) The marital estate: separate and community property defined

A marriage has three estates: the separate property of husband, the separate property of wife, and community property belonging to both. While a divorce decree should clarify the separate property of each spouse, only community property (CP) needs to be divided in a divorce, since separate property (SP) already belongs to each spouse individually. The first step, then, is to determine what property in the marital estate is CP, SP, or a combination of the two. In section 4, we discuss how CP is divided.

Checklist. Use the checklist shown here to organize your thinking about the property and bills in your marital estate. Make a few blank copies before you start filling it out. Better yet, our companion CD has the same checklist in the Forms Etc folder, a PDF version with fields that you can fill out on any computer.

Community property is any property other than SP, no matter where it is located, that was acquired by either spouse during the marriage. Property owned by either spouse during the marriage or at the time of the dissolution is **presumed** to be community property. Even if the spouses have been separated for years, the earnings and debts of each spouse are community property until the divorce is ordered.

Property checklist and worksheet

Item	Market value	Amount owed	Net value	Proposed division
1. Real Estate family home rental property recreation property other				
2. Household goods, furniture, and appliances				
3. Jewelry, antiques, art, collections, coins, etc.				
4. Vehicles, boats, trailers (get license and ID numbers)				
5. Cash on hand, and savings, checking, credit union accounts (get account numbers)				

Property checklist and worksheet (continued)

Item	Market value	Amount owed	Net value	Proposed division
6. Life insurance with cash value (get policy numbers)				
7. Equipment, machinery, and livestock				
8. Stocks, bonds, secured notes				
9. Retirement/pension plans, profit-sharing plans, annuities				
10. Tax refunds due, accounts receivable, unsecured notes				
11. Partnerships, business interests				
12. Other assets				

13. List all other debts, taxes due, bills:

To whom due	What for	Balance

Separate property is property owned before marriage, acquired during marriage by gift or inheritance directed to just one spouse, and recovery for injury suffered during marriage, except recovery for loss of earning capacity during the marriage. Without some clear agreement otherwise, SP that is mixed and mingled with CP tends to lose its separate quality. For the sake of clarity, SP of significant value or personal meaning should be listed in your Petition and in any agreement between the spouses.

If there's a disagreement as to what is SP, the degree of proof required to establish that the property is separate is "clear and convincing evidence." This means you must be able to trace and clearly identify property claimed as separate, say by showing that it was purchased with SP funds. If the identity of SP is ambiguous or intermingled with CP, you will probably need the assistance of a family law attorney (see chapter A8).

b) When funds flow between marital estates

During marriage, it is not uncommon for funds to flow between marital estates, that is, from separate to community or vice-versa. Unless there is a pre- or post-marital contract that states otherwise, then to the extent it can be made clear with records, one marital estate might have a claim against another for reimbursement that matures on dissolution. Prior to September 1, 2009, Texas had a complicated law called "Economic Contribution," which has been repealed and now applies only to cases filed before the new law took effect. If your case was filed before that date and you think you might have a claim not covered below, get help. See chapter A8.

Reimbursement. Think of the three estates: (1) the separate income and assets of one spouse; (2) the separate income and assets of the other spouse; and (3) community income and assets. Not everyone has them all but they are potentially there for everyone. Reimbursement is about settling up for the uncompensated flow of value from one estate to another. Here are some examples:

 • Using marital income or assets to pay down one spouse's debts, or using the separate income or assets of one spouse to pay down the debts of the other spouse or the community.

 • Compensation for time, toil, talent and effort of one spouse that benefitted only that spouse. The community is entitled to share.

 • Using the income or assets of the community or of one spouse for capital improvements to the separate property of the other spouse.

The whole story is in the somewhat impenetrable Family Code sections 3.401 to 3.409.

To get a judge to order reimbursement you have to have records to show where the money or effort came from, how it was used, and what value was derived. This is one of those things lawyers can argue about endlessly. The best course, as always, is to work things out between you, perhaps with the help of a mediator. Taking the issue to court can be very expensive because this is one of those things lawyers can argue about endlessly.

Claims for reimbursement can be offset against each other if the parties agree or a court decides it is appropriate. Any benefit for the use and enjoyment of property may be offset against a claim for reimbursement for expenditures to benefit a marital estate, except a separate estate of a spouse may *not* claim an offset for use and enjoyment of a primary or secondary residence owned wholly or partly by the separate estate against contributions made by the community estate to the separate estate. If reimbursement is sought for funds used to improve another marital estate, the court is to use the standard of enhancement of value.

Claims are determined on equitable principles and it is entirely in the discretion of the judge whether to recognize a claim, taking into account all circumstances and having due regard for the rights of each spouse and any children of their marriage—another reason why it's better and safer to settle it between you.

Non reimbursable claims. The court will not recognize a marital estate's claim for reimbursement for:

1. The payment of child support, alimony, or spousal maintenance;
2. The living expenses of a spouse or child of a spouse;
3. Contributions of property of little value;
4. The payment of a liability of small amount; or
5. A student loan owed by a spouse.

If you suspect you have a potential claim for reimbursement but find this difficult, you might want to get legal advice from a family law specialist. See chapter A8.

c) Bills and liabilities of the spouses

If you or your spouse, or both of you, accumulated debts during your marriage, these are community debts that will have to be valued and divided along with the property.

Important. Orders of the court and agreements between spouses about who is to pay bills do not in any way affect people you owe. If you owed money to someone before the divorce and your spouse is ordered to pay the bill but does not, then you still owe the money. The creditor can come after you or repossess the property. Your spouse may be in contempt of court, for all the good that does you.

Between marriage and divorce, spouses are liable for each other's debts. This means that if your spouse moved away five years ago, hasn't been heard from since, and bought some shoes last month, the shoe store can come to you for payment if the bill is not paid by your spouse. This unnecessary and unfortunate rule is the reason many people are in a big hurry to get their divorce over with.

As soon as you separate, close all joint accounts and notify all creditors in writing that you will no longer be responsible for the debts of your spouse.

d) Pension and retirement plans

There are often benefits to employment beyond wages, including accrued rights in a profit-sharing plan, company or government pension plans, Keoghs, 401(k) and 403(b) plans, Individual Retirement Accounts (IRAs), SEP IRAs, Tax Sheltered Annuities (TSAs), and Employee Stock Option plans (ESOPs). If either spouse was a participant in such a plan during the marriage, then some part of that plan is community property that *must* be dealt with as part of the divorce.

This area can be difficult, so if you read through the material below and get confused, don't feel bad—it confuses most lawyers too! After you read this section, if you have questions or want advice, read chapter A8.

Social Security is not community property and not subject to division by a court. It is a federal program with its own rules, so contact the Social Security Administration about your rights after divorce. Note that benefits accrue to spouses of a marriage that lasted at least 10 years, so if you are approaching that deadline, don't rush into a Judgment that could conveniently be postponed.

Military and Federal Pensions. Military retirement pay and federal civil service benefits can be community property and subject to division in state courts. Spouses of marriages that last through 10 years or more of military service gain advantages in the enforcement of pension awards. Former spouses of marriages that lasted through at least 20 years of active military service are entitled to commissary and PX benefits. Don't be hasty with your divorce if you are approaching a 10- or 20-year deadline. A retiring military spouse can be bound by a written agreement to designate a former spouse as beneficiary under a Survivor Benefit Plan (SBP) if the agreement is incorporated, ratified, or approved in a court order incident to divorce, and if the Secretary concerned receives a request from the former spouse, along with the agreement and court order.

Must be valued correctly. If the community has an interest in a retirement fund or plan, you need to know how much that interest is worth.

- If your plan is a tax-deferred savings account like a 401(k), the total value is probably the figure shown on the summary statement. *The community share* in such a fund is equal to the number of married years the employee-spouse was part of the plan, divided by the total number of years of employment when the marriage is dissolved. Multiply the current worth of the pension plan at time of divorce by this ratio to determine the current value of the community interest—that is the amount subject to division at the time of divorce.

- For defined benefit plans where you have to wait for a certain age or number of years of employment to begin receiving payments, it requires an expert to say how much the plan and the community interest are worth. You must have your plan appraised by a professional pension actuary—it will be money well spent! If you call around to find one, be sure to ask if they do "present buy-out appraisals of community interest in a pension plan." You might also ask how many they do each year. Most lawyers would not be capable of doing it correctly, nor would most accountants. If you need an appraisal of a pension plan, read chapter A8.

Joinder. If the community has an interest in one or more pension plans or retirement funds, then unless you are already completely certain that the entire plan or fund will be awarded to the employee-spouse, you need to join each plan or fund to your case to freeze the funds and make sure they are not improperly withdrawn or transferred before the matter is settled correctly in a judgment. So, with the exception of federal government plans and individual IRA accounts (not including SEP IRAs), when you file your Petition, or as soon after as possible, you should also join each plan or fund. You will need help from a family law attorney to do this. Read chapter A8.

How to deal with a pension plan when doing your own divorce. Because of the complexities involved with retirement and pension funds, if you are going to have a settlement agreement, we recommend that you use DealMaker instead of the simple sample agreement in chapter 6.

The following methods can be used either to settle the pension matter now or to put it off for later.

1) The waiver can be used if the community interest is truly worth very little. The non-employee-spouse simply gives up, in a settlement agreement, all interest in the employee's pension fund.

2) The trade-off (present day buy-out) is a clean and easy way to divide a pension fund; courts like it, and it has no immediate tax consequences. By this method, one spouse trades his/her interest in the employee-spouse's pension plan for something else of equal value, such as a larger share of the family home or a promissory note. Be careful—insist that any note be secured, preferably with a Trust Deed on real property.

Note that the employee-spouse trades hard dollars in the present for something that *might* be collected if he or she stays employed long enough and lives long enough to collect. The employee-spouse will pay taxes on that future income while the other spouse pays no taxes on the trade. However, the employee-spouse may need the entire pension to live on after retirement, so it may be better to pay now rather than have less to live on later. Or maybe the community interest is relatively low and easy to pay for now, just to get things wrapped up cleanly.

3) The payoff (division into two accounts) awards present ownership of a share of *future* pension rights (when they come due) to the non-employee-spouse. Transfers following a payoff *must* be done in strict accordance with IRS rules, or you might suffer an *immediate* tax liability. This method costs several hundred dollars for a special order called a QDRO (see below). The non-employee-spouse may have to wait for his/her share, and the employee-spouse will have a smaller pension check to live on. It is most appropriate in long marriages where the pension is the only or largest asset. Sometimes the employee-spouse will use it to reduce or eliminate spousal support payments.

QDROs. To divide a pension plan or retirement fund, you need a Qualified Domestic Relations Order (QDRO), which is like an official title or "pink slip" to a share of the pension fund, 401(k), or annuity. This *must* be done at the same time or before the Judgment is signed or the non-employee-spouse could lose out. Besides, plan or fund administrators will probably not release funds without a proper order that meets their highly specific requirements.

Two different plans require two joinders (see above) and two QDROs. One pension plan with multiple parts may require more than one QDRO. QDRO orders are difficult to draft and any mistake could be very expensive, so we *strongly* recommend that you call an attorney with a lot of pension fund experience to see if there is some way to get what you want *safely* without having to prepare a QDRO, or to prepare a QDRO for you. Don't take a chance with such an important matter—get expert assistance . It will be worth it. See chapter A8.

Death benefits. Divorce automatically removes a spouse as beneficiary under some plans but not others, so the employee-spouse should notify the plan of the divorce and name a new beneficiary. The non-employee-spouse may want to be continued under the plan, but it is usually better to value this part of the plan separately and replace it with an annuity or life insurance of equal value and cover the cost in the settlement agreement, perhaps with a small increase in spousal support.

Be careful with pension plans and retirement funds as there are often tax consequences and penalties if pensions or 401(k)s are not correctly divided or if withdrawals are made before retirement age. Don't touch a fund without making sure your changes won't end up costing you. If you want advice about how to deal with pensions or retirement funds, or help deciding what's best for you, talk to an accountant or, better yet, a family law attorney (see chapter A8).

e) The family home and other real estate

If you and your spouse own your home or other real property, then you must decide how to divide it. Some likely alternatives are to sell it and split the proceeds; have one spouse transfer it outright to the other; or have one spouse transfer it to the other in return for something, such as other property, or a note for some amount to be paid in the future (at some specific date or upon some specified event, such as when the kids are grown, if and when the house is sold, the spouse moves out of it, or any other that you can agree to). In a slow market, you can defer the sale and own it together as tenants-in-common until you decide the time is right to sell it.

Before deciding what to do about real property, you need to know how much of it you actually own—your "equity," which is the difference between what you can get for it on the current market less mortgages, liens, and the cost of selling it. You can find out the current market value of your property by consulting a professional real estate appraiser. This will cost some money, so call around for prices. You would also do fairly well by calling in a few local real estate agents, but this may not be as accurate. Once you have figured the market value, deduct the amounts you owe on it and the commission for the real estate agents. If you don't sell it yourself, they will get six to eight percent. Add on a few hundred dollars for miscellaneous expenses.

The divorce will be much easier if you can settle the matter of the real estate and transfer it before you file the Petition. That way you won't have to list the house and make orders about it in your Decree. Agreements about real property are not enforceable unless they are in writing. In order to actually transfer the home from joint ownership by both spouses into sole ownership of one spouse, you need to make a deed from one spouse to the other, then have that deed signed before a Notary and recorded in the county where the property is located. Similarly, if a note is to be assumed, then it too must be properly drawn up, signed, and recorded. There will be a small fee for recording and maybe a transfer tax. If you cannot make up your own deed or note from forms available at a stationer's, then you should seek assistance from a title company, bank, real estate broker, or attorney. Call around. A form for transferring the property between spouses is included with the forms in the back of this book.

If you do not transfer the home before the Petition is filed, then it must be listed with your other property. If it is still not transferred by the time of the hearing, or settled by written agreement, the judge will divide it along with all the other listed property. In the Petition and Decree, the property should be listed by both its common address and legal description (as on the deed). The judge can award the house to one spouse, or order it sold and the proceeds divided in some particular way. It is much better if the spouses take care of it their own way before the Petition is filed.

Because the time and manner of transfer can have tax consequences, it can benefit spouses to cooperate over the transfer to arrange it to their own advantage. See a tax expert if you have enough income and property to benefit from tax games.

f) Income tax

Any income taxes owed or refunds due should be divided with the rest of your property. Most people split these 50-50, but you can agree to any division you want. If you settle division of taxes in a settlement agreement (chapter E), you do not need to list them in your Decree. You also need to decide how to divide any income tax that you *will owe* or refunds you *will receive* for the year of the divorce itself. The easiest way is to agree that each of you will be responsible for taxes incurred on his or her own income only. If your divorce is completed before December 31, you will file taxes as "single" or "head of household."

If you do not have your Decree by December 31, you have the option of filing as "married filing jointly" or "married filing separately." If you and your spouse are in agreement, work up the tax forms both ways to see which form of filing is most advantageous to both of you and share the benefit.

Keep in mind that if you and your spouse owe back taxes, the IRS may still hold you liable even if the debt is assigned to your spouse in your divorce. Tax problems are beyond the scope of this book. You should contact a tax lawyer, CPA, or an enrolled IRS agent before you go to court if you have questions.

4. When property is divided by the court

If there is community property or debts of any significance at the time of your divorce, then it must be properly divided. Property can be divided either by agreement of the spouses, or by the judge according to his or her own standards. There are many advantages to working things out by agreement. These are discussed in section 5 below, but first it might help to understand how things work when left to the court to divide.

The judge has a great deal of discretion, as the law specifies only a division that is "just and right, having regard for the rights of each party and any children." This makes it very important to get an agreement with your spouse, otherwise some stranger (the judge) who knows nothing about you or your family will decide and no one can predict how it will come out. If required to decide at trial, judges tend to look at a variety of factors, including fault in the breakup if fault was alleged. This is unfortunate, as it encourages angry spouses to fight about fault in order to grab for a larger share.

Apart from fault and other wrong-doing, a judge will consider the health, education and experience of the spouses, their incomes and earning capacity, who raised the kids, disparity of ages, size of their separate estates, business opportunities, tax issues and debts of the parties. These factors nicely anticipate lawyer's arguments that can come up at trial, but they do not help to predict what a judge will decide.

The profound uncertainty and huge expense of taking a case to trial makes it extremely important for you to do everything in your power to negotiate an agreement. If you anticipate any difficulty, be sure to read my book *How to Make Any Divorce Better*, which gives you many specific steps to take to resolve differences and negotiate an agreement.

Where there is significant property, other than personal possessions, that is not divided by the time the Petition is filed, then *all* the valuable property and debts of the spouses should be listed in the Petition. The Petition should indicate which is community and which is separate property. It is also a very good idea to indicate how the Petitioner wishes the property and debts to be divided.

If there is still no agreement by the time of the hearing, the court has almost complete discretion as to how it will divide your property. This leaves things pretty wide open, so anything can happen. The court is supposed to consider the property, the children, earning ability of each spouse, and any other circumstances the judge thinks relevant, then the judge will make a decision that is difficult to reverse. The judge will be strongly influenced by the Petition and by the words of the Petitioner at the hearing, and very likely will decide as requested. But there is no guarantee. Even attorneys are sometimes surprised by the judge's decision.

The judge will usually divide *only* the community property, and will clarify who owns which items of separate property. However, in rare cases where it seems necessary, the judge may invade a spouse's separate property for the benefit of children.

Here are some general rules of thumb for you to consider, but you must keep in mind that there is no certainty as to what kind of order a judge will make.

    a) An approximately equal division of the property and debts will most likely be ordered where there are no children and the spouses have equal earning abilities and equal circumstances. This is especially true in short marriages. Where an item has a debt attached to it—if it was mortgaged or bought on time—the spouse getting the item will most often get the debt too.

    b) An unequal division of the property and debts may be ordered in favor of the spouse with:
- custody of the child/ren
- greater need,
- lesser earning ability, or
- favorable circumstances of fairness.

    c) The judge can, and you should, consider taxes on property and when the tax will have to be paid; say where a spouse gets the house intending to sell it, thus incurring capital gains tax.

    d) **Fraud.** If the court finds fraud on the community estate, the court will calculate the value of the estate as it would have been had there been no fraud, then divide it as the judge thinks is just, including an award to the wronged spouse of an extra share, money damages, or both.

Where there are children, the family home and furnishings are almost always kept together for the benefit of the children and awarded to the spouse with custody. The wage-earner spouse may be ordered to pay debts on items he or she does not possess (if he or she fails to pay, the creditor may come and get the stuff anyway).

If the court awards you property that is still in the possession of your spouse, you have to figure out how to get it. If you can't get it peacefully, then you will need an attorney to help you get it, if it is worth the money and trouble.

5. Dividing it by agreement

If your property is minimal, you can just go ahead and divide it up, and that will be that. If there are items of some value, it is usually better to make a written agreement, just to help you keep track of what it was you actually agreed to. If there is any real estate, or if you are dividing a pension plan, then any agreement *must* be in writing.

In uncontested divorces, a judge will almost always follow your agreement, so long as it appears to be generally fair, but the judge is not legally bound to follow your contract. Especially in matters of child custody and support, a judge will want to make sure that your terms are reasonable and fair and children are protected.

Chapter E discusses written agreements and shows you how to make one.

6. How to transfer titles to property

Some property is held under a document or written indicator of ownership, called "title." This includes real estate, motor vehicles, boats, trailers, bank accounts, investment accounts, stocks, and bonds. In such cases, ownership after divorce is not complete until title has been properly transferred or otherwise dealt with.

As with every other part of your divorce, it is always much easier if your spouse will cooperate with you. If this is not possible, you can usually accomplish your goal some other way, but not always. If your spouse is not cooperative, then getting title is merely the first step—you still have to get possession. In some cases, it means a lot to have possession first, as with bank accounts that could be spent while you are waiting around to get title. If you can't get possession in any peaceful way, you may have to seek the help of an attorney.

a) Real estate is easy to transfer if your spouse will sign a warranty deed, which is included with the forms on the CD in the back of this book. The deed is then recorded at the Clerk's Office in the county where the land is located. There will be a very nominal recording fee of a few dollars. It is very helpful to have this done before the hearing; if possible, even before you file your Petition.

If the transfer is not made by the time you file your Petition, you must list it, being careful to use the exact legal description of the property, which you can copy from your deed, which you can find at the Clerk's Office in the county where the land is located. If the transfer is still not voluntarily made by the time of your hearing, the property must be awarded as part of the Decree. If the land is in Texas, title can be transferred merely by filing a certified copy of the Decree with the Clerk's Office in the county where the land is located. If the land is not in Texas, make sure your Decree specifically orders your spouse to make a transfer by deed to you. Then you have to try to enforce the order by contempt proceedings. This will require the service of an attorney.

b) Vehicles can be transferred by a cooperative spouse merely by the signing of the form on the back of the vehicle title slip. You can also have your spouse sign a Power of Attorney to Transfer Motor Vehicle in front of a Notary Public. A copy of that form is in on the CD in the back of this book. Take this to the auto transfers office in your county within 10 working days of the date of the signature. If the title slip has been lost, you will need to pick up a special form at that office to replace the lost one. If your spouse will *not* cooperate, then the vehicle must be listed and awarded to you in the Decree. The description must be very complete, including make, model, year, license plate number, and motor or vehicle I.D. number. Take a certified copy of the Decree to the auto transfers office and they will have you fill out a couple of forms, pay a few dollars, and the transfer will be made.

Any way you do it, if there is a lien on the auto (where you owe money on it), the lien must be brought forward on the new title.

c) Bank accounts are commonly held in one of three ways: (i) in an individual name, (ii) in the names of "H or W," (iii) in the names of "H and W." If the account is in your own individual name, it is yours and you don't have to worry about it. If it is in the individual name of your spouse, then even an attorney would have a hard time doing much about it. The easiest thing to do is to list it on the Petition at its value at that time, and have it awarded to your spouse as a setoff for something else that you want. If the account is in the name of you *or* your spouse, as is most common, this means either one of you can withdraw it at any time. You might want to take out as much as you wish to protect and put it into an account in your own name. Joint accounts in the name of one spouse *and* the other are probably rare. This would mean that the signatures of *both* spouses are required to make a transfer. In such a case, if your spouse will not cooperate, take a certified copy of the divorce Decree to the bank and see if that does the trick. If not, a court order will be required and you will need an attorney's services to get it. Until then, the money is safe, since your spouse can't get it either.

This discussion applies also to other types of property and instruments, such as stocks and bonds which, like bank accounts, can be held individually or jointly. Possession of the paper means a great deal, especially with "bearer" instruments such as government bonds, which can be negotiated by whoever has possession.

d) Tax refunds are easy with the cooperation of your spouse, and fairly easy in any event if you have possession of the refund check. Either get your spouse's signature when and where required, or take the check along with a certified copy of the divorce Decree to the nearest IRS office. If you do not have possession of the check, then use your innate cunning to get it peacefully, or forget it. A lawyer has a few tricks that sometimes work, but it's rarely worth it, since the check is usually not even big enough to pay the lawyer's fee.

e) Insurance policies can be transferred merely by sending the insurance company a certified copy of the Decree awarding the policy or any covered property to you.

7. Wills, trusts, and beneficiaries

After a divorce, you should definitely make a new will—or better yet, a living trust. Be sure to review the people you previously named as beneficiaries in wills, trusts, insurance policies, bank or investment accounts, or named in a pre-divorce Health Care Directive.

C. Children: Custody and Visitation

1. Generally

When you have children, a divorce never completely ends the relationship. You no longer live together, but chances are you will still be involved because of the children. This makes it extremely important that you try to keep things as calm as possible. It is not good for the children or their parents if you can't get over your differences at least enough to permit the parental relationship to continue and grow.

Managing and Possessory Conservators. Sometimes it's easy to believe that lawmakers have a special department to figure out how to make simple things complicated. In Texas, what normal people call custody, the law calls "conservatorship." The parent with custody is the "managing conservator" and the other parent (the one who visits) is the "possessory conservator." What people call "visitation," the law calls "possession." It takes practice, but you will get the hang of it, eventually.

The divorce Petition *must* list all children of the marriage under 18 and not married, including any child natural-born to the spouses or adopted by both. Include stepchildren only if legally adopted by the stepparent. If the wife is pregnant, you have to wait until the child is born to finish your divorce. Any child born to the wife between marriage and divorce is presumed to be her husband's.

Not my kid? If any child born during marriage is not husband's, or if the wife is pregnant by another man, get help. You **must** establish paternity before you try to complete your divorce.

Other cases? If custody of a child has come before any court before now, get help, as your case is too complicated to do yourself. See chapter A8. If you're not sure—if there's even a slight chance that a Texas court has been involved with a child's custody—then use form VS-168 (on the CD in the Forms Etc. folder) to find out if any court has continuing jurisdiction over the child. Follow the simple instructions on that form. If they reply that the child is not under the jurisdiction of any court, then you are free to go ahead with your case, but be sure to take their response to the hearing with you and put it into evidence.

Modification. Orders about custody, visitation, and support of children are subject to modification. If circumstances change significantly, either parent can go back into court to seek a change in the court orders.

History of family violence. A history of family violence, abuse or neglect will play a very large role in any judge's determination of custody and visitation (conservatorship and possession), especially if there's evidence of it within the previous two years. If you want restricted visitation, take evidence to your court hearing.

2. Custody (conservatorship)

There are two forms of custody for children in Texas. The law gives preference to *joint managing conservatorship* (JMC), which normal people would call "joint custody." In a JMC, the parents share the duties and responsibilities of raising the child(ren). However, those duties and responsibilities are spelled out very specifically in your Decree, so you can tailor your conservatorship to fit the agreement between you and your spouse. JMC does not have to mean equal or even near-equal periods of custody. It also does not eliminate the requirement for child support. In a joint conservatorship, one parent is selected to provide the primary residence, or domicile, for the child and is called the "home parent" and the other is the "Co-Parent."

Another arrangement is *sole managing conservatorship*, where one parent gets primary custody and responsibilities, while the other parent has more limited duties plus visitation (possession). This used to be the norm, but should now be used only when you can show a judge that joint custody is not in the best interest of your child/ren. Some examples of reasons that sole custody would be best include: the other parent can't be located, or has a history of substance abuse, or committed family violence against you or the children, or has a criminal record, or has physical or mental disabilities. Things like that. In case you get a judge who is reluctant to order sole managing conservatorship, you should put together the best evidence you can find (documents, witnesses, your own story) to bring to court when you have your hearing.

Right now is a good time to go to the back of this book and take a close look at the Conservatorship Order, an Exhibit that goes with the Decree. This form shows you the choices you have to make when you define a child's custody.

Here are some points of law a judge must consider when deciding custody if parents are unable to agree and the matter comes to court:

- Parents are preferred over third parties.
- Joint custody (JMC) is presumed best, but this presumption can be rebutted with evidence. A history of domestic violence removes the presumption.
- The law requires that no preference be given due to marital status or gender of a parent or child. However, for young children there is still a cultural bias in favor of mothers, so if the parents can't agree a father can win custody more easily when the children are older or it is clear that the mother is unfit.
- Split custody (one for me and two for you) is to be avoided.

- Children 12 years of age and older have the right to express a preference to the judge in chambers who he/she wants to live with. The judge can go along with the child's choice, but is not required to. At the judge's discretion, younger children can express a preference in chambers.

If there is a custody battle, in most cases a social study of the family will be ordered. A social worker will be appointed to "study" your family and talk to you and everyone you know and don't know in order to send a report back to the judge, stating facts uncovered and advising what the social worker thinks is best for your child(ren). The lawyers on each side will probably try to make the other side look like a disaster for the kids, and there's even a chance that an older child could end up talking to the judge. Whoever wins, the kids usually lose. Don't do it unless you have no other choice. It is far better to work it out outside of court, if you can do it peacefully. In tough cases, consider using a trusted friend, member of the clergy, mediator, or counselor for help.

You would be foolish to attempt to be your own lawyer if your spouse opposes you legally. Get help; see chapter A8.

3. Visitation (possession)

Divorce is not the end of the relationship between parents, as there is still the continuing need—duty, in fact—for both to be involved regularly in the lives of their children. Studies have shown that children of divorced parents are most badly damaged when hard feelings and conflict continue long after the divorce, while children adjust fairly nicely if the heat and smoke clear away soon after the Decree. For the sake of your children, make your co-parenting as smooth and comfortable as possible. In conversations with the other parent, talk less about who has custody and more about how you can share the care and parenting of your child(ren).

"Reasonable visitation" is no longer used because no one knows what it means, so the parents have to constantly work out who has the kids at which times, and this is not easily done when parents are not getting along. Vast experience shows that if negotiating a detailed plan is something you can do, you and your children will be far better off because everyone will know exactly what the schedule is when the parents can't agree. Parents can arrange visitation any way they like by agreement, without regard for the terms of the Decree, but when relations become strained, the visitation terms define the schedule very clearly, so there's less to argue about.

Standard Possession Order (SPO) and variations

Texas has standard terms for possession—the parenting schedule—that are presumed by law to be in the child's best interest. This is the Standard Possession Order (SPO), which is an Exhibit that goes with the Decree. After you finish this section, go to the back of the book and take a close look at the SPO.

If parents can't agree about their parenting schedule and go to court, they will definitely get the SPO, so why bother going to court? If you can't agree, just do the SPO. On the other hand, if you *can* agree, you can have almost any reasonable Possession Order you like, so long as you specify which parent has the right to designate the primary residence of the child, either anywhere or within a specific geographical area. In our forms, this is done by reference to the Conservatorship Order, where rights and duties are defined.

The SPO is really just for backup, to cover times when you can't agree. You aren't required to rigidly follow the SPO. The very first paragraph says that you can follow any schedule you like by mutual agreement, but if you can't agree, you *must* follow the Possession Order. Ideally, parents will discuss the SPO and decide which responsibilities to share and what schedule is best for their circumstances. Any Possession Order can be changed by mutual agreement or when circumstances change, such as a child growing older, but if you change the SPO significantly, drop the word "Standard" from the title and just call it "Possession Order."

Joint custody. Where the parents are joint managing conservators (JMC), the SPO is presumed to be the *minimum* amount of possession for the visiting parent, but you can add additional care time to it. Some parents use the Standard Possession Order rigidly, while others prefer to change visits regularly. It is advisable for the children's sake that once you settle on dates and times, you stick to them, as children require stability to feel secure. It would be very unsettling for you not to know until Friday where you were spending the night—think about how your child feels!

Any schedule or written agreement for JMC *must* (1) state which parent has the right to designate the primary residence of the child within a specified geographic area—in our forms, this is done by reference to our Conservatorship Order; (2) specify the rights and duties of each parent, as in our Conservatorship Order form; and (3) include provisions to minimize disruption of the child's education, daily routine, and friendships (what, exactly, this means is not specified, so just use our SPO as a guide).

Variations. Some set of detailed terms *must* be part of any Decree involving custody of children. You can alter the terms of the SPO to fit your work schedules, preferences, or special needs of the parents or child, but there are only two ways to get completely different terms—you can enter into a written agreement with almost any reasonable terms you like, subject to the court's approval; or, without an agreement of the parents, something different from the SPO can be ordered if you can give the court a very good reason for it. If your Possession Order varies more than a little from the SPO in the back of the book and on our CD, remove "Standard" from the Possession Order so the judge will know it is not the standard order.

It is very unusual, but still possible, that the judge will find that your agreement is not in the best interest of the children. If this happens, the judge will either issue orders of his own design, or perhaps request a revised agreement.

Children under three. You should prepare a different schedule for them that is more suitable to their needs, and include an order in your Decree that they will automatically graduate to an attached possession order for older children on their third birthday. In the Forms folder on the CD, Exhibit 05-Ex3A is a Possession Order for children under three and the adjacent file, 3B, has suggested terms for babies of various ages. You can use the RTF file "05-Ex3B.rtf" to edit the terms to suit your own needs.

Virtual visitation means staying in touch with your children via video calls, e-mail, instant messaging, and cell phones. Video calls are free or very inexpensive and they allow you to hear and see each other, share documents, help with homework, play games, bring friends or grandparents into the visit, and so on. It is not a substitute for quality time spent together, but rather an extremely valuable supplement. Virtual visitation benefits all parties, as it allows the custodial parent to stay in touch with the child during extended summer or holiday visits with the non-custodial parent, and the child never has to feel cut off from either parent at any time. If requested, Texas judges have the discretion to make such orders (Family Code § 153.015). Family Codes are on the companion CD in the Forms Etc. folder. For more information, tales of personal experience, tips on how to do it, and suggestions for virtual visitation language in your settlement agreement, go to **www.internetvisitation.org**.

Visitation problems

Visitation is not tied to support. The parent who has custody is not allowed to forbid visiting because support money is not coming in or because the parents are angry with one another. Visitation is not a weapon to be used against the visiting spouse. But visitation can be refused if it is clear that the child's safety is involved; for example, if the visiting spouse shows up drunk and wants to drive away with the child.

Counties have been authorized since 2001 to set up visitation centers to facilitate visitation or exchange for parents who have (or anticipate) visitation problems. Check with your county to see if they have this service. If they do, pay them a visit to discuss how they can help you.

You should know that there are criminal sanctions against a person who keeps or conceals a child in order to frustrate visitation orders. For example, if the visiting parent just decides to keep the child for awhile and not bring the child home when due, there would be a strong reaction from the authorities if they are called in.

In very rare cases, it may be clear that it is dangerous for the court to permit any visitation at all. To get such an order, you will have to present clear, strong evidence that some specific harm is likely to come to the children if visitation of any kind is allowed. This means showing a pattern of behavior such as heavy use of drugs or alcohol, sexual abuse, or violence toward the children. If you are determined to prevent visitation altogether, you would be better off with an attorney.

4. Class required for parents?

Many counties in Texas now require divorcing parents to take a course on how divorce affects the children and how best to share parenting. These courses are part of a nationwide trend to soften the impact of divorce on children. Both parents must take this course and present proof that you did it to the judge at the final hearing. If you do not know where your spouse is, the court may waive the requirement that your spouse attend the class, but you still have to attend. The course is usually four hours long and the average cost is about $30.

Check with the District Clerk's Office in your county to see if you are required to take a parenting course and, if so, get the cost, schedule, location, and other details. Take a look at **www.texasafcc.org** for parenting and co-parenting resources.

D. Child Support and Alimony

Child Support

Child support services. The Office of the Attorney General, Child Support Division, provides services for parents who wish to obtain or provide support for their children. Their services include (1) locating a noncustodial parent; (2) establishing paternity; (3) establishing and enforcing child support orders; (4) establishing and enforcing medical and dental support orders; (5) reviewing and adjusting child support payments; and (6) collecting and distributing child support payments.

Get an account. Support payments will be ordered through the Attorney General's Support Disbursement Unit (SDU), so you might as well set up an account now. Ask the court clerk for information about support services in your county or look on the Attorney General's web site at **www.oag.state.tx.us**.

Duration. The duty of support lasts until the child marries, dies, becomes self-supporting, begins active service in the U.S. military, or reaches his/her 18th birthday or beyond his/her 18th birthday until high school graduation **if** enrolled in an accredited program leading to a high school diploma and complies with the school's attendance requirements. Support can continue indefinitely for a child who is handicapped and unable to provide for him/herself. In any case, unless otherwise agreed in writing or expressly stated in a court order, child support terminates on the marriage, emancipation, or death of the child. Support survives the death of the obligor and the unpaid amount due becomes a lump sum charge against the obligor's estate.

Amount set by guidelines. Texas has statewide child support guidelines that judges are required to consider in every case. While not quite mandatory, they are *presumed* to be in the best interest of the child. Without a written agreement with your spouse, if you want to get a different amount ordered, you have to present evidence to show a good reason for departing from the guidelines (section 4 below). Then a judge *may* decide to order a different amount. Here's how the guidelines work:

1. Framework for child support guidelines

    a) The **"obligor"** (the parent who pays) will pay a percentage of his/her **"monthly net resources"** (net income) to the **"obligee"** (recipient).

    b) Parents can agree to any amount of support, even if it varies from the guidelines, but subject to approval of the court. The court will probably approve any *reasonable* agreement of the parties.

    c) On *written* request of either party within *10* days of the child support order, the judge must state the basis for the order, and if the award varied from the guidelines, the reason for the departure must be given.

d) The guidelines are applied without regard to gender of the obligor, obligee, or child. In setting child support, the judge may consider the needs of the child, the ability of the parent to contribute to the support of the child, any financial resources available for the support of the child, and the amount of possession of and access to a child by the parties.

2. Figuring obligor's monthly net resources (income)

Step 1. Figure Obligor's total gross annual income and divide by 12 to get a monthly average. "Gross resources" is much broader than the income figure used for tax purposes. It includes all benefits from personal effort—*everything*: (1) wage and salary income *before* deductions, and including overtime, commissions, tips, bonuses; (2) interest, dividends, royalties; (3) self-employment income; (4) net rental income (deducting only operating expenses and mortgage payments but not non-cash items such as depreciation); and (5) all other income—severance pay, retirement benefits, pensions, trust income, annuities, capital gains, Social Security benefits *other* than supplemental security income, unemployment benefits, disability and worker's compensation, gifts, income from notes, prizes, and spousal maintenance and alimony. Child support actually being received by an obligor (person paying support) is added to the obligor's resources. The only income *not* considered is public assistance received for children, payments for foster care, accounts receivable, and return of principal or capital.

When figuring income from self-employment (includes partnerships, joint ventures, close corporations), include all income and the value of benefits of any kind, allowing deductions only for ordinary expenses and amounts necessary to produce income, but not such things as depreciation, tax credits, or other non-cash deductions.

If Obligor has a spouse, his/her income is not included and needs of the spouse or step-children are not deducted.

Gone? If Obligor is gone, or you just can't get any information about his/her income, the law says wages shall be presumed to be equal to the prevailing federal minimum wage for a 40-hour week. So, get your child support order with this figure and when income information becomes available, you can apply for a modification. When you get an order for a missing spouse, the Attorney General's office can get involved in trying to find the obligor to get the support paid.

Step 2. Subtract allowed deductions. From total resources, subtract permitted deductions: (1) Social Security taxes; (2) federal income tax based on the tax rate for a single person claiming one personal exemption and the standard deduction; (3) state income tax; (4) union dues; and (5) expenses for health and dental insurance coverage for the obligor's child. If other minors are covered by the same plan, divide the total cost for the insurance by the total number of minors and apply the amount attributed to children of this case. The result after all deductions is the **monthly net resources.**

Tax charts. The Attorney General publishes tax charts for both employed and self-employed people to help you figure Obligor's after-tax income. First, read the instructions, then locate Obligor's monthly gross income in the left column and the chart gives you the monthly resources after taxes are paid. The 2013 charts are on the companion CD in the Forms folder. Look for updated or past charts at **www.oag.state.tx.us/cs/attorneys/attorneys_other_tax.shtml**. Unless Obligor lives out of state, the charts are reasonably accurate. **Note** that the charts give you after-tax inome—there might be additional deductions to take, as described in step 2 above.

Unemployed? Under employed? A judge can consider additional factors that increase or decrease Obligor's ability to pay. This includes valuable assets that do not produce an income, income-producing assets that have been voluntarily shifted to produce less income, and income that is significantly less than Obligor *could* earn because Obligor is voluntarily unemployed or underemployed. In such cases, the court can use at least the federal minimum wage or Obligor's earning potential—what he/she *could* earn.

3. Applying the guidelines

Guideline child support is a percentage of obligor's **net** monthly resources (income) as figured in steps 1 and 2 above. The percentage you apply depends on how many children the obligor and obligee have together and how many other children obligor has by other relationships, as shown in the table below. Here's how you use it.

No other children. Find the number of children you have and look on the first line below that (zero other children) to find the percentage of obligor's net monthly resources that must be paid for child support. For more than 5 children, the amount to be paid is "not less than" the amount for 5 children.

Other children. Use the left column to find the number of children from other relationships that obligor supports and follow that line across to the column under the number of children in the current case. This is the percentage of obligor's net monthly resources that must be paid for child support for the children of *this* case.

| | | Number of children in this case |||||||
		1	2	3	4	5	6	7
Number of	0	20.00%	25.00%	30.00%	35.00%	40.00%	40.00%	40.00%
other children	1	17.50	22.50	27.38	32.20	37.33	37.71	38.00
obligor has	2	16.00	20.63	25.20	30.33	35.43	36.00	36.44
a legal duty	3	14.75	19.00	24.00	29.00	34.00	34.67	35.20
to support	4	13.60	18.33	23.14	28.00	32.89	33.60	34.18
	5	13.33	17.86	22.50	27.22	32.00	32.73	33.33
	6	13.14	17.50	22.00	26.60	31.27	32.00	32.62
	7	13.00	17.22	21.60	26.09	30.67	31.38	32.00

If the obligor receives Social Security old age benefits, subtract from the guideline support the value of benefits paid to the child through Social Security old age benefits.

Income cap. The court will apply the guidelines to the obligor's first $7,500 of net monthly resources. If there is more, the court can order additional child support as appropriate, depending on the income of the parties and *proven* needs of the child.

Agreements of the spouses will be given great weight and consideration in court, but the judge has the power to make a different order if he/she thinks it is in the best interest of the child. The judge is especially likely to interfere if the support amount seems too low and the custodial parent also has low income.

When hearing your case, the judge is likely to want income tax returns for the past two years and current wage stubs, so take these with you to the hearing. Though not required, it is a good idea to take a financial statement to the hearing that shows the incomes and expenses of yourself and, if possible, your spouse. We provide a Financial Information worksheet in the forms section at the back of the book and on the CD that you can use to speak from and offer to the judge.

4. Factors for departing from the guideline

A judge can depart from the guideline only if shown evidence that the guideline amount would be unjust or inappropriate. The judge must consider all relevant factors, including those below. The full list is in Texas Family Code § 154.123, which can be found on the CD.

    a) the amount of the obligee's net resources, including the earning *potential* if the obligee is intentionally unemployed or underemployed, and any property the obligee may own;

    b) the age and needs of the child;

    c) child care expenses incurred by either party to maintain employment;

    d) whether either party has custody or support of another child, and amounts actually being paid under another child support order;

    e) whether either party has a car, housing, or other benefits furnished by an employer, a business, or another person;

    f) other deductions from wages or other compensation of the parties;

    g) cost of health insurance and dental insurance and any uninsured medical or dental expenses;

    h) extraordinary educational, health care or dental care, or other special expenses of the parties or of the child(ren);

    i) cost of travel to exercise access to or possession of a child;

    j) debts assumed by either party; and

    k) whether Social Security, disability or SSI benefits are received by a party on behalf of the child(ren).

5. Health care and dental care as additional support

Health care for a child, including dental care and vision care, is an essential part of the child support obligation, *in addition to* guideline support. The judge *must* see that the child's health and dental care has been provided for and must also consider how accessible the child's health and dental care is from the child's primary residence.

a) If health insurance and/or dental insurance is available for the child through the obligor's employment or membership in a union, trade association, or other organization at reasonable cost, the court **must** order the obligor to include the child in the obligor's health and/or dental insurance.

b) If not available under (a) above, but available through the obligee's employment or membership in a union or other organization at reasonable cost, the court **may** order the obligee to provide health and dental insurance for the child and order the obligor to pay additional child support for the actual cost of the health and dental insurance for the child.

c) If not available under (a) or (b) above, the court shall order obligor to provide health and/or dental insurance for the child if the court finds that such insurance is available to obligor from another source at reasonable cost.

d) If neither parent has access to private health or dental insurance at reasonable cost, the court shall order the custodial parent (or, to the extent permitted by law, the noncustodial parent) to immediately apply on behalf of the child for participation in whatever public medical and dental assistance program for which the child might be eligible, and that the obligor pay additional child support for the actual cost of such program.

e) If none of the above is available, the court shall order obligor to pay a reasonable amount (as determined by the court) each month for medical and dental support.

Reasonable cost. In the sections above, "reasonable cost" means that the cost of health insurance for all children the payer is required by court order to cover cannot exceed 9% of payer's **gross** annual income (see section 2, step 1, above) and dental insurance cannot exceed 1.5% of payer's gross annual income.

The court will require the parent who is ordered to provide health and/or dental insurance to produce evidence to the court's satisfaction that the parent has applied for and/or secured such insurance, or has otherwise taken action to provide health care and dental care coverage, as ordered by the court. A parent ordered to provide health or dental insurance who fails to do so is liable for necessary medical and dental expenses of the child, and the cost of health and dental insurance premiums, if any, paid on behalf of the child.

6. Method of payment and income withholding

Payments to the SDU. Judges will **always** order that child support must be paid through the State Disbursement Unit (SDU). The SDU will keep an accounting of payments, so either party can easily show what payments were made. Ask the court clerk for information about contacting them and setting up a support account.

Important! Payments that are not made through the SDU will not be not be counted and are generally considered gifts. So don't make informal payments to the receiving parent or the child and expect to get credit for it.

Income withholding. An income withholding order (IWO) is *required* in every case where there is child support.

The withholding order remains on file with the court until you ask the clerk's office to issue it to the obligor's employer, which will cost you a small fee. The court retains continuing jurisdiction until all support is paid.

If the obligor is unemployed, self-employed, or can't be located, you obviously need not bother having the order issued until circumstances change. You also have the option of agreeing not to have the order issued as long as support payments do not fall too far behind. But in cases where the children are receiving public assistance, the withholding order *must* be issued and delivered to Obligor's employer.

After support is ordered, it still remains to be collected. Call the Clerk's office in your county and ask for the location of the nearest support enforcement office and call that office to arrange to set up an account. Payment through the registry protects both parents because it gives an unbiased record of payment amounts and dates received. If you are not receiving your child support, the Attorney General's office provides collection services, and larger counties have domestic relations offices that enforce child support for county residents. To enforce child support, tax returns can be intercepted, licenses suspended, wages garnished, and the nonpaying parent can be jailed.

The withholding order requires the name, address, and phone number of the obligor and the obligor's employer, if known; the obligor's Social Security number and driver's license number; and Social Security numbers for the child(ren). Each parent is required to give written notice to the other, to the court, and to the State Case Registry Office 60 days in advance of changes. If you don't know 60 days in advance, you *must* notify the other party within five days of the date you find out. If you have a good reason why you don't want your spouse to know where you are, you do not have to list your own address in public documents.

An alternative. In cases where it seems appropriate, the judge has the power to order any parent's property set aside and administered in a trust for the benefit of the child. The court can also order any parent to make a lump-sum payment in addition to or in lieu of periodic payments. These are unusual steps, so if you wish something along these lines, you should consult an attorney.

Life insurance. Parents can agree or the judge can order that the obligor obtain life insurance to secure support in the event of his/her death.

Retroactive child support. The court can make an order for retroactive child support if a petition requesting it is filed not later than the child's 22nd birthday.

Modification. Either party can come back to court to modify the support order if circumstances have changed significantly since the previous order was made. The Attorney General's Office provides a free review of child support for possible modification once every three years, or more often if there has been a change in circumstances. This service may also be available through the Domestic Relations Office in larger counties. Contact these offices for information.

The IRS test for who qualifies to take the dependency exemption depends on who has provided the most financial support. The IRS usually presumes that the "domicile" parent, the one the child lived with most of the year, qualifies to take the exemption. The "non-domicile" parent can claim the exemption only if he or she contributed over half of the child's support *and* the domicile parent agrees to sign IRS Form 8332, which turns over the dependency exemption to the non-domicile parent. In families where the obligor earns a lot more than the obligee, it makes sense to do this, because the family will save on the obligor's taxes and can agree to share the tax savings the obligor realizes. Run the taxes both ways and share the amount saved.

Spousal maintenance (alimony)

Spousal maintenance (alimony) can be ordered for any amount and for any length of time if both parties agree to it in a written marital settlement agreement (chapter E), but absent agreement of the parties, the power of a court to order alimony is limited.

Factors. In determining eligibility, duration and amount of alimony, the court will consider all relevant factors, including: (a) recipient's financial resources after the divorce; (b) time necessary to acquire education and employment skills, and availability and practicality of such education and training; (c) duration of the marriage; (d) age, employment history, earning ability, and physical and emotional condition of recipient; (e) effect of child support payments, if any, on each spouse's ability to be self-supporting; (f) wrongful acts of either spouse affecting their jointly held property; (g) contributions by one spouse to the education, training or earning ability of the other spouse; (h) property brought to the marriage by either spouse; (i) contributions of a spouse as homemaker; (j) marital misconduct, including adultery or cruelty during the marriage; (k) any history of family violence.

Eligibility for alimony. For an ex-spouse, "self-supporting" means being able to meet minimum reasonable needs. Absent agreement of the parties, alimony can be awarded **only** if the recipient lacks sufficient property after divorce to be self-supporting **and** (1) the marriage lasted 10 years or longer and the recipient lacks the ability to be self-supporting, **or** (2) the recipient has an incapacitating mental or physical disability, or is the custodian of a child of the marriage of any age who requires substantial personal care due to mental or physical disability, **or** (3) if, within two years of the divorce suit, payor was convicted of or received deferred adjudication for violence during the marriage against recipient or recipient's child. **But**, unless the recipient can show a good reason why it should not apply, it is presumed that alimony is not warranted unless the recipient has been diligent in earning sufficient income or developing necessary skills to become self-supporting during the period since separation.

Duration. The duration of alimony should be the shortest reasonable period to allow the recipient to become self-supporting unless the recipient's ability to do so is substantially diminished due to physical or mental disability, or recipient is the custodian of a young or disabled child of the marriage, or some other compelling impediment, in which case the duration can be for as long as the condition continues.

Unless the parties have a written settlement agreement that states otherwise, a court can't order alimony that lasts longer than:

- 5 years if the marriage lasted less than 10 years, but **only** if the payor was convicted of or received a deferred adjudication for violence against the recipient or recipient's child that took place during the marriage.

- 5 years if the marriage lasted from 10 to 20 years

- 7 years if the marriage lasted from 20 to 30 years

- 10 years if the marriage lasted more than 30 years

Of course, the court can decide to order alimony for a shorter time than these limits.

Amount. A judge can't order monthly maintenance that is more than (a) $5,000 per month, or (b) 20% of the obligor's average monthly gross income, whichever is less. Even then, the judge is to order an amount only sufficient to cover minimum reasonable needs of the recipient, considering employment and property owned after marriage. Gross income for spousal maintenance includes all wage and salary income and any other compensation for personal services (including commissions, overtime pay, tips, and bonuses); interest, dividends, and royalty income; self-employment income; net rental income (defined as rent after deducting operating expenses and mortgage payments, but not non cash items such as depreciation); and all other income actually being received, including severance pay, retirement benefits, pensions, trust income, annuities, capital gains, unemployment benefits, interest income from notes regardless of the source (but not the repayment of principal), gifts and prizes, maintenance, and alimony. Gross income does **not** include return of principal or capital; accounts receivable; benefits from federal public assistance programs; benefits paid under Temporary Assistance for Needy Families program; payments for foster care of a child; Veterans service-connected disability compensation; supplemental security income (SSI), social security benefits, and disability benefits; or workers compensation benefits.

Termination. Alimony terminates on death of either party or the remarriage of the recipient. Except as stated in the Decree, all other terminations require a motion and a hearing, including allegations of cohabitation or romantic relationship. Unpaid arrears remain in effect.

Income withholding (IWO). The court *may* issue an order for income withholding for spousal maintenance, but even if the amount is based on a written agreement of the spouses, the IWO cannot be for more than the amount and duration that a court could have ordered (as described on the previous page).

Health insurance for spouses

Under federal law (COBRA), spouses and children who will lose their health coverage due to divorce or legal separation from the primary wage-earner are entitled to continued coverage and benefits for up to three years at similar rates (100% of what the employer pays), but now at their own expense. The wage-earner may be required to pay for the insurance of the children (see page 61), but the spouse will have to pay for his or her own coverage.

Limitations. Among other things, COBRA does not apply to the federal government, church related organizations, or employers with fewer than 20 employees. Also, if you are presently covered by a health plan provided through *your* employer and it provides coverage comparable to your spouse's plan, your spouse's employer is not required to offer you COBRA coverage.

To find out if you are covered by COBRA, contact the administrator of the health care plan that provides the employed spouse's insurance. Alternatively, you can call the Employee Benefits Security Administration toll-free at (866) 444-3272 if you have questions about your COBRA rights. In either case, you'll first want to have a copy of the health care policy or your proof of coverage card so the person you speak to can identify the exact employer and policy involved.

You must give notice. To exercise your COBRA right, you *must* give written notice of the divorce or legal separation to the health care plan administrator within 60 days after your Decree is signed by the judge. The plan must then give you notice within 14 days of your right to elect COBRA coverage. The plan *cannot* insist on new evidence of insurability. Compare rates for coverage available to you under other alternatives before you decide.

E. Marital Settlement Agreements

We have several times discussed the impressive advantages of a divorce by agreement, and now it is at last time to show you how this is actually done.

Marital settlement agreements are subject to the approval of the court. Judges are especially likely to take a close interest in the arrangements you have made for the custody and support of your child/ren, if any. Still, assuming that the agreement appears to be generally fair, it is almost certain that it will be approved.

In matters of child support and custody, the court retains its power to modify its orders no matter what the parties have agreed. This means that in the future, should circumstances change in some important way, either party can come back into court for a different order concerning the best interests of the minor children.

For a marital agreement to be enforceable in the future, it must fulfill two minimum conditions:

- The agreement must be generally fair.
- It must have been made without undue pressure, force, mistake, or fraud. No bullying or cheating, in other words.

We are going to show you two different ways to go about a divorce by agreement. The first is the Approved Decree, and then there is the full-blown marital settlement agreement.

1. The approved Decree

This is an easy way to do an agreed divorce. By this method, you prepare the Decree well ahead of time (chapter 7), and both parties sign their approval of it. Under this method, your property, if there is any, should be itemized in the Petition.

Read the rest of this book until you understand when and how the Decree is used, then prepare a Decree that is agreeable to both you and your spouse. Then, on the last page, both parties date and sign their approval of the Decree. You will need the original and three copies: two to take to court and a copy of the signed Decree for Respondent after it has been filed and stamped. Best to make an extra in case you need it later. Follow all the other instructions in this book, and when you get to the hearing, present the approved Decree to the judge. Tell the judge that the Decree has been agreed to and approved by both of you and you recognize your spouse's signature (or saw him/her sign it). After the hearing, give the Respondent a certified (stamped) copy of the Decree to show that the agreement was completed.

2. The marital settlement agreement

A settlement agreement is like any other contract. It will be valid and binding so long as the meaning is clear and unambiguous and it is entered into freely and voluntarily with **full disclosure** of all facts made by both parties well before signing, and it does not appear on the face of it to be shockingly unfair.

Disclosure. If you have property or debts of much value, you should each complete a list of all assets and debts with approximate values. You can use the property checklist on the CD. Give each other a copy of your list at least a week before signing the agreement so you each have time to think about it. Failure to give full disclosure could lead to trouble in the future and possible invalidation of your agreement.

If you have real estate or a significant amount in a pension plan or retirement fund, use DealMaker software (see inside front cover) instead of this simple agreement. If you have trouble understanding this agreement, or have questions, or uncertainty about what to do, get help from a family law attorney. See chapter A8 about how to find the right kind of help.

Every situation is different, so there is no one form that will be just right in every situation. The simple contract here is included so you can see what one looks like, how it works. You can use it as a guide in preparing your own agreement. Use parts that apply to you and disregard others, and change it to suit your own case, but do **not** leave out paragraphs VIII, IX, X, or XI.

Joint custody (Joint Managing Conservatorship). A written agreement for JMC *must* (1) state which parent has the right to designate the primary residence of the child and state whether that right is limited to a specified geographic area; (2) specify the rights and duties of each parent toward the child; and (3) include provisions to minimize disruption of the child's education, daily routine and friendships (what this means is not specified). The easiest way to do this would be to attach a completed Conservatorship Order and Standard Possession Order to your agreement, initialed by both parents, and incorporated into your agreement by reference. The forms are in the back of this book and on the companion CD. See chapter 7 for more about these exhibits.

If you decide to make your own contract, study the Decree first and see if there are any terms in the Decree that you want to include in your agreement. When done, make an original, a copy for your spouse, and three copies to take to the hearing with you. Get it signed before you go to court, of course.

For your convenience, the agreement in this chapter is also found in the MSA folder on our CD so you can edit it to make your own agreement.

Marital Settlement Contract

I,   , Husband,

and I,   , Wife, agree as follows:

I. GENERALLY: We are now husband and wife. We were married on   , and separated on   . We make this agreement with reference to the following facts:

    A. Children: There are

        ☐ no children, and none are expected.

        ☐ the following minor children of the parties
           (list by full name and give sex and birth date for each child).

    B. Our marriage has become insupportable because of discord or conflict of personalities such that there is no reasonable expectation for reconciliation. For this reason, we now desire to settle our mutual rights and duties as set forth below.

II. SEPARATION: We agree to live separately and apart, and, except for the duties and obligations imposed and assumed under this agreement, each shall be free from interference and control of the other as fully as if he or she were single. We each agree not to molest, interfere with, or harass the other.

III. CUSTODY OF CHILDREN:

☐ The (Wife/Husband) shall be the Managing Conservator of the child/ren, to have full parental rights, duties, and powers, subject only to the rights of the (Husband/ Wife), as Possessory Conservator, to visit with and temporarily take possession of the child/ren as specified in the Possession Order, attached to and incorporated herein.

☐ The Wife and Husband shall be Joint Managing Conservators of the child/ren, to have full parental rights, duties and powers as specified in the Conservatorship Order and Possession Order, attached to and incorporated herein.

    (Complete those forms, attach to this agreement, both parties initial each page.)

IV. SUPPORT OF CHILDREN: Subject to the power of the court to modify these terms, (Husband/Wife) shall pay to (Wife/Husband), as and for child support, the sum of $ per month, beginning on the   day of   , 20   , and continuing until the first to occur of the following: the child reaches the age of 18, except that if the child is fully enrolled in an accredited program leading to a high school degree and the child complies with the attendance requirements of the school, then child support shall continue until the end of the month in which the child graduates; the child marries; the child dies; the child becomes self-supporting; enlists in the U.S. armed forces or is otherwise emancipated.

(If there is more than one child, repeat the next sentence as many times as necessary until only one child is left to support. The amount paid after each reduction of support must equal or exceed the child support guidelines for the number of children still being supported.)

Thereafter, (Husband/Wife) shall pay to (Wife/Husband) as and for child support the sum of $ per month beginning on the   (same as above) day of the first month following the occurrence of any of the above described events.

This obligation shall survive the death of the obligor. This clause of our agreement shall end if obligor becomes the Managing Conservator.

If there is a handicapped child, add this: Support for *(name of child)* shall continue beyond the age of eighteen, as said child requires continuous care and personal supervision and is unlikely to become self-supporting.

Optional terms:

In addition, during the term of the support obligation for the child/ren, (Husband/Wife) shall

☐ carry and maintain life insurance in the amount of $, naming the child/ren as beneficiary(ies).

☐ carry and maintain ☐ medical ☐ dental ☐ hospital insurance for the child/children's benefit.

☐ pay for ☐ required ☐ extraordinary medical and dental expenses.

V. PAYMENTS TO SPOUSE: In order to fully discharge all obligations arising from the marriage, other than division of property, (Husband/Wife) agrees to pay to (Wife/Husband) the sum of $ per month, payable on the   day of each month, beginning on   , 20   , and continuing until:

- ☐ the death of (you can name one or both parties)
- ☐ the remarriage of the recipient
- ☐ some other date or condition (*specify*)

These spousal maintenance payments ☐ may be ☐ may not be the subject of an income withholding order.

VI. DIVISION OF PROPERTY AND DEBTS:

We have each made a full and honest disclosure in writing to the other of all current finances and assets, and each enters into this agreement in reliance thereon. Each warrants to the other and declares under penalty of perjury that the assets and liabilities divided in this agreement constitute all of their marital assets and liabilities.

We each declare that we understand that failure to make a full and accurate disclosure as required by law could result in the Decree being set aside and that if a motion to set aside the Decree is brought by either of us, each must provide the Court with copies of his/her disclosure.

- A. Property Transferred to Wife: Husband transfers and quitclaims to Wife as her sole and separate property the following items: (*list—include items that are already Wife's separate property. How to list property, see notes for page 6 of the Petition in chapter 5*).

- B. Property Transferred to Husband: Wife transfers and quitclaims to Husband as his sole and separate property the following items: (*list—include items that are already Husband's separate property*).

Note: If there is a community interest in a pension plan, be sure to list and dispose of it in this section. To divide a pension or retirement fund you will need the help of an attorney who specializes in dividing pensions.

Note: Here is an alternative way to deal with property for small estates: Husband and Wife agree that they have already divided the property to their mutual satisfaction, and each hereby transfers and quitclaims to the other any and all interest in any property in the possession of the other, and agrees that whatever property the other may possess is now the sole and separate property of the other.

C. Insurance: Wife (or Husband) is expressly retained as the beneficiary of the following insurance policies: (*description*)— *or*—Wife (or Husband) is no longer the beneficiary of any insurance policy carried by Husband (or Wife).

D. Debts Assumed by Husband: Husband shall pay and hold Wife harmless from the following debts: (*list and give specific description of each one*).

E. Debts Assumed by Wife: Wife shall pay and hold Husband harmless from the following debts: (*list and give specific description of each one*).

VII. TAXES: The parties agree that:

Any tax refunds for the current tax year will be distributed as follows: (*specify*).

Any tax deficiencies for the current tax year shall be paid as follows: (*specify*).

VIII. EXECUTION OF INSTRUMENTS: Each party agrees to execute and deliver any documents, make all endorsements, and do all acts that are necessary or convenient to carry out the terms of this agreement.

IX. APPROVAL BY COURT: At the divorce proceeding, this agreement shall be presented to the court for incorporation into the Decree, and the parties shall, by the terms of the Decree, be ordered to comply with all terms of this agreement.

X. DISCLOSURES: Each party has made a full disclosure to the other of his or her current assets and income, and each enters into this agreement in reliance thereupon.

XI. BINDING EFFECT: This agreement, and each provision of it, is expressly made binding upon the heirs, assigns, executors, administrators, representatives, and successors in interest of each party.

Dated: _____   _____
                                                        Husband

Dated: _____   _____
                                                        Wife

Part Two

How to Do
Your Own Divorce

1. Introducing the Forms

A complete set of forms for doing your own uncontested divorce is in the back of this book. The same forms, plus several others, are on the companion CD, for easy use on a Windows or Mac computer.

Good news! There are **a lot** of forms in this book, but the good news is that no one uses them all—just use the ones you need.

Here is a list of forms you are likely to use:

Every case

> **Petition** — *Basic info about your marriage, tells the court what you want*
> **Case Information Sheet** — *A statistics form*
> **Statistics Form** — *Another statistics form*
> **Final Decree of Divorce** and exhibits — *The whole enchilada: findings of facts and orders*
> and
> **Waiver of Service** — *If Respondent will sign, it says "I got the Petition, go ahead without me"*
> or **Information for Server** — *If Respondent is served with the Petition*

Special situations

> **Orders Re Property and Debts** — *If you need orders about property or debts*
> **Certificate of Last Known Address** — *Default cases (see chapter A5)*
> **Military Status Affidavit** — *Default cases (see chapter A5 and Checklist C below)*
> **Income Withholding Order** — *If child or spousal support is ordered*

Cases with minor children

> **Conservatorship Order** — *Custody and visitation*
> **Standard Possession Order** — *The care schedule for who gets child/ren when*
> **Child Support Order** — *Who pays, how much, how long*
> **Medical Support Order** — *Health care and insurance for children*
> **Dental Support Order** — *Dental care and insurance for children*
> **Out of State Parent Affidavit** — *If a parent lives outside TX*
> **Property Owned by Children** — *If a child owns significant property*
> **Family Information** — *Information about parents and child/ren*

Other useful forms

The book and CD have additional forms that will be useful to some people, including a property checklist, an information sheet for the officer serving the Petition, kits for publishing your notice when your spouse is missing or evasive, a financial information form to take to the hearing, a power of attorney to transfer title to a vehicle, and a warranty deed to transfer title to marital real estate.

2. Checklists

A. Preplanning Checklist

Here's how you go about getting your divorce:

1. Divorce by agreement or by default?

It is much easier and better if you can divorce by agreement, but more common for it to be done by default. Review chapters A 5 and 9 and chapter E. Try to work toward an agreed divorce, but if it can't be done, or if you do not want to try, proceed by default.

2. Decisions that must be made

- How to divide the property (chapter B), *and*

- Arrangements for child custody, visitation, and support and spousl support, if any (chapters C and D).

3. Plan how to give notice to your spouse

If you can proceed by agreement, you will also have your spouse sign the Waiver of Service and the Decree, most conveniently done when you sign your agreement. Even without an agreement, see if your spouse will sign the Waiver. If not, have the Petition served personally (chapter 6).

If your spouse successfully evades service, or if you can't find your spouse, you have to serve notice by publication or posting (chapter 6). A kit with forms and instructions for doing this are on the companion CD or you can get them separately at **www.nolodivorce.com/TX**.

The Agreed Divorce

This is by far the best, smoothest way to get a divorce. In an agreed divorce, Respondent must be willing to sign the Waiver of Service and a written agreement and/or the Decree. If you have kids, real estate, a lot of property or the desire to know ahead of time what a judge will order, you'll be better off with a written agreement. Review chapter E, decide whether to use the approved Decree or a written agreement, then prepare the forms you need to use. Best actually to sign the agreement and/or the Decree as early in your case as possible, but later is better than never.

B. Checklist for the Agreed Divorce

1. Prepare: Petition (chapter 5)
    Case Information Sheet
    Got kids? Ask clerk if parents have to attend a class.
    A parent lives outside TX? Out of State Parent Affidavit

2. Notice to spouse. Ideally, you'll get signatures on the Waiver of Service, your agreement, and the Decree as early as possible—in that order of importance if you can't get them all done at once. The Waiver of Service has to be signed before a notary. If you have an agreement, Respondent *must* also sign the Decree—so, if possible, sign the settlement agreement and the Decree at the same time.

3. File your Petition and pay the filing fee with cash or a money order (chapter 4). Ask the clerk if your county has Standing Orders (page 100) that must be attached to the Petition.

4. Prepare: Decree signed by both parties
    and attachments as needed (chapter 7)
    Got kids? Exhibits 2–6 Orders re: children
    and the Family Information Form
    Property or debts? Orders Re Property and Debts
    Child or spousal support? Income Withholding Order
    and maybe a Request to Issue Withholding Order (ch. 9)
    Statistics form (chapter 8)

    Optional, but recommended when support is requested:
    the Financial Information form.

5. At least 61 days after you filed your Petition, set a court date and go to the Hearing (chapter 11).

The Default Divorce

Respondent was properly served (chapter 6) but filed no documents with the court: no Answer, no Waiver; nothing.

C. Checklist for the Default Divorce

1. Prepare: Petition (chapter 5)
   Case Information Sheet
   Got kids? Ask clerk if parents have to attend a class.
   A parent lives outside TX? Out of State Parent Affidavit

2. File your Petition and pay the filing fee with cash or a money order (chapter 4). Ask the clerk if your county has Standing Orders (page 100) that must be attached to your Petition

3. Notice to spouse. See if your spouse will sign the Waiver of Serivice. If not, arrange for the Petition to be served. Ask the clerk if they can help with this (chapter 6B).

4. Prepare: Decree and attachments as needed (chapter 7)
   Certificate of Last Known Address
   Military Status Affidavit (chapter 10)
   Got kids? Exhibits 2–6 Orders re: children
       and the Family In Formation form.
   Property or debts? Orders Re Property and Debts
   Child or spousal support? Income Withholding Order
       and maybe a Request to Issue Withholding Order (ch. 9)
   Statistics form (chapter 8)

   Optional, but recommended when support is requested: the Financial Information form.

5. At least 61 days after you filed your Petition, set a court date and go to the Hearing (chapter 11).

3. How to Use the Forms

Good news! Don't be put off by the large number of forms in this book—you won't need them all. Many forms are for different kinds of cases or special situations. Just use the forms you need. In chapters that follow, you'll find a description of each form with detailed instructions on how to fill it out. But first, here are some general instructions that apply to all forms.

There are paper forms in the back of this book and computer forms on the companion CD. They are completely legal and they will work for you. This book and our forms have been working just fine throughout Texas since 1980!

Our forms bear a strong resemblance to other sets of forms that judges are used to seeing. This is intentional as there is some advantage to this. Texas judges are buried to their ears in divorce cases, so it always goes much easier when your forms resemble forms they are used to and your case looks pretty much like all the others before and after it. This lets the judge settle into a comfortable routine and move along quickly.

If any of your requests are unusual (giving custody of a child to a non-parent, or asking to change the husband's name to Florence, or taking $250 for support from a person who makes $100,000), then you are inviting some extra questions and explanations. It always goes much easier when your case is pretty much like all the others before and after it.

A. General instructions

These instructions show you how to use the forms that come with this book. Follow them carefully and they will help eliminate errors.

Using the forms

1. Keep all papers and receipts orderly, neat, and in one safe place.

2. First make a copy of the complete set of computer or paper forms so you'll have a work set and a blank set. Additional sets of forms can be purchased and downloaded at **www.nolodivorce.com/TX** or by using the coupon in the back of this book.

3. **Computer forms.** You'll find a complete set of forms on the CD that comes in the back of this book. They are PDF files that can be filled out and printed on any computer. They have been specially enabled so that, if you use Adobe Reader 8.0 or later, you can save the data you enter by using the File > Save As function. **Highlighted fields** make forms much easier to use. If fields are **not** highlighted when you open a form, just click the "Highlight" button in the upper right corner of the window.

To use the PDF forms, all you have to do is check boxes and enter information as instructed. Additional sets of fillable PDF forms can be purchased separately at our site or by using the order coupon in the back.

4. **Paper forms.** Tear out the forms and make two or three good, clear copies of the blank forms. You want to fill out and file a set of the copies so they will all be an exact 8.5 x 11 in size. Use a blue ballpoint pen and print very neatly so the judge doesn't have to strain to read your forms. Just follow our instructions to check boxes and fill in blanks by hand. Before you use ink, you might work on a set in pencil and then make a clean set, filled out very neatly for the court.

5. When your forms are accurate and complete, make three copies of your completed forms. Take the originals and the copies when you file them and ask the clerk to file stamp your copies to show proof that they were filed and when.

Notarizing documents

At least two documents you are likely to use will need to be notarized when signed, including the Waiver of Service, which is commonly used and very important. A notary can be located in the yellow pages or at most banks and many real estate offices or copy shops; call around, ask what they charge to notarize a document.

Military Personnel. Military people on duty overseas will probably not be able to find a notary, but they can have documents notarized by any of the many officers in their command structure who have been given notary powers.

B. The caption

At the top of each legal document is a heading, called a caption, which is filled out like this:

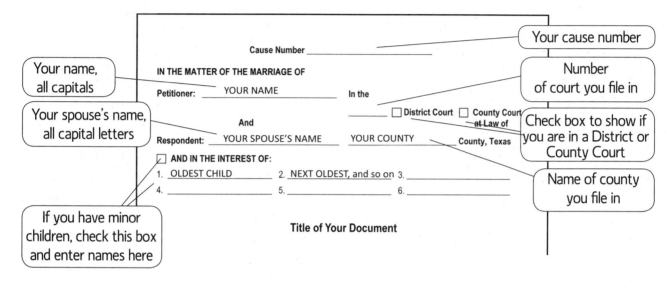

The Cause Number (case number) and the Judicial District Number (number of your court) are assigned when you file the Petition, and after that must be filled in exactly the same on any document you file. The Court Number identifies your court, the one that will be handling and hearing your case. The Cause Number is their identification for your file and case.

If there are minor children of this marriage, check the box "And In The Interest Of:" and enter their names in the numbered spaces, oldest to youngest in order. If there are no minor children, do not check that box and leave the lines blank. Include any legally adopted children. If the wife is pregnant, do not start your own divorce until the child is born.

C. Petitioner/Respondent

The Petitioner is the spouse who files the papers and goes to court. The Respondent is the other spouse. Apart from possibly signing a Waiver and/or written agreement, the Respondent does nothing—files no papers, does not go to court.

D. Pro Se

This term appears in a few places on the forms and you may hear it in court. It is a legal Latin term meaning "for self," which indicates that you are appearing as your own attorney.

E. Names

Use the full legal names of parties and children. You must be consistent, so names will appear exactly the same way each time, including signatures. The court will not know, for instance, that John Smith, J. W. Smith, John W. Smith, and J. Wilson Smith are different names for the same person. It is good form to type the names in capitals. Use the names in normal order—last names go last. Use the wife's married name unless the form requests her maiden name.

F. Protecting privacy

You can omit private information in cases if you can present the judge with **facts** that give rise to a reasonable concern for the safety of yourself or a child. In this case, check the information you want to protect at item 8 on your Petition and omit that information from documents you file. Information that might be sensitive includes such things as your home address, home phone, mailing address, work phone, employer's name, work address, social security number, and driver's license number. At your hearing, the judge is likely to require some factual evidence, at least your testimony, to show your concern is reasonable.

Sealing documents. In order to protect the parties and children from the threat of identity theft, in your Petition you can ask the judge to seal from public view the attachments to the Decree that contain identifying information. It is entirely up to the judge's discretion whether to grant this request, as it is not mandated by law.

G. Copies

Type each form neatly, check for errors, then make four copies of each page on a high-quality copy machine. When there is more than one page to a document, staple the pages together in the upper left-hand corner.

The court always gets the original of each form, the Respondent gets a copy, and you keep a copy for your files. Thus you need an original and two copies of each document, but you should make two extra copies in case you want them later. It is an especially good idea to have extra copies of the Decree. When you file the Decree, have the clerk certify your copies, and keep them for future use.

H. Change of contact information

After you file your Petition, if any of your contact information changes, it is **essential** to notify the court and serve the other side by mail with notice of the change. Use the form "Notice of Change of Address," number 14 on the CD.

4. How to File Your Papers

A. The courts, the clerks and the fees

The county in which you file is determined by which spouse satisfies residency requirements (chapter A, section 3c) and is usually the county you live in, but it could be the county where Respondent lives. In most counties, your papers will be filed at the District Clerk's Office, but in a few counties family cases are handled in County Courts at Law and papers would be filed at the County Clerk's Office.

Locating your court. If you have access to the Internet, see if your county and your court have a web site where you will find the address and phone number, and possibly they will post important information like local forms and rules that you will want to know about. Start by looking on our companion CD, where we keep a list of District Courts sorted by county, with addresses, phone numbers and links to web sites. Or, go to your nearest courthouse and ask around, or look in the phone book and call. They will be listed under the name of your county, or under "Government."

Filing. Filing papers is easy. Just take them to the District Clerk's Office and hand them to the clerk and pay the filing fee. You could mail them in with a self-addressed stamped envelope, but doing it in person saves you wondering if they got there, if they are acceptable, and when they are coming back.

When you file your Petition, the clerk will give you a cause number and fill in the number of the Judicial District in your caption. From this time on, all documents must have your cause number and the court number on them.

Standing Orders. Ask the clerk if your county has standing orders (see page 100). If so, a copy of it must be attached to your Petition when you file it and serve it. Ask if there are any local rules you should know about. Always ask the clerk to file stamp your copies of whatever documents you file.

e-filing. Texas courts are moving steadily into the modern world by phasing in mandatory electronic filing (e-file), starting January 2014 for the largest counties. People doing their own divorce *may* file electronically, but are not required to. Not yet, not real soon. So, for the foreseeable future you can continue to file as instructed in this book. However, if you might want to try e-filing, visit **www.texfile.com** and view the video showing how to register as an independent (self-represented) user and how to file documents electronically.

Fees. When you have the clerk's Office on the phone, ask how much the filing fee will be. Fees depend on whether there are children and whether Respondent will sign a

Waiver or if a Citation will have to be issued. Tell the clerk you want to file a divorce petition with or without children, and whether there will be a Waiver or if instead you want a Citation to be served. Then ask the filing fee.

Fees must be paid by cash, money order, or a bank check made payable to "District Clerk, (name of county), Texas." Be sure to get a receipt and keep it in your file. If you can't afford the fees, you can file an Affidavit of Inability to Pay—a sworn statement about your finances—and the fees might be waived. See Appendix A.

If your case will not have a Waiver signed by Respondent, a Citation will have to be prepared and issued by the clerk, and forwarded to an officer for service. Unless you want to hire a professional, ask if they will forward the Citation for service.

Clerks can't give legal advice because they are not attorneys. But if they want to, they can be very helpful with matters related to filing papers and how procedures are handled in their office. Don't be afraid to ask questions. You should also remember that most employees of the clerk's offices are (or feel they are) overworked and underpaid. A big smile and politeness on your part can go a long way toward getting your questions answered.

The Case Information Sheet. When you file your Petition and other documents, you must also file a Case Information Sheet, used by courts for statistical purposes.

B. The Case Information sheet

When you file your Petition, you must also file this form. Get it from the clerk or use the fillable form on the CD. If filing electronically (chapter 4), this can **not** be the top sheet. The form can't be used for any other purpose and it can't be admitted as evidence. You probably won't need them, but for your convenience the official instructions for this form are on the companion CD.

How to fill it out

Note 1. <u>Left column</u>. Enter your contact information and sign where indicated. If you don't have e-mail or fax, enter "N/A." <u>Right column</u>. Enter the names of the parties named in the caption of your case and check the box "*Pro Se* Plaintiff/Petitioner."

Note 2. At the top of the 4th column, under "Marriage Relationship," under "*Divorce*," check the box "With Children" or "No Children," whichever describes your case.

Note 3. Leave this blank. None of the choices are applicable to the kind of divorce case described in this book.

Note 4. Leave this blank. It does not apply to family law cases.

The Case Information Sheet

CIVIL CASE INFORMATION SHEET

CAUSE NUMBER *(FOR CLERK USE ONLY)*: _____ COURT *(FOR CLERK USE ONLY)*: _____

STYLED _____
(e.g., John Smith v. All American Insurance Co; In re Mary Ann Jones; In the Matter of the Estate of George Jackson)

A civil case information sheet must be completed and submitted when an original petition or application is filed to initiate a new civil, family law, probate, or mental health case or when a post-judgment petition for modification or motion for enforcement is filed in a family law case. The information should be the best available at the time of filing.

Note 1

1. Contact information for person completing case information sheet:		Names of parties in case:	Person or entity completing sheet is:
Name:	Email:	Plaintiff(s)/Petitioner(s):	☐Attorney for Plaintiff/Petitioner ☐*Pro Se* Plaintiff/Petitioner ☐Title IV-D Agency ☐Other: _____
Address:	Telephone:		Additional Parties in Child Support Case:
City/State/Zip:	Fax:	Defendant(s)/Respondent(s):	Custodial Parent:
Signature:	State Bar No:		Non-Custodial Parent: Presumed Father:
		[Attach additional page as necessary to list all parties]	

Note 2

2. Indicate case type, or identify the most important issue in the case *(select only 1)*:

Civil			Family Law	

Contract	Injury or Damage	Real Property	Marriage Relationship	Post-judgment Actions (non-Title IV-D)
Debt/Contract ☐Consumer/DTPA ☐Debt/Contract ☐Fraud/Misrepresentation ☐Other Debt/Contract: *Foreclosure* ☐Home Equity—Expedited ☐Other Foreclosure ☐Franchise ☐Insurance ☐Landlord/Tenant ☐Non-Competition ☐Partnership ☐Other Contract:	☐Assault/Battery ☐Construction ☐Defamation *Malpractice* ☐Accounting ☐Legal ☐Medical ☐Other Professional Liability: ☐Motor Vehicle Accident ☐Premises *Product Liability* ☐Asbestos/Silica ☐Other Product Liability List Product: ☐Other Injury or Damage:	☐Eminent Domain/ Condemnation ☐Partition ☐Quiet Title ☐Trespass to Try Title ☐Other Property: **Related to Criminal Matters** ☐Expunction ☐Judgment Nisi ☐Non-Disclosure ☐Seizure/Forfeiture ☐Writ of Habeas Corpus— Pre-indictment ☐Other:	☐Annulment ☐Declare Marriage Void *Divorce* ☐With Children ☐No Children **Other Family Law** ☐Enforce Foreign Judgment ☐Habeas Corpus ☐Name Change ☐Protective Order ☐Removal of Disabilities of Minority ☐Other:	☐Enforcement ☐Modification—Custody ☐Modification—Other **Title IV-D** ☐Enforcement/Modification ☐Paternity ☐Reciprocals (UIFSA) ☐Support Order **Parent-Child Relationship** ☐Adoption/Adoption with Termination ☐Child Protection ☐Child Support ☐Custody or Visitation ☐Gestational Parenting ☐Grandparent Access ☐Parentage/Paternity ☐Termination of Parental Rights ☐Other Parent-Child:

Employment	Other Civil	
☐Discrimination ☐Retaliation ☐Termination ☐Workers' Compensation ☐Other Employment:	☐Administrative Appeal ☐Antitrust/Unfair Competition ☐Code Violations ☐Foreign Judgment ☐Intellectual Property	☐Lawyer Discipline ☐Perpetuate Testimony ☐Securities/Stock ☐Tortious Interference ☐Other:

Tax	Probate & Mental Health	
☐Tax Appraisal ☐Tax Delinquency ☐Other Tax	*Probate/Wills/Intestate Administration* ☐Dependent Administration ☐Independent Administration ☐Other Estate Proceedings	☐Guardianship—Adult ☐Guardianship—Minor ☐Mental Health ☐Other:

Note 3

3. Indicate procedure or remedy, if applicable *(may select more than 1)*:

☐Appeal from Municipal or Justice Court ☐Arbitration-related ☐Attachment ☐Bill of Review ☐Certiorari ☐Class Action	☐Declaratory Judgment ☐Garnishment ☐Interpleader ☐License ☐Mandamus ☐Post-judgment	☐Prejudgment Remedy ☐Protective Order ☐Receiver ☐Sequestration ☐Temporary Restraining Order/Injunction ☐Turnover

Note 4

4. Indicate damages sought *(do not select if it is a family law case)*:
☐Less than $100,000, including damages of any kind, penalties, costs, expenses, pre-judgment interest, and attorney fees
☐Less than $100,000 and non-monetary relief
☐Over $100, 000 but not more than $200,000
☐Over $200,000 but not more than $1,000,000
☐Over $1,000,000

Rev 2/13

5. The Petition

The Petition states basic information about your marriage and tells the court what you want done. When it is served on the Respondent, it gives notice of what is happening in court. If the Respondent declines to respond, then the judge is free to assume that all the facts stated in it are true, and the Petitioner's requests are very likely to be granted.

How to fill it out

Fill out the Petition as shown in the illustrations.

The caption

Fill out the caption just as for all your other forms (see page 81).

Page numbers

In the lower right corner of each page you will see "Page 1 of ___" or "Page 2 of ___" for the first five pages. The remaining pages show "Page ___ of ___." This is because we don't know ahead of time how many pages you will use. If you do **not** have children, you will omit all four pages that concern children, then continue with the rest. If you have children, you will use all pages. So, with no children, the total number of pages would be 5. If you have children, the total number will be 8 .

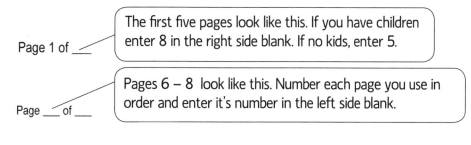

Page 1 of ___
The first five pages look like this. If you have children enter 8 in the right side blank. If no kids, enter 5.

Page ___ of ___
Pages 6 – 8 look like this. Number each page you use in order and enter it's number in the left side blank.

❶ Notes for page 1 of the Petition

Fill it out as shown in the illustration and these notes.

Caption. The Cause Number and the court's district number are left blank, just this once. These will be assigned by the clerk when you file the Petition. From that point on, you must put the cause number and court number in all captions.

Children in the caption. If you have minor children, you must name them here. Include all children born to or adopted by you and your spouse who are under 18 or 18+ and still in high school, or disabled adult children who cannot care for themselves. If the wife is pregnant, do not do your own divorce until the child is born.

Item 3, Out-of-State Parent? If either parent resides outside of Texas and you have minor children named in this case, you *must* fill out and attach the Out-of-State Parent Affidavit, found in the back of this book and on the companion CD.

❷ Notes for page 2 of the Petition *(not shown)*

Item 4, Protective Orders. Also called "restraining orders." Check the 1st box if you do **not** have a protective order in effect or pending. If you do have one, or if one has been applied for, check the 2nd box and enter the county where the order or application was filed, the state, the case or cause number. Below that, indicate with the check boxes if the order is attached to your Petition, or will be filed before your hearing, or will be filed if a pending order is actually issued.

Item 5, Marriage and Grounds for Divorce.

Enter your date of marriage and the date when you stopped living together as husband and wife. For date of marriage, the exact date is best, but in either case get as close as you can. If you had a common-law marriage, check that box.

> **Common-Law Marriage.** You **must** file for divorce **within two years** of separation. If you wait longer, it is presumed that the marriage never existed, and you can't go through a regular divorce. If that happens, you will have to find another way to divide property and establish paternity of children born during the relationship in order to collect support and arrange for visitation.

Item 6, Children

If you have **no** minor children, check this 1st box. Do not check this box if even one statement below it is **not** true: say, if Wife is pregnant or if during the marriage she gave birth to a child and Husband was not the father.

If you check this box, no children, do **not** use the next 3 pages in the Petition. Continue on below with instruction for page 6, the one that starts with item 7, about property.

If you **do** have children, leave this box blank and go on to page 3. You will use all of the pages in the Petition form.

How to fill out the Petition

Page 1

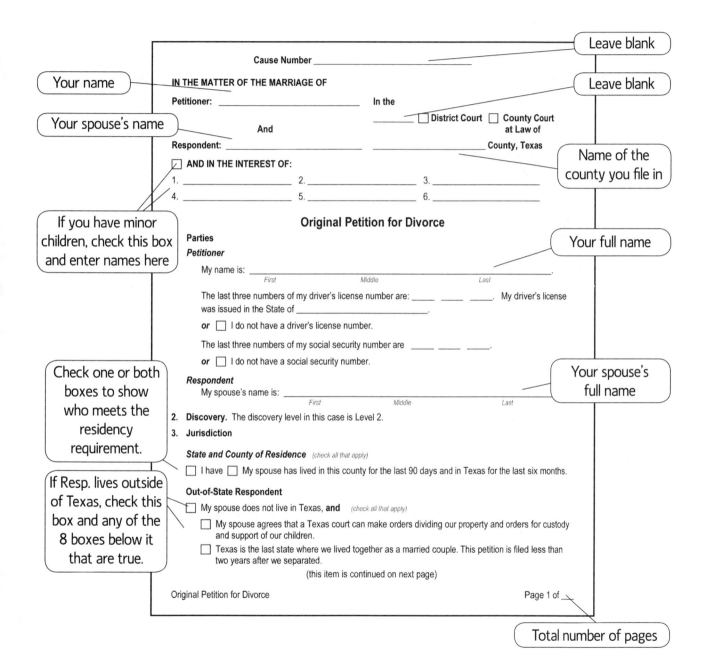

Leave blank

Your name

Your spouse's name

Leave blank

Name of the county you file in

If you have minor children, check this box and enter names here

Your full name

Check one or both boxes to show who meets the residency requirement.

Your spouse's full name

If Resp. lives outside of Texas, check this box and any of the 8 boxes below it that are true.

Total number of pages

Cause Number _____

IN THE MATTER OF THE MARRIAGE OF

Petitioner: _____   In the

_____ ☐ District Court ☐ County Court at Law of

And

Respondent: _____   County, Texas

☑ AND IN THE INTEREST OF:

1. _____   2. _____   3. _____
4. _____   5. _____   6. _____

Original Petition for Divorce

Parties

Petitioner

My name is: _____.
        First   Middle   Last

The last three numbers of my driver's license number are: ____ ____ ____.   My driver's license
was issued in the State of _____.

or ☐ I do not have a driver's license number.

The last three numbers of my social security number are   ____ ____ ____.

or ☐ I do not have a social security number.

Respondent

My spouse's name is: _____
        First   Middle   Last

2. **Discovery.** The discovery level in this case is Level 2.

3. **Jurisdiction**

State and County of Residence (check all that apply)

☐ I have ☐ My spouse has lived in this county for the last 90 days and in Texas for the last six months.

Out-of-State Respondent

☐ My spouse does not live in Texas, **and** (check all that apply)

    ☐ My spouse agrees that a Texas court can make orders dividing our property and orders for custody and support of our children.

    ☐ Texas is the last state where we lived together as a married couple. This petition is filed less than two years after we separated.

(this item is continued on next page)

Original Petition for Divorce   Page 1 of ____

❸ Notes for page 3 of the Petition – Cases with children

Note 1. Check the 1st box and enter the name, age, sex (M or F), the birthdate (day/mo/year), and the birthplace of each child. Include all children born to or adopted by you and your spouse who are under 18 or 18+ and still in high school, or disabled adult children who cannot care for themselves. Do not include stepchildren who have not been legally adopted by the stepparent.

Note 2, Husband not bio-dad? If a child born during marriage is not the biological child of the husband, check this box and for each such child, enter the name, age, sex (M or F), the birthdate (day/mo/year), and the birthplace.

Note: If husband claims not to be the father of any child born during marriage, or if the wife is pregnant and husband claims not to be the father, you can't finish your divorce until paternity is legally settled by either a court order or the filing of an Acknowledgment of Paternity signed by the genetic father **and** a Denial of Paternity signed by the husband.

Paternity established. In the boxes below, check the 1st box if paternity has **not** been established. Note that you won't be able to finish your divorce until this has been done.

If paternity **has** been established, check the 2nd box and one of the two boxes below to indicate if (a) there was a court order, or (b) an Acknowledgement was signed by the genetic father and a Denial by Husband. In either case, you must attach these documents to your Final Decree.

Item A, Disabled child. If you do **not** have a disabled child, check the 1st box. If you **do** have a disabled child who will require care and not be capable of self-support, check the 2nd box and enter that child's name here.

Item B, Pregnancy. If Wife is **not** pregnant, check the 1st box. If Wife **is** pregnant, check the 2nd box and check one of the boxes below to indicate if Husband is or is not the father of that child.

How to fill out the Petition

Page 3

Note 1

☐ **Children of the marriage**

The following children now under eighteen years old were born to or adopted by the parties:

	Name	Age	Sex	Birth date	Birthplace
1.					
2.					
3.					
4.					
5.					
6.					

Note 2

☐ **Children born during marriage but husband is NOT the father**

  ☐ The wife did not have children with another man while married to the husband.

  ☐ All children born during the marriage that are NOT the husband's adopted or biological children are listed below.

	Name	Age	Sex	Birth date	Birthplace
1.					
2.					
3.					
4.					

  ☐ Paternity of children listed above **has not** been established. I understand that paternity must be established before I can finish my divorce.

  ☐ Paternity of children listed above **has** been established.

    ☐ A court order has determined the father of each child named above. I understand that I must attach a file-stamped copy of the order to my Final Decree of Divorce.

    ☐ An Acknowledgment of Paternity signed by the genetic father **and** a Denial of Paternity signed by Husband herein has been filed with the Bureau of Vital Statistics for each child listed above. I understand that I must attach a copy of these documents to my Final Decree of Divorce.

A. Disabled child

  ☐ My spouse and I do not have any disabled children.

  ☐ _____, a child of this marriage named above, requires continuous care and personal supervision because of a disability and will not be capable of self-support. The Court is requested to order that payments for the support of this child be continued after the child's eighteenth birthday and extended for an indefinite period.

B. Pregnancy. ☐ The wife in this marriage **is not** pregnant

    ☐ The wife in this marriage **is** pregnant **and**

      ☐ The husband **is** the father. ☐ The husband **is not** the father.

Original Petition for Divorce

Page 3 of ___

Total number of pages

❹ Notes for page 4 of the Petition – Cases with children

Item C, Court orders concerning children. The judge needs to be sure that no child is the subject of another court action or order. So, regarding your children listed at the top of page 3 . . .

If there are **no** court orders now in effect for any of them, check the 1st box.

If there **are** court orders in effect for your child/ren, check the 2nd box and, in that same line, check a box to indicate if the orders affect **all** listed children or just some. Enter the requested information about the order as shown in the illustration.

Join the cases? If you have a child support or custody case pending in another court, you will probably want to file a motion to consolidate the two cases into one action. Forms and instructions for doing this are in the Forms Etc. folder on the CD.

Item D, Custody, visitation and support.

Joint custody. Check the 1st box if you want joint custody, and in the blank space indicate which party will have the right to establish the child's primary residence. This might matter for such things as school zone or applications for assistance, etc. The law presumes that it will be best for the children if parents have Joint Managing Conservatorship (JMC). The hope is to provide the children with a stable, ongoing relationship with both parents. It does *not* mean that the children spend half of their time with each of you. It *does* mean that you will both spend substantial time with them and both will have a voice in decisions affecting them. The rights and responsibilities of both parents will be spelled out by you in detail in your Decree.

Sole custody. Check the 2nd box if there are reasons why you think Joint Managing Conservatorship will not work for your children (chapter C), but be prepared to explain to the judge what those reasons are. Indicate if you want Petitioner or Respondent to have sole custody (be the Sole Managing Conservator), and name the other party as Possessory Conservator.

Item E(1-4), Children's health and dental insurance. Private insurance means insurance that is not from a government aid program like Medicaid or C.H.I.P.

If private **health** insurance for your child/ren **is** in effect, check E1 and enter requested information. If private **dental** insurance **is** in effect, check E3 and enter requested info.

If private insurance is **not** in effect, check E2 and/or E4, indicate whether children are covered under a government program, and whether private insurance is available at reasonable cost to the parent who pays support. "Reasonable" means no more than 9% of total gross income for all kids for health insurance, 1.9% for dental insurance.

How to fill out the Petition

Page 4

C. Court orders involving children (check one box)

☐ There are no court orders in effect now for any of the children listed above.

☐ There is a court order in effect for ☐ all of the above named children ☐ the following children

_____

County/State where order was made _____

Date of order _____ Cause number _____

Name of order _____

This order is ☐ temporary ☐ final

> If you check the 2nd box, enter the county and state, date, cause number, kind of order it is, and check a box to show if the order is temporary or final.

D. Custody, visitation, and child support

I will try to make an agreement with my spouse about custody, visitation, and support for our children. If we cannot make an agreement by the time of the hearing, I ask the court to make the following orders:

1. Custody

☐ Petitioner and Respondent should be appointed Joint Managing Conservators of the child/ren and_____ will have the right to establish the child/ren's primary residence.

☐ _____ to be appointed the Sole Managing Conservator of the child/ren and _____ to be appointed Possessory Conservator of the child/ren.

2. Support

☐ Petitioner ☐ Respondent should be ordered to make payments for the support of the children in the manner specified by the Court.

E. Children's health and dental insurance

1 ☐ **Private health insurance IS in effect.**

Name of insurance company _____

Policy number _____ Cost of premium $_____

Name of person who pays for the insurance _____

This insurance policy ☐ is ☐ is not available through the parent's work

2 ☐ **Private health insurance is NOT in effect.**

The children ☐ do ☐ do not receive medical insurance through CHIPS or Medicaid.

Cost of premium (if any) $_____

Health insurance ☐ is ☐ is not available at reasonable cost to the parent who pays child support.

(continued on next page)

Original Petition for Divorce

Page 4 of ___

> Total number of pages

❺ Notes for page 5 of the Petition – Cases with children

Item F – Children's property. If the child/ren do not own any significant property other than their personal effects, check the 1st box. If any child does own significant property, check the 2nd box and list the property in the space below. If you need more room, on the last line enter "See attachment for Item 6F," complete your list on a separate page with the heading "Attachment for Item 6F" and attach it to your Petition.

Item G – Family Information – Attachment to the Decree. If you have children, you must attach the Family Information form to your Decree—it's in the back of this book and on the companion CD. For both parents and each child you enter a lot of personal information, including addresses, social security and driver's license numbers, phones, employer's name and address, etc. Any bit you don't know, enter "Unknown." Both parents are ordered to notify the other parent, the Court, and the Case Registry Office of any **intended** change at least 60 days in advance, or no later than 5 days after you know of such change. Send all notices by registered or certified mail, return receipt requested. Notice to the Registry Office goes to: State Case Registry, Contract Services Section, MC046S, P.O. Box 12017, Austin, Texas 78711

Check the 1st box if you will file this form with your Decree.

But wait! Check the 2nd box if you believe you or a child will be at risk if you give the info to Respondent, then check any or all of the boxes to show which information you want held back. If you do this, you will need to present facts at your hearing to show that your concern is reasonable. Take a look at chapter 7, notes for page 5 of the Decree.

There's more! Check the 3rd box if you want personal information kept from public view for fear of identity theft. The judge might not order it, but you have nothing to lose by asking for protection. Offer some facts about identity theft: it can only help.

Order to Keep Family Information Confidential. Get it from the CD, bring the completed form to your hearing and ask the judge to sign it when you get to this part.

Item H – Out of State Parent Affidavit – Attachment to the Petition. If either parent resides outside of Texas, you must attach the Out of State Parent Affidavit to your Petition. It must be **signed and sworn** before a notary. The form is in the back of this book and on the companion CD. **Item 2:** For each child, you enter the name, current address, who the child currently lives with and for how long, followed by similar information for the past 5 years. **Item 3A:** If you have participated in any custody proceeding involving any child, enter the details here. **Item 3B:** If you know of any person not a party to your divorce who has physical custody of any child, or claims any rights to physical or legal custody, identify them here.

As with item G, above, if you can present facts at your hearing to show that revealing personal information might put you or your child at risk, you can omit it. But bring a completed form to your hearing, just in case and also the Order to Keep Confidential.

How to fill out the Petition

Page 5

3 ☐ **Private dental insurance IS in effect.**
Name of insurance company _____
Policy number _____ Cost of premium $_____
Name of person who pays for the insurance _____
This insurance policy ☐ is ☐ is not available through the parent's work

4 ☐ **Private dental insurance is NOT in effect.**
The children ☐ do ☐ do not receive dental insurance through CHIPS or Medicaid.
Cost of premium (if any) $_____
Health insurance ☐ is ☐ is not available at reasonable cost to the parent who pays child support.

F. Children's property
☐ The children do not own any property.
☐ The children own the following property:

_____
_____
_____
_____

> Check this box if children do not own any property.

> If any child owns property other than personal effects, name child and list property.

G. Family information
☐ I will fill out and file the Family Information form when I file the Final Decree of Divorce, as required by section 105.006 of the Texas Family Code.
☐ **Potential harm.** I believe my children or I will be harassed, abused, seriously harmed, or injured if I am required to give my spouse the information checked below for myself and the children.

☐ home address ☐ mailing address ☐ employer ☐ work address,
☐ home phone # ☐ work phone # ☐ social security # ☐ driver's license #.

I ask the Court to Order that I not have to give this information or notice of changes in this information to my spouse.

☐ **Identity theft.** I ask the Court to seal and keep confidential this information, any attachment to the Final Decree, and any Orders to Withhold Earnings that the court might issue, that disclose the Social Security and driver's license numbers, current address, and telephone numbers of parties or children in order to protect parties and children from exposure to identity theft. Such information will be provided to parties and the court but should not be made part of files to which the public has access.

> Check the 1st box if you will file the Family Info Form with the Decree. Check the 2nd box if you do not want to furnish personal info to the other parent. Check the 3rd box if you want that info sealed from public view.

H. Out of state parent information
The information required by Texas Family Code § 152.209 (check one box)
☐ Is not required because both parents reside in Texas.
☐ Is submitted in an attached affidavit.
☐ Is not provided because the health, safety, or liberty of a party or child would be jeopardized by disclosure of identifying information.

> See note for item H and check the box that applies to your case.

Original Petition for Divorce   Page 5 of ___

> Total number of pages

❻ Notes for page 6 of the Petition

Item 7, Property and debts.

Note 1, Agreement anticipated. It's a good idea to check this box as it signals to Respondent that you hope to work things out. But, if you don't also check the box asking the Court to divide property and also list all CP assets and debts, then you can't complete your divorce unless you actually get an agreement. Maybe that's a good way to reassure Respondent, but if no agreement, you'll have to file and serve an amended petition listing your property. You've lost a bit of time. Does that matter?

Note 2, Divided by the court. Unless you have no marital property to divide or are certain you will get an agreement, check this box and list your community property and debts so the judge will be able to divide them at the hearing.

How to list property. There are many ways you could list your community property, but we suggest you do it something like this:

1. Personal effects of the Petitioner $465
   Personal effects of the Respondent 875
   (covers clothing, ordinary jewelry, hair brushes, etc.)
2. Sable stole 650
3. Household goods, furnishings, appliances 1,200
4. 1958 Edsel, license no. HOG 101, vehicle I.D. No. 24564R556, encumbered by debt to Good Guy Finance Co. in amount of $853, payable $75 per month 1,400
5. Ameritrade acct. # 34-5678, 22 shares of XYZ 1,350
6. The Respondent's vested retirement account, Teacher's Union Retirement Account no. 76R456 8,000
7. House and lot located at 10 Downing Street, Clyde, Texas, described as Lot 1, Section 3, on Map 33, Page 4, Plat Records, Cork County, Texas, encumbered by:
   Mortgage, loan no. 54-56-78900, Lubbock First National Bank, Lubbock, Texas in the amount of approximately $33,654, payable at $144 per month 40,500

How to list debts. Any debt not already listed as secured by some property item should be listed separately, together with a word or two about what it's for, the amount, payment schedule, and to whom owed. For example: .... *(it went that a'way)* .... ➡➡➡

How to fill out the Petition

Page 6

Check this box if there is no community property to be divided.

Check this box if you expect an agreedment.

Check this box if you already have a written settlement agreement.

Check this box if you want the Court to divide your CP and list it all here.

This requests an equal division of the property.

This requests an unequal division. Indicate which party should receive the larger share.

Check this box to ask the Court to order your spouse to pay debts.

7. **Property and debts**

☐ **No property.** To Petitioner's knowledge, other than personal effects there is no community property of any significant value which is subject to division by the Court at this time.

☐ **Agreement anticipated.** Petitioner believes the parties will reach an agreed property division and ask the Court to approve that agreement when presented to the Court or, absent agreement, divide the assets and debts of the parties according to Texas law.

☐ **Marital Settlement Agreement.** The parties have entered into a Marital Settlement Agreement, a copy of which is attached and incorporated by reference.

☐ **Community property and debts to be divided by the Court**
To Petitioner's knowledge and belief, community property owned by the parties consists of the following assets and debts that were acquired during the marriage.

Item #	Description	Value

Division: Petitioner requests the Court to order a division of the community property in a manner that the Court deems just and right, as provided by law.

☐ It would be fair to divide the property into approximately equal portions.

☐ There are many equities which the court should consider making it fair that

☐ Petitioner ☐ Respondent be awarded a substantial portion of the property.

☑ It will be fair and equitable for the Court to order Respondent to assume and to pay without any right to contribution or reimbursement from Petitioner the debts described in the above list, namely items numbered: _____.

Original Petition for Divorce   Page 6 of ___

Total number of pages

Debts:

8. Home Finance Co., for dental work, $75 per month............................ $839

9. J. Jones, Respondent's father, for vacation, no fixed
   schedule of payments 950

❼ Notes for page 7 of the Petition

Note 1, Separate property to be confirmed.

If you or your spouse own separate property or owe separate debts, like maybe a loan on a separate house or car or a separate credit card account, it is a good idea to have the Court confirm the property or debt as belonging to one spouse or the other. This will help to make things clear in the future. This is especially important for items of value or special meaning to you, like Grandma's locket, or family photos, etc. List those items separately even if they are of no great value other than in a personal way.

Check the 1st box to list separate property or debts you want confirmed to Petitioner and the 2nd box to list separate property or debts you want confirmed to Respondent.

Listing the property and debts. Check the notes for the previous page to see how to list assets and debts.

Note 2, Spousal Maintenance (alimony). Check the 1st box if you do not want spousal maintenance. Check the 2nd box if you have already arranged for it in a Settlement Agreement. Check the 3rd box if you want the court to award alimony based on facts that you will present in your court hearing or in an agreement that you will file or present to the court at your hearing. Review chapter D to see what you must prove to the court (if there is no agreement) to get spousal maintenance and how much you can hope for.

How to fill out the Petition

Page 7

Separate property to be confirmed by the Court

☐ I request that the following items be confirmed as Petitioner's separate property as they were owned before the marriage or acquired during marriage by inheritance, gift to Petitioner only, or represents the proceeds, other than lost wages, of a personal injury lawsuit:

Item #   Description   Value

_____

_____

_____

_____

_____

_____

_____

_____

_____

☐ I request that the following items be confirmed as Respondent's separate property as they were owned before the marriage or acquired during marriage by inheritance, gift to Respondent only, or represents the proceeds, other than lost wages, of a personal injury lawsuit:

Item #   Description   Value

_____

_____

_____

_____

_____

_____

_____

8. **Spousal Maintenance**

☒ Spousal maintenance is not requested.

☐ The parties have entered into a Marital Settlement Agreement regarding maintenance, a copy of which is attached and incorporated by reference.

☐ Petitioner requests that this court award spousal maintenance according to Texas law.

Original Petition for Divorce   Page 7 of ___

Callout notes:

- Check these if there is separate property you want confirmed to Petitioner or to Respondent.
- Check this if you do **not** want alimony.
- Check this if alimony agreed to in MSA
- Check this if you want alimony.
- Total number of pages

❽ Notes for page 8 of the Petition

Note 1, Name change.

You can ask the Court to change your name but only to a name that you had before you were married and only if you are not changing your name to avoid creditors or criminal prosecution.

Now what?

When your Petition and attachments are completed, check them for accuracy. Make three copies and take the original and all copies to the District Clerk's Office with the filing fee (cash or money order, no personal checks). The clerk will assign a cause number and court number at this time. Ask the clerk to file-stamp your copies. If you are going to serve your spouse personally, ask the clerk what information they have for getting this done. The clerk can send papers out for service or you can get a set to send yourself to a sheriff or professional server (chapter 6).

Standing Orders

Courts in over a dozen Texas counties have a set of orders called "standing orders" that must be attached to all copies of your Petition. Ask the clerk if your county has standing orders and get a copy if they do and attach them to your Petition.

These are automatice restraining orders that are designed to keep the peace, protect children and preserve marital property. Standing Orders become active the moment the Petition is filed and they apply to *both* parties. If such orders are required in your county, read them very carefully and be very careful to do as they say.

Filing an amended petition

If you later find you made a mistake, or left something out, or changed your mind, you can file an amended (changed) Petition so long as the Decree hasn't been filed, only this time you title it "Amended Petition for Divorce." Very neatly, in blue ballpoint ink, print the word "Amended" in the title. You won't have to pay another filing fee, but you have to follow all the same instructions as if you were starting over again, because that is exactly what you are doing, so serve your Amended Petition on your spouse and follow the checklist in Chapter 2.

How to fill out the Petition

Page 8

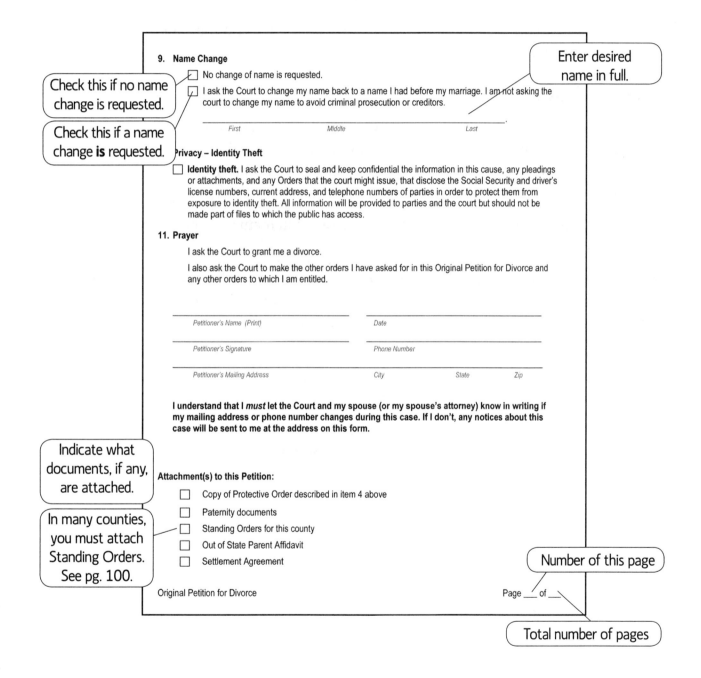

Check this if no name change is requested.

Check this if a name change is requested.

Enter desired name in full.

9. **Name Change**

☐ No change of name is requested.

☐ I ask the Court to change my name back to a name I had before my marriage. I am not asking the court to change my name to avoid criminal prosecution or creditors.

_____
First   Middle   Last

Privacy – Identity Theft

☐ **Identity theft.** I ask the Court to seal and keep confidential the information in this cause, any pleadings or attachments, and any Orders that the court might issue, that disclose the Social Security and driver's license numbers, current address, and telephone numbers of parties in order to protect them from exposure to identity theft. All information will be provided to parties and the court but should not be made part of files to which the public has access.

11. **Prayer**

I ask the Court to grant me a divorce.

I also ask the Court to make the other orders I have asked for in this Original Petition for Divorce and any other orders to which I am entitled.

_____   _____
Petitioner's Name (Print)   Date

_____   _____
Petitioner's Signature   Phone Number

_____   _____
Petitioner's Mailing Address   City   State   Zip

I understand that I *must* let the Court and my spouse (or my spouse's attorney) know in writing if my mailing address or phone number changes during this case. If I don't, any notices about this case will be sent to me at the address on this form.

Indicate what documents, if any, are attached.

In many counties, you must attach Standing Orders. See pg. 100.

Attachment(s) to this Petition:

☐ Copy of Protective Order described in item 4 above

☐ Paternity documents

☐ Standing Orders for this county

☐ Out of State Parent Affidavit

☐ Settlement Agreement

Number of this page

Total number of pages

Original Petition for Divorce   Page ___ of ___

The Family Information form

You must attach this form to your Decree unless you claim in the Petition that to do so would endanger a parent or child. If you make this claim, you'll have to present facts at your hearing to show that this is a reasonable concern.

It orders both parents to notify the other parent, the Court, and the state case registry office of any changes.

The Out of State Parent Affidavit

If either parent lives outside Texas, you must attach this form to your Petition unless you claim in the Petition that to do so would endanger a parent or child. The form provides the court with information about where the child has lived and with whom over the past five years.

Signed and sworn before a notary. This is a sworn statement under oath and must be signed before a notary.

Item 2. For each child, enter the the name, current address, who the child currently lives with and for how long, followed by similar information for the past five years. If you don't know any bit of information requested, put "unknown."

Item 3A. Tell the court whether or not you have participated in any custody proceedings involving any child, or know of any such proceedings. If you do, enter the court, case number and nature of the proceeding.

3B. If you know of any person who is not a party to the current suit for divorce who has physical custody or claims any rights of physical or legal custody, identify them here and enter their name and address.

6. Notice to Your Spouse

Proper notice to Respondent is essential as that is what gives the court power to act in your case. Chapter A3(d) explains why this is so, and here we show you how it is done.

When you go to the hearing, it *must* appear in the court's file that notice was properly given. This can be shown by:

1. Respondent's signed Waiver of Service (section A below), or
2. Official personal service with a Return of Citation filed by the server, stating that he/she served papers on the Respondent (section B below), or
3. Substituted service, by publication or posting. This is used when, after a diligent search, you can't find your spouse. Search very hard because (a) the law requires it, and (b) service by the first two methods gives the court far more authority over Respondent. A kit for doing publication or posting is in the Forms folder on the companion CD.

Military spouse? If your spouse is on active military duty, the Waiver is the *only* way you can proceed without an attorney. If your military spouse won't sign the Waiver, get help (see chapter A8).

A. The Waiver

What it is

The Waiver is a statement signed by your spouse under oath before a notary, which states that the Petition was received and that the case can proceed without further notice to the Respondent. It is, in effect, a consent to an uncontested divorce.

Using the Waiver is the easiest way to proceed because you don't need to have the Citation issued and papers served. It helps to smooth the way at the hearing, because the judge can see that your spouse is in the picture and agreeable to the case being completed without him/her. However, there are some limitations.

Limitations
- The Waiver *must* be signed after the date your Petition is filed;
- Best to avoid the Waiver if there has been domestic violence in your marriage;
- If your spouse won't sign the Waiver before a notary and is *not* on active military duty, have the Petition served personally as explained in section B below.

If your spouse won't sign a Waiver *and* successfully evades service, you'll need to serve notice by publication or posting. A kit for doing this is in the Forms folder on the CD.

How to fill it out

Fill it out as if you were Respondent. Do the first page as shown in the illustration and the notes below. For any information you do not have, ask Respondent to finish the form neatly by hand with a blue ballpoint pen and initial his/her entries.

First page

Note 1. Enter Respondent's full name, address, and best contact phone number.

Note 2. If you know it, enter the last three digit's of Respondent's driver's license and the state that issued it, or check the box if he/she doesn't have one.

Note 3. If you know it, enter the last three digit's of Respondent's social security number or check the box if he/she doesn't have one.

Second page (not shown).

• The first set of checkboxes indicates either that Respondent is not on active military duty or, yes, is on active military duty but waives all rights due to him/her under the Servicemember's Civil Relief Act that are contrary to the Waiver.

• The second set of checkboxes tells the Court whether Respondent wants his/her name changed. If yes, enter the full name exactly as it is requested.

• The Waiver should not be signed and dated until Respondent is before a notary.

Then what?

1. Check it over, then make three copies.
2. Send your spouse:
   • The original and one copy of the Waiver, *and*
   • One copy of the Petition with any attachments.
3. The Waiver must *not* be signed before the Petition is filed. File the Petition first, then give the Waiver to your spouse.
4. Tell your spouse that the Waiver *must* be signed before a notary. The *original* signed and notarized copy, is to be returned to you as soon as possible.
5. If your spouse is also going to approve the Decree as described in chapter E1, this is the best time to get that done. Prepare the Decree (chapter 7), send the original and one copy with the other papers, and make sure the *original* Decree is returned to you after Respondent signs the last page. If any parts of your Decree are crossed out, then your spouse should initial each and every cross-out in the margin.
6. Take the original signed Waiver to the District Clerk's Office and file it.

How to fill out the Waiver

Page 1

Cause Number _____

IN THE MATTER OF THE MARRIAGE OF

Petitioner: _____   In the

                                            _____ ☐ District Court ☐ County Court
                And   at Law of

Respondent: _____   _____ County, Texas

☐ AND IN THE INTEREST OF:

1. _____ 2. _____ 3. _____
4. _____ 5. _____ 6. _____

Waiver of Service

The person who signed this affidavit appeared, in person, before me, the undersigned notary, and stated under oath:

"I am the Respondent in this case.

"My name is: _____.
         First   Middle   Last

"My mailing address is: _____.
              Address   City   State   Zip

"My phone number is: (_____) _____.

"The last three numbers of my driver's license number are: ___ ___ ___.

My driver's license was issued in *(State)*: _____.

☐ " I do not have a driver's license number.

"The last three numbers of my social security number are: ___ ___ ___.

☐ " I do not have a social security number.

" I have been given a copy of the *Original Petition for Divorce* filed in this case. I have read it and understand what it says. I do not give up my right to review a different *Petition for Divorce* if it gets changed *(amended)*.

" I understand that I have the right to be given a copy of the *Original Petition for Divorce* and official notice of this case by an official process server. I do not want to be given official notice. I give up my right to issuance and service of citation in this case and enter my appearance in this case for all purposes.

"I also give up my right to be notified of any and all hearings in this case.

"I agree that a Judge or Associate Judge in the county and state where this case is filed may make decisions about my divorce, even if the divorce should have been filed in another county. I do not want a court reporter to make a record of the testimony in this case.

Waiver of Service   Page 1 of 2

Fill out the caption as shown on page 81.

Note 1

Note 2

Note 3

B. Official service in person or by mail

When you file your Petition (or later if you like), tell the clerk that you want to have your spouse served. The clerk will then print a Citation form and attach a copy of your Petition to it.

Ask the clerk how they can help you arrange for service, what the options are, and what it costs as there will be a fee at this point. Tell the clerk whether you want an officer (constable, sheriff) or private process server to serve the papers. In many counties the clerk will have a list of private servers who will cost more, but they can usually serve papers faster than public officers. If you are in a hurry, ask the clerk for their list.

Service by mail. You can ask the clerk or the officer to send papers to Respondent by certified mail, return receipt requested, but **do not serve by mail** unless you are **very** sure that Respondent will sign the receipt of mail at the given address. If someone else signs, it's no good and you'll have to do it all over again. Do not serve by mail if Respondent is in jail—forward the papers to a sheriff or constable near the jail.

If Respondent is in a different county or not in Texas, you'll probably have to arrange for service of papers yourself. It's easy: just call the sheriff in the county where Respondent can be found, give them details of where Respondent is located, and ask for their fee and the address where you forward the papers.

Information for server. It is not required, but we strongly recommend that you send along an information sheet with the Petition, giving as much information as you can get about Respondent's whereabouts and habits, with a complete description and, if possible, a recent clear photograph. An Information for Server form is in the back of this book and on the CD.

When service is made inside the county, the serving officer has two ways to get papers served: they can be personally carried out and handed over, or mailed by registered or certified mail, delivery restricted to addressee only. Unless you can be sure that Respondent will sign the receipt for mail received (and not try to avoid signing), tell the server not to serve by mail.

The serving officer is unlikely to do anything creative about finding and serving your spouse. It is *your* responsibility to give the best and most complete information you can about how to locate and identify your spouse. Dig hard. Talk to people; write, call, be a detective. Make your information sheet very complete, clear, and specific.

Lost spouse? If you have no idea where your spouse is, you can do the Citation only by Publication or Posting. See Chapter A3(d) and the Forms folder on the CD.

3. The Return of Service form

Whoever serves the Petition should fill out a Return of Service form stating where, when, with what, and how your spouse was served. They might file the form or give it to you. If service was by mail, the return receipt (green card) is what you need to prove that notice was given.

The Return of Service is extremely important as it is the only way the Court knows for sure that notice was given and the case is good to go. Without it, you're stuck. Also, you can't have your hearing until 12 days after the Return of Service (or the return receipt by mail) is filed with the clerk, so you must make doubly sure that it gets filed. Go down to the clerk's office and check to make sure. If it is on file, ask for a file-stamped copy of the Return (or the mail receipt) so you can take it to your hearing.

The Return of Service options:

- It will be returned blank if service was not made. It will be filled out and signed if service was successful.

- If your papers were forwarded to the sheriff by the clerk, it will be returned to the clerk, with notice by post card to you. You should go down to the Clerk's office to make sure it is on file, accurately filled out, and signed by the officer.

- If forwarded to the sheriff by you, it will come back to you. You should check it over, make a couple of copies, and quickly get it on file at the District Clerk's office.

- If service was not made, contact the sheriff to find out what the problem was. You can either send out a new Citation and try one more time, or try a professional process server, or refer the case to an attorney for help (see chapter A8).

7. The Decree

What it is

After listening to your testimony at the hearing, the judge will verbally make findings and issue orders; that's your judgment. The clerk will take notes of the decision.

Since you usually get what you ask for in uncontested cases, you prepare the Decree and necessary Exhibits before the hearing and take them with you so the Decree can be signed right there. If the judge orders something different, go home and prepare a Decree to match the judge's orders and send it in (through the clerk) for signing.

Exhibits

In cases with children, or property or debts to be divided, the Decree uses attachments, called Exhibits, to make orders on those subjects. Use the ones that are relevant to your case. When you use orders in your Decree, name them in order: Exhibit A, Exhibit B, and so on. There are seven possible Exhibits:

Children's Property	Used if a child owns property
Conservatorship Order	Used in cases with a minor child
Standard Possession Order	Used in cases with a minor child
Child Support Order	Used in cases with a minor child
Medical Support Order	Used in cases with a minor child
Dental Support Order	Used in cases with a minor child
Family Information	Used in cases with a minor child
Orders Re Property and Debts	Used for orders about property or debts

How to fill it out

Fill out the Decree and any necessary exhibit attachments as described in the illustrations and the notes below.

The caption

Fill out the caption just as for all your other forms (see page 81).

Page numbers

In the lower right corner of each page you will see "Page 1 of ___" or "Page 2 of ___" for the first two pages. The remaining pages show "Page ___ of ___." This is because we don't know ahead of time how many pages of the Decree you will use. If you do not have children, you will omit all four pages that concern children, then continue with the rest. If you have children, you will use all pages. So, with no children, the total number of pages will be 5. If you have children, the total number will be 9.

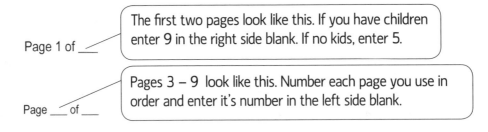

Page 1 of ___ — The first two pages look like this. If you have children enter **9** in the right side blank. If no kids, enter **5**.

Page ___ of ___ — Pages **3 – 9** look like this. Number each page you use in order and enter it's number in the left side blank.

Check boxes

To show an item or section is being used. Boxes are checked to indicate that a section or item in the Decree is being used. For example, the caption. If you have children, you check the box next to "AND IN THE INTEREST OF" and enter their names. If you do not have children, you do not check the box and you leave the entries fields blank.

To make a choice. Boxes are checked to show that one item or the other is true. For example, on page 1 at the bottom, you check one of 5 boxes to show which choice best describes Respondent's presence or absence at the hearing.

❶ Notes for page 1 of the Decree

Note 1. Check a box to indicate if you are the Husband or Wife. Below that, check the first box to show that you were present at the hearing.

Note 2. If you know for sure ahead of time, check the box that best shows Respondent's appearance at the hearing (read them carefully). If not sure, leave this blank and either complete it at the hearing or ask the judge to check the appropriate box.

❷ Notes for page 2 of the Decree *(not shown)*

Several pages are not illustrated, but it will help to have the pages in front of you when you go over these instructions. Get it from the back or print it from files on the CD.

Item 2. Leave it blank. The Court will fill this out.

Item 3 – Jurisdiction. Check the first box to show that your hearing is being held at least 60 days after the Petition was filed.

Item 5 – No children. If you have **no** minor children, check this box. Do not check this box if even one statement below it is **not** true: say, if Wife is pregnant or if during the marriage she gave birth to a child and Husband was not the father and did not adopt.

If you check this box, no children, do **not** use the next 4 pages in the Decree. Continue on below with instructions for page 7, the one that starts with item 6, about property.

If you **do** have children, leave this box blank and go on to page 3. You will use all of the pages in the Decree form.

How to fill out the Decree
Page 1

Fill out the caption as shown on page 81.

Date of hearing

Your name

Spouse's name

Note 1

Note 2

Cause Number _____

IN THE MATTER OF THE MARRIAGE OF

Petitioner: _____ In the

_____ ☐ District Court ☐ County Court at Law of

And

Respondent: _____ _____ County, Texas

☐ AND IN THE INTEREST OF:

1. _____ 2. _____ 3. _____
4. _____ 5. _____ 6. _____

Final Decree of Divorce

A hearing took place on _____. There was no jury. Neither party asked for a jury.
Date

1. Appearances

Petitioner
Petitioner's name is: _____
First   Middle   Last

The Petitioner is the ☐ Husband ☐ Wife
(check one box)
☐ The Petitioner **was present**, representing him/herself, and has agreed to the terms of this Final Decree of Divorce *(called "Decree" throughout this document)*.
☐ The Petitioner **was not present** but has signed below, agreeing to the terms of this Decree.

Respondent
Respondent's name is: _____
First   Middle   Last

(check one box)
☐ The Respondent **was present**, Pro Se, and announced ready for trial.
☐ The Respondent **was present**, Pro Se, and has signed below agreeing to the terms in this Decree.
☐ The Respondent was **not present** but filed an Answer or Waiver of Service and has signed below, agreeing to the terms in this Decree.
☐ The Respondent was **not present** but filed a Waiver of Service that waived Respondent's right to notice of this hearing and did not otherwise appear.
☐ The Respondent was **not present** but was served and has defaulted. The Petitioner has filed a Certificate of Last Known Address and a Military Status Affidavit.

Final Decree of Divorce   Page 1 of ___

❸ **Notes for page 3 of the Decree – cases with children**   *(page not shown)*

If you don't have kids, skip to instructions for page 7 below. That will be your page 3.

Top of the page. Check the box to show that you have minor children.

List kids. In order of birth, oldest first, enter each child's name and other information.

More than six children? In the blank for the 6th child's name, enter "Continued on Attachment for Item 5" and attach a page right behind this page with the heading "Continuation of List of Children" and enter the same information as for the other children.

Got property? Below the list of children is a list of facts the Court finds to be true. If any of the listed findings are **not** correct, be sure to tell the judge at your hearing. The last finding is about the children's property. If any child owns anything other than personal effects, check the box and attach an Exhibit that list's each child's property. Call it Exhibit A, because this will be your first Exhibit. There's a form for this in the back or use 05-Ex1 on the CD. It's simple to fill out. Enter significant items separately and combine similar items. Review how property was listed on page 6 of the Petition.

Item 5A – They're all ours? If Wife did **not** have children with another man while married to the Husband, check the first box.

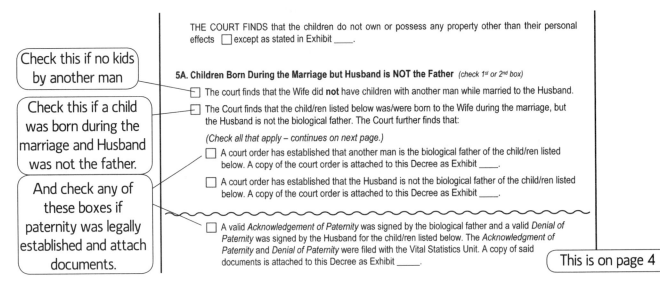

But . . . If during the marriage Wife **did** have a child by another man, check the second box and check any of the 3 boxes below (3rd one is on the next page) that are true. Read them carefully—these are the three ways of establishing parentage legally.

Got documents? If parentage has not been established legally, you can't finish your divorce until it has. If parentage has been established by any of the three ways described in those check boxes, you'll need to attach such documents as Exhibits to the Decree.

❹ Notes for pages 4-6 of the Decree – cases with children *(pages not shown)*

Items 5C, 5D, 5E, and 5F – Conservatorship, Possession, Support, Medical Support and Dental Support. If you have a minor child, these Exhibits are all required. Enter the numbers for each of these Exhibits. The Exhibit numbers you enter depend upon what other Exhibits you named before these. Say you've already indicated that an Exhibit A will be attached, then these would then be Exhibits B, C, D, E and F. They are all in the back of the book *and* on the CD.

Item 5D. Check the box under 5D if you want a different parenting schedule for a child under three and enter the Exhibit number for that alternate Possession Order.

And here's how to fill out your Exhibits . . .

Top. On the **first** page of each Exhibit, enter the cause number and the Exhibit number. **Footers.** At the foot of **each page**, enter the Exhibit number.

Exhibit: Conservatorship Orders

This Exhibit is where you define the rights and duties of each parent.

Page 1, item A spells out parents' rights and duties in detail, so read it very carefully and, if possible, discuss it with the other parent. No choices to make on this page.

Page 2, item B1 – Joint Custody. Check B1 if you want joint custody and check the first box below to indicate which parent will have the right to decide where the child/ren will live and whether that choice is limited to a specific school zone, county, state or region. If neither parent will have that right exclusively, the Court will order the child/ren to be kept in a specific zone or region that you define by checking boxes.

Page 3. Check one box in each of the 9 rows to show how the parents will share various rights and one duty. Read carefully and for each item, indicate whether the matters described will be the right (or duty) of one parent alone, the other parent, both together, or each to have authority without consulting the other.

Item B2 – Sole custody and visitation. Fill in the names to indicate which parent has sole custody (the Managing Conservator) and which parent has visitation (the Possessory Conservator).

Page 4. Nothing to do on this page, just enter the Exhibit number at the bottom.

Exhibit: Possession Order

This Exhibit is the Standard Possession Order (SPO). Read chapter C3 and study this Exhibit (back of book) carefully. Notice the places with blanks or check boxes where you must indicate times or make choices. Think about it and fill it out.

Whatever your custody order says, it is the Possession Order that determines when each parent will have the child. Notice that the second paragraph says that parents can have the child any time by mutual agreement in advance—it is only when there is no agreement that parents must abide by the SPO. The SPO will be issued in every case. If you want restricted visitation or no visitation at all, consult an attorney (see chapter A8), or ask at the Clerk's Office if there are local resources for help with visitation.

It is probably a good idea to create a separate schedule for a child under three, in which case you would prepare two schedules. The first one is the Standard Possession Order, and the second is the Possession Order for Children Under Three. You'll find one on the CD. There is also a file with suggestions for suitable posssession terms for infants. The Standard Order automatically takes over when a child reaches its 3rd birthday.

Exhibit: Child Support Order

Page 1, item 1. Check boxes to indicate which party pays (the Obligor) and which party receives (the Obligee) child support payments.

Page 1, item 2 – Amount. In most cases, use the guideline amount (chapter D).

If just one child is being supported, check the 1st box. Enter the amount due and the date for the first payment. Choose a date after the date the Decree is signed.

For more than one child, check the 2nd box. On the first line enter the total amount for all children and the date for the first payment (after the date the Decree is signed). On the lines that follow, enter the amount that will be due for one less child. Say you have three children: you would enter the amount for all three on the first line, then the amount for two on the second line and the amount for one child on the third.

Page 3, item 6 – Child Support Guideline. Check the 1st box if your support order is about the same as recommended by Texas guidelines (see chapter D). If your order is quite different, check the 2nd box and enter the information requested. Net resource figures (income) are described in chapter D2. The last entry wants a brief list of facts that would make the guideline amount unfair or inappropriate.

Page 3, item 7 – Disabled Child. Check this box if you have a disabled child that will need support indefinitely. Enter the amount you want ordered and be prepared to explain your situation and needs at your hearing. Bring documentation if you have any.

Exhibits: Medical Support Order and Dental Support Order

You need both. The two forms are identical so follow the same instructions for each.

Names. At items B1 and B2, enter the name of Obligor (person who pays) and Obligee (recipient) the same way those names appear in the caption of your documents.

Page 1, item A – Availability of Health/Dental Insurance. Check box A1 if health and/or dental insurance **is** available *at a reasonable cost* (see page 61). Check any of the next four boxes below to show the ways that such insurance is available to Obligor. Check A2 if health/dental insurance is **not** available to either parent at reasonable cost. Check boxes to indicate whether your children are currently covered by Medicaid or by C.H.I.P. If they are, enter the cost.

Under A2: Priorities not followed? The Court is supposed to follow a list of priorities in ordering health insurance for children: 1st choice should be insurance available through a parent's work or membership; 2nd choice is insurance available through another means; and 3rd would be government assistance. If you want an order that does not follow these priorities, check this box and explain your reasons. Fam Code 154.182.

Page 1, item B1 – Obligor to Provide Health Insurance. Check B1 if Obligor is ordered to provide health and/or dental insurance. Enter Obligor's name, then check a box to show where the insurance will come from: through work, etc, or some other source.

Page 2, item B2 – Obligee to Provide Health/Dental Insurance and Be Reimbursed. Check B2 if Obligee is ordered to provide health and/or dental insurance. Enter Obligee's name, then check a box to show where it will come from: through work, etc, or some other source. Then, on page 3, enter Obligor's name and the amount of additional support to be paid per month as reimbursement to Obligee for health insurance premiums. Enter the date the first payment is due (some time after the date the Decree is signed).

Page 3, item B3 – Obligee to Apply for Assistance. If medical and/or dental coverage is available to Obligee under a government program like Medicaid or C.H.I.P., and if there's no chance of getting it through any other means available to either party at a reasonable cost, check B3 and enter Obligee's name. Read the rest of this part carefully.

Then, on page 4, enter Obligor's name and the amount of additional support to be paid per month as reimbursement to Obligee for health and/or dental insurance premiums. Enter the date the first payment is due (some time after the date the Decree is signed).

❺ Notes for page 5 of the Decree – cases with children

Item 5H, Required Information. In cases with children, a final order has to contain personal information about each parent and each child, including: current residence and mailing addresses, home phone, name of employer and employer's address and work phone, and social security and driver's license number if they have them. Each party **must** notify the other parent, the court and the state case registry of an intended change in any of the personal information.

In your Petition (page 5, item 7) you might have asked the court to excuse you from giving this information to the other parent due to risk of harassment, abuse or harm, or you might have asked for the information to be made unavailable to the public. If so, here's how you deal with personal information at your hearing.

1. If you plan to attach the required information, check this box, enter the number of the Family Information form (described below) and attach it to the Decree.

2. Sealing personal information is good common sense, but not required by law. It might be best to leave this paragraph in your Decree with the boxes blank, and at the hearing remember to ask the judge to protect your family from identity theft by ordering your information to be sealed from public view.

3. If you can present facts to show the judge that giving personal information to Respondent would expose a party or child to harassment or abuse, check the third box and do not attach the Required Information exhibit. But bring it to court in case the judge doesn't think your evidence is convincing. If that happens, refer the judge to item 2 above and ask to order the information sealed.

If you choose option 2 or 3 or both, bring a completed Order to Keep Family Information Confidential (on the CD) and ask the judge to sign it.

Exhibit: Family Information

Enter cause number and Exhibit number at the top. Enter requested information for each party and child. Try to get it all, as it will help if enforcement is required.

If you don't know an item, put "unknown." If a child has no Social Security number, contact the Social Security office to get one, as it is necessary for the enforcement of support orders. Enter driver's license numbers for children who have them, otherwise type in "none."

❻ **Page 6.** Nothing to do here but enter the correct page number at the bottom.

❼ Notes for page 7 of the Decree

Item 6, Property and Debts.

1st box: No property. If your Petition did not list any community property (CP) or separate property (SP) for the Court to deal with, check the 1st box under item 6.

2nd box: Agreement. If you have a written settlement agreement, check the 2nd box and attach your agreement to the Decree. It will then become part of the Court's orders.

3rd box: Divided by the Court. If your Petition listed separate property or debts (SP) or community property or debts (CP), check the 3rd box, enter the Exhibit number, and attach the Orders Re Property and Debts exhibit.

Exhibit: Orders Re Property and Debts

How to list property and debts. Look at the checklist in chapter B3 and review the notes for page six of the Petition in chapter 5 (page 96).

Page 1, item A1. Check this box to confirm ownership of separate property and debts to the Petitioner and list the separate property and debts being confirmed.

Page 1, item A2. Check this box to confirm ownership of separate property and debts to the Respondent and list the separate property and debts being confirmed.

Page 1, item B1 - Pension plan. If you can't manage to award all of a defined benefit pension plan to the employee-spouse, check this box and the court will retain jurisdiction over the plan, and the employee is ordered not to apply for or accept benefits under the plan without notifying the other spouse. **Warning!** You *must* seek to clarify or divide rights in the plan within two years or lose the right. You'll need the help of an attorney to correctly divide a pension or retirement fund (see chapter A8).

Enter the employee's name on the first line, then enter the account number and exact name of the plan. Then enter the name of the employee on the last line in B1.

Page 2, item B2 - Community property awarded to Petitioner. Check this box if any CP is being awarded to Petitioner. Check boxes and list property as indicated by the other items below.

Page 3 item 3 - Petitioner's Debts. Check boxes at this item to identify the debts that Petitioner will be responsible to pay.

Page 3, item 4 - Community property awarded to Respondent. Check this box if any CP is being awarded to Respondent. Check boxes and list property as indicated by the other items below.

Page 4 item 5 - Respondent's Debts. Check boxes at this item to identify the debts that Respondent will be responsible to pay.

Note about debts. Ordering one spouse or the other to pay a debt is effective between the spouses but it does not affect the rights of creditors. If you were liable for a debt before you divorced, you will still be liable for it afterward. If your spouse doesn't pay, the creditor can come after you. So, it might be best to take debts you think your spouse might not pay in exchange for a larger share of some other property.

Item 9, Spousal Maintenance. Check this box if there will be an order for spousal maintenance, then check a box to show which party will receive it. Check one or more of the first two boxes below to show grounds for a support order, then check any of the last three boxes to show reasons that justify it. Review chapter D for a discussion of the requirements for spousal maintenance in Texas.

(this item continues onto page 8)

❽ Notes for page 8 of the Decree. Fill it out as shown on the next page.

At the top of page 8, continue the order for spousal maintenance. Check a box to show who will pay it and who will receive it. Enter the amount per month and the date the first payment is to be made, some date after the Decree is signed. Enter the number of months spousal maintenance will continue.

❾ Notes for page 9 of the Decree.

In every case, you will sign the Decree on this page. Enter your name and phone number on the first line, date and sign the second line, and enter your address below that.

If your spouse will sign it (see chapter E1), enter his/her name and phone number, get his/her signature on line 2, then make three or four copies of the signed Decree.

You sign on this side.	By signing below, the Petitioner agrees to the form and substance of this Decree.	By signing below, the Respondent agrees to the form and substance of this Decree.
	Petitioner's Name (print) Phone number	Respondent's Name (print) Phone number
	Petitioner's Signature Date	Respondent's Signature Date
	Mailing Address	Mailing Address
	City State Zip	City State Zip

Then what?

Check all of your forms for accuracy, make three or four copies of each, and take all originals and copies with you to the hearing. When they are filed, ask the clerk to file-stamp your copies and ask the clerk for one or two certified copies of the Decree.

How to fill out the Decree
Page 8

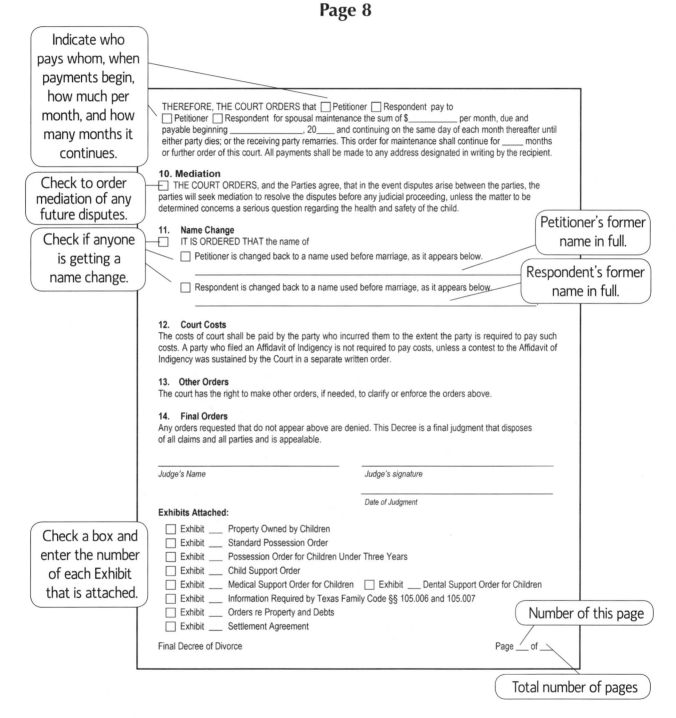

Indicate who pays whom, when payments begin, how much per month, and how many months it continues.

THEREFORE, THE COURT ORDERS that ☐ Petitioner ☐ Respondent pay to ☐ Petitioner ☐ Respondent for spousal maintenance the sum of $_____ per month, due and payable beginning _____, 20____ and continuing on the same day of each month thereafter until either party dies; or the receiving party remarries. This order for maintenance shall continue for _____ months or further order of this court. All payments shall be made to any address designated in writing by the recipient.

10. Mediation

Check to order mediation of any future disputes.

☐ THE COURT ORDERS, and the Parties agree, that in the event disputes arise between the parties, the parties will seek mediation to resolve the disputes before any judicial proceeding, unless the matter to be determined concerns a serious question regarding the health and safety of the child.

11. Name Change

Check if anyone is getting a name change.

☐ IT IS ORDERED THAT the name of

☐ Petitioner is changed back to a name used before marriage, as it appears below.

Petitioner's former name in full.

_____

☐ Respondent is changed back to a name used before marriage, as it appears below.

Respondent's former name in full.

_____

12. Court Costs

The costs of court shall be paid by the party who incurred them to the extent the party is required to pay such costs. A party who filed an Affidavit of Indigency is not required to pay costs, unless a contest to the Affidavit of Indigency was sustained by the Court in a separate written order.

13. Other Orders

The court has the right to make other orders, if needed, to clarify or enforce the orders above.

14. Final Orders

Any orders requested that do not appear above are denied. This Decree is a final judgment that disposes of all claims and all parties and is appealable.

_____   _____
Judge's Name   *Judge's signature*

                                      _____
                                      Date of Judgment

Exhibits Attached:

Check a box and enter the number of each Exhibit that is attached.

☐ Exhibit ____ Property Owned by Children
☐ Exhibit ____ Standard Possession Order
☐ Exhibit ____ Possession Order for Children Under Three Years
☐ Exhibit ____ Child Support Order
☐ Exhibit ____ Medical Support Order for Children   ☐ Exhibit ____ Dental Support Order for Children
☐ Exhibit ____ Information Required by Texas Family Code §§ 105.006 and 105.007
☐ Exhibit ____ Orders re Property and Debts
☐ Exhibit ____ Settlement Agreement

Final Decree of Divorce   Page ____ of ____

Number of this page

Total number of pages

8. The Statistics Form

Information on Suit
Affecting the Family Relationship

What is it?

Although the court already has a file full of information about your divorce, they need this additional form to track and report the basics of your case to the Bureau of Vital Statistics. When there are children, the State Case Registry uses it for tracking support orders and payments. The Bureau of Vital Statistics uses the basic information about your divorce for their periodic statistical reports.

Like all the forms in these chapters, this form is in the back of the book and on the companion CD. You probably won't need them, but for your convenience we also included on the CD the official instructions for filling out this form.

How to fill it out

Fill it out as shown on the next three pages.

Then what?

Make one copy of the completed form for your own files and take the original with you to the hearing. The clerk will ask for it at the right time.

Note! This form *must* be printed on two sides of one page, not two separate pages.

Notes for the front side

There is no need to cross out unused sections on this form.

Section 1. The information for item 1 comes from the caption on your divorce forms. At item 3, check one of the top boxes to indicate whether or not your divorce involves children. At item 4, because you are representing yourself, enter your own name, phone, and address. Your name should be followed by a comma and the words Pro Se. Leave box 4b blank.

Section 2. Fill in all requested information. If no children, enter "0" at item 17.

Section 3. Fill in as many segments as you have children. If more than four children, attach an additional form marked "continuation" at the top and attach it to the original form. As children of divorce do not typically get new names, nor are they typically known by a prior name (a.k.a.), most people will leave items f and g blank.

Notes for the back side

Section 4. Must be completed if there is child support. "Obligee" is the parent receiving support and "obligor #1" is the parent who pays support. Check box 25c or 25d to show if obligee is the husband or wife, then complete only items 31 and 32. Next, check box 33b or 33c to show if obligor #1 is the husband or the wife, then complete only items 39 to 43.

Section 5. Leave blank.

Section 6. Leave blank.

Information on Suit
Affecting the Family Relationship

Front side

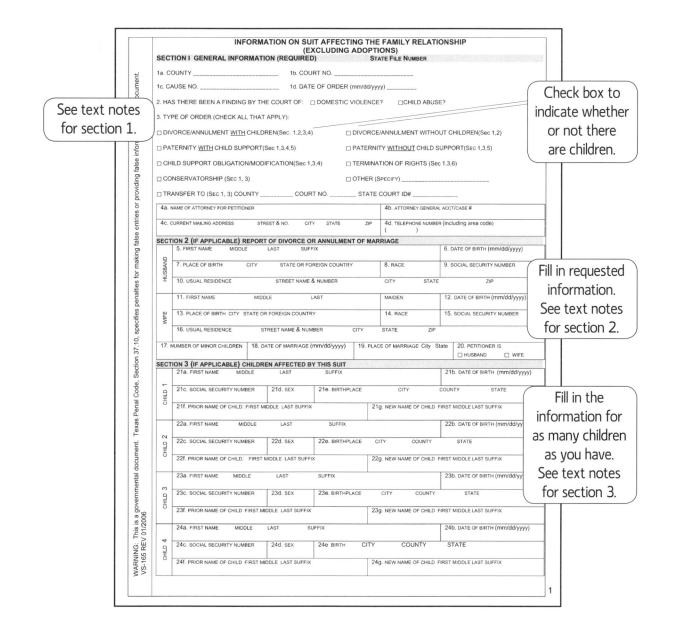

See text notes for section 1.

Check box to indicate whether or not there are children.

Fill in requested information. See text notes for section 2.

Fill in the information for as many children as you have. See text notes for section 3.

Information on Suit
Affecting the Family Relationship

Back side

See text notes for filling out section 4.

Leave this part blank.

Leave the rest blank.

SECTION 4 (IF APPLICABLE) OBLIGEE/OBLIGOR INFORMATION

THIS PARTY TO THE SUIT IS (CHECK ONE)	☐ 25a. TDPRS	☐ 25b. NON-PARENT CONSERVATOR – COMPLETE 26 – 32
☐ 25c. HUSBAND AS SHOWN ON FRONT OF THIS FORM – COMPLETE 31 – 32 ONLY		☐ 25d. WIFE AS SHOWN ON FRONT OF THIS FORM – COMPLETE 31 – 32 ONLY
☐ 25e. BIOLOGICAL FATHER – COMPLETE 26 – 32		☐ 25f. BIOLOGICAL MOTHER – COMPLETE 26 – 32

26. FIRST NAME MIDDLE LAST SUFFIX		MAIDEN
27. DATE OF BIRTH (mm/dd/yyyy)	28. PLACE OF BIRTH CITY STATE OR FOREIGN COUNTRY	
29. USUAL RESIDENCE	STREET NAME & NUMBER CITY COUNTY STATE ZIP	
30. SOCIAL SECURITY NUMBER	31. DRIVER LICENSE NO & STATE	32. TELEPHONE NUMBER ( )

THIS PARTY TO THE SUIT IS (CHECK ONE)	☐ 33a. NON-PARENT CONSERVATOR – COMPLETE 34 – 43
☐ 33b. HUSBAND AS SHOWN ON FRONT OF THIS FORM – COMPLETE 39 – 43 ONLY	☐ 33c. WIFE AS SHOWN ON FRONT OF THIS FORM – COMPLETE 39 – 43 ONLY
☐ 33d. BIOLOGICAL FATHER – COMPLETE 34 – 43	☐ 33e. BIOLOGICAL MOTHER – COMPLETE 34 – 43

34. FIRST NAME MIDDLE LAST SUFFIX	MAIDEN
35. DATE OF BIRTH (mm/dd/yyyy)	36. PLACE OF BIRTH CITY STATE OR FOREIGN COUNTRY
37. USUAL RESIDENCE	STREET NAME & NUMBER CITY COUNTY STATE ZIP
38. SOCIAL SECURITY NUMBER	39 DRIVER LICENSE NO. & STATE 40. TELEPHONE NUMBER ( )
41. EMPLOYER NAME	42. EMPLOYER TELEPHONE NUMBER
43. EMPLOYER PAYROLL ADDRESS STREET NAME & NUMBER CITY STATE ZIP	

(OBLIGOR #1)

THIS PARTY TO THE SUIT IS (CHECK ONE) ☐ 44a. NON-PARENT CONSERVATOR – COMPLETE 45 – 54	
☐ 44b. HUSBAND AS SHOWN ON FRONT OF THIS FORM – COMPLETE 50 – 54 ONLY	☐ 44c. WIFE AS SHOWN ON FRONT OF THIS FORM – COMPLETE 45 – 54 ONLY
☐ 44d. BIOLOGICAL FATHER – COMPLETE 45 – 54	☐ 44e. BIOLOGICAL MOTHER – COMPLETE 45 – 54

45. FIRST NAME MIDDLE LAST SUFFIX	MAIDEN
46. DATE OF BIRTH (mm/dd/yyyy)	47. PLACE OF BIRTH CITY STATE OR FOREIGN COUNTRY
48. USUAL RESIDENCE	STREET NAME & NUMBER CITY COUNTY STATE ZIP
49. SOCIAL SECURITY NUMBER	50. DRIVER LICENSE NO & STATE 51. TELEPHONE NUMBER
52. EMPLOYER NAME	53. EMPLOYER TELEPHONE NUMBER
54. EMPLOYER PAYROLL ADDRESS STREET NAME & NUMBER CITY STATE ZIP	

SECTION 5 (IF APPLICABLE) FOR ORDERS CONCERNING PATERNITY ESTABLISHMENT OF BIOLOGICAL FATHER

55. BIOLOGICAL FATHER'S NAME FIRST MIDDLE LAST	56. DATE OF BIRTH (mm/dd/yyyy)
57. SOCIAL SECURITY NUMBER	58. CURRENT MAILING ADDRESS STREET NAME & NUMBER CITY STATE ZIP

DOES THIS ORDER REMOVE INFORMATION PERTAINING TO A FATHER FROM A CHILD'S CERTIFICATE OF BIRTH? ☐ NO ☐ YES

SECTION 6 TERMINATION OF RIGHTS – INFORMATION RELATED TO THE INDIVIDUAL(S) WHOSE RIGHTS ARE BEING TERMINATED IN THIS SUIT.

FIRST NAME MIDDLE NAME LAST NAME SUFFIX	60b. RELATIONSHIP
61a. FIRST NAME MIDDLE NAME LAST NAME SUUFIX	61b. RELATIONSHIP
62a. FIRST NAME MIDDLE NAME LAST NAME SUFFIX	62b. RELATIONSHIP

COMMENTS: _____

_____

I CERTIFY THAT THE ABOVE ORDER WAS GRANTED ON THE
DATE AND PLACE AS STATED.

_____
SIGNATURE OF THE CLERK OF THE COURT

9. The Income Withholding Order (IWO)
and the Request to Issue IWO

A. The Income Withholding Order (IWO)

You prepare this form whenever income withholding will be ordered in your Decree for child support, cash for medical support, dental support, or spousal maintenance.

When ordered by a court, any employer that gets served with an Income Withholding Order (IWO) must withhold a percentage of Obligor's pay and send it to the person or agency named in the order.

Child support. Every child support order must contain a provision for income withholding, no exceptions. If the Obligor is self-employed, unemployed, or can't be found, the IWO will remain on file until it can be used. If the Obligor changes employment, just fill out a Request to Issue an IWO (section B below) and take it to the clerk's office to get a new IWO issued and served.

IWO for spousal maintenance. The court can issue an order for income withholding for spousal maintenance, but even when the Decree contains an order based on a written agreement of the spouses, the IWO cannot be for more than the amount and duration that a court could have ordered under Texas law if there were no agreement. See chapter D for the limits on court ordered spousal maintenance.

Suspension of the IWO. If the parties agree, and the Court approves, the Decree can order that no income withholding order will be issued or served on the employer unless: 1) child support payments are more than 30 days late, or 2) the past due amount is the same or more than the monthly child support amount, or 3) another violation of the child support order occurs or 4) another court or agency is already providing child support services to the support recipient.

Cooperation. If you and your Ex are on good terms, you can agree informally that you will not request the clerk to issue and serve the IWO so long as support payments are not more than a certain number of days late. Best to do this in writing, at least a signed letter, so you can remind one another later what you agreed to. However, if the children are receiving public assistance, or if the Office of the Attorney General is managing your child support case, this might be out of your hands.

How to fill it out

Note 1. Check the first box for an "Original" IWO, assuming this is your first IWO. Check the second box if this IWO amends a previous IWO. Check the third box if this is for a one-time lump sum payment. Check the fourth box if this terminates an IWO.

At the far right, leave the date blank. It will get entered when the judge signs it.

In the box below the caption, the box for Court is checked to indicate that the IWO will be issued by the court after the judge signs it.

Note 2. Left column. On the second line, under "Texas," enter the county where your Petition was filed. Right column. Leave "Remittance Identifier" blank unless you happen to know it. For "Order Identifier" enter your cause number as it appears on your Decree. For "CSE Agency Case Identifier," if you have an Attorney General case number or a State Disbursement Unit case number, enter that, otherwise leave it blank.

Note 3. Left column. Top line, Employer: enter "Any Employer or Income Withholder of Obligor named in this order." If you have it, bring the Employer's name and address with you to your hearing. After the IWO is signed and filed, ask the clerk to send it to the Employer. Below the address, enter Employer's FEIN number if you have it. You can leave this blank, or call their accounting department or person and ask for their Federal EIN tax number. Right column. Top line, "RE:" enter Obligor's full name, last name first. Below that, Obligor's Social Security number, and on the bottom line, enter your full name, last name first.

Note 4. List the children for whom support has been ordered, last name first, and enter their birth dates. If more than six, enter additional children's names and birthdates on page 3 under "Additional Information."

Note 5. Top line, enter the total amount of monthly child support as was ordered in your Decree. If an amount has been ordered for past due child support enter it on the 2nd line and check a box to indicate if the arrears are greater than 12 weeks' worth. Enter an amount on the 3rd and 4th lines only if you have an order for cash medical or dental support or past-due cash medical or dental support. **Spousal support:** If spousal maintenance has been ordered, enter the **monthly** amount on the 6th line. **Total:** At the bottom, "Total Amount to Withhold," enter the total of all monthly support that has been ordered.

Terminate withholding. To have your IWO terminate withholding, enter $0 for the amount of support.

Note 6. Enter the amount to be withheld to match any pay cycle.
- Weekly: Multiply the total monthly amount by 12 then divide by 52.
- Biweekly: Multiply the total monthly amount by 12 then divide by 26.
- Semi-monthly: Divide the total monthly amount by 2.

Income Withholding Order
Page 1

INCOME WITHHOLDING FOR SUPPORT

Note 1

☐ ORIGINAL INCOME WITHHOLDING ORDER/NOTICE FOR SUPPORT (IWO)
☐ AMENDED IWO
☐ ONE-TIME ORDER/NOTICE FOR LUMP SUM PAYMENT
☐ TERMINATION of IWO

Date: _Leave this blank_

☐ Child Support Enforcement (CSE) Agency ☒ Court ☐ Attorney ☐ Private Individual/Entity (Check One)
NOTE: This IWO must be regular on its face. Under certain circumstances you must reject this IWO and return it to the sender (see IWO instructions http://www.acf.hhs.gov/programs/cse/forms/OMB-0970-0154_instructions.pdf). If you receive this document from someone other than a State or Tribal CSE agency or a Court, a copy of the underlying order must be attached.

Note 2

State/Tribe/Territory _Texas_
City/County/Dist./Tribe _Your County_
Private Individual/Entity_____

Remittance Identifier (include w/payment) _If you know it_
Order Identifier _Cause number of your case_
CSE Agency Case Identifier _AG case # or SDU Case # if you know it_

Note 3

Any Employer or Income Withholder of Obligor named in this order
Employer/Income Withholder's Name

Employer/Income Withholder's Address

Employer/Income Withholder's FEIN _Blank if not known_

RE: _Obligor's full name — last name first_
Employee/Obligor's Name (Last, First, Middle)
Obligor's full Social Security Number
Employee/Obligor's Social Security Number
Recipient's full name — last name first
Custodial Party/Obligee's Name (Last, First, Middle)

Note 4

Child(ren)'s Name(s) (Last, First, Middle)   Child(ren)'s Birth Date(s)

Note 5

ORDER INFORMATION: This document is based on the support or withholding order from _Texas_ (State/Tribe). You are required by law to deduct these amounts from the employee/obligor's income until further notice.
$_____ Per month_____ current child support
$_____ Per month_____ past-due child support - **Arrears greater than 12 weeks?** ☐ Yes ☐ No
$_____ Per month_____ current cash medical support
$_____ Per month_____ past-due cash medical support
$_____ Per month_____ current spousal support
$_____ Per month_____ past-due spousal support
$_____ Per_____ other (must specify) _____
for a **Total Amount to Withhold** of $_____ per month_____.

Note 6

AMOUNTS TO WITHHOLD: You do not have to vary your pay cycle to be in compliance with the _Order Information_. If your pay cycle does not match the ordered payment cycle, withhold one of the following amounts:
$_____ per weekly pay period $_____ per semimonthly pay period (twice a month)
$_____ per biweekly pay period (every two weeks) $_____ per monthly pay period
$_____ **Lump Sum Payment:** Do not stop any existing IWO unless you receive a termination order.

REMITTANCE INFORMATION: If the employee/obligor's principal place of employment is Texas, you must begin withholding no later than the first pay period following the date this Order/Notice was delivered to the employer. Send payment on the same day as the pay date/date of withholding. If you cannot withhold the full amount of support for any or all orders for this employee/obligor, withhold up to 50% of disposable income for all orders. If the employee/obligor's principal place of employment is not Texas, obtain withholding limitations, time requirements, and any allowable employer fees at http://www.acf.hhs.gov/programs/cse/newhire/employer/contacts/contact_map.htm for the employee/obligor's principal place of employment.

Document Tracking Identifier _Leave this blank_   OMB 0970-0154

The Income Withholding Order — page 2

There is nothing for you to fill out on page two. The court will handle it.

The Income Withholding Order — page 3

Note 7. Enter the Employer's name if you know it. Enter the Employer's FEIN number if you know it. If convenient, call the Employer's accounting department or person and ask for their Federal EIN tax number. Or leave it blank.

Note 8 – Contact Information. What you enter here depends upon who is managing your support payments.

If you already have a support account, enter the contact information for the office that handles your account.

If you don't already have a support account, ask the court clerk how you should go about setting up an account in your county. Contact that office, start setting up an account, and get from them the contact information to enter on this form.

Income Withholding Order

Page 3

Note 7

Employer's Name:_*Leave this blank if not known*_____ Employer FEIN: _*Blank if not known*____

Employee/Obligor's Name: _*Full name of Obligor — the person ordered to pay support*_____

CSE Agency Case Identifier: _*AG or SDU case number if you know it*_ Order Identifier: _*Cause number of your divorce case*_____

Withholding Limits: You may not withhold more than the lesser of: 1) the amounts allowed by the Federal Consumer Credit Protection Act (CCPA) (15 U.S.C. 1673(b)); or 2) the amounts allowed by the State or Tribe of the employee/obligor's principal place of employment (see *REMITTANCE INFORMATION*). Disposable income is the net income left after making mandatory deductions such as: State, Federal, local taxes; Social Security taxes; statutory pension contributions; and Medicare taxes. The Federal limit is 50% of the disposable income if the obligor is supporting another family and 60% of the disposable income if the obligor is not supporting another family. However, those limits increase 5% - to 55% and 65% - if the arrears are greater than 12 weeks. If permitted by the State or Tribe, you may deduct a fee for administrative costs. The combined support amount and fee may not exceed the limit indicated in this section.

For Tribal orders, you may not withhold more than the amounts allowed under the law of the issuing Tribe. For Tribal employers/income withholders who receive a State IWO, you may not withhold more than the lesser of the limit set by the law of the jurisdiction in which the employer/income withholder is located or the maximum amount permitted under section 303(d) of the CCPA (15 U.S.C. 1673 (b)).

Depending upon applicable State or Tribal law, you may need to also consider the amounts paid for health care premiums in determining disposable income and applying appropriate withholding limits.

Arrears greater than 12 weeks? If the *Order Information* does not indicate that the arrears are greater than 12 weeks, then the Employer should calculate the CCPA limit using the lower percentage.

Additional Information:

_____

NOTIFICATION OF EMPLOYMENT TERMINATION OR INCOME STATUS: If this employee/obligor never worked for you or you are no longer withholding income for this employee/obligor, an employer must promptly notify the CSE agency and/or the sender by returning this form to the address listed in the Contact Information below:

☐ This person has never worked for this employer nor received periodic income.

☐ This person no longer works for this employer nor receives periodic income.

Please provide the following information for the employee/obligor:

Termination date: _____ Last known phone number: _____

Last known address: _____

Final payment date to SDU/ Tribal Payee: _____ Final payment amount: _____

New employer's name: _____

New employer's address: _____

CONTACT INFORMATION:

Note 8

<u>To Employer/Income Withholder:</u> If you have any questions, contact _____ (Issuer name)

by phone at _____, by fax at _____, by email or website at: _____.

Send termination/income status notice and other correspondence to:

_____(Issuer address).

<u>To Employee/Obligor:</u> If the employee/obligor has questions, contact _____ (Issuer name)

by phone at _____, by fax at_____, by email or website at:_____.

IMPORTANT: The person completing this form is advised that the information may be shared with the employee/obligor.

B. The Request to Issue Income Withholding Order

When you file your Decree ordering support, you'll want to ask the clerk to issue a certified copy of the IWO and deliver it to the Obligor's employer. If the obligor changes jobs, you'll need to ask the clerk to issue another certified copy of the IWO and deliver it to the new employer. You might need to file a form to get this done.

First, ask the court clerk if they want you to file a request form in order to get an IWO sent to the Obligor's employer right after the Decree is filed. If not, ask if they will want you to file a request form if you need to have an IWO served on new and different employers in the future.

Next, ask if they have a local form they want you to use. If so, get it and use it. If they don't have a local form but they do want a written request, use this form.

Ask if you can mail the form or fax it and how then to arrange payment of their fee. Finally, ask how much they charge to get a certified copy of the IWO issued and sent.

How to fill it out

First, make a copy of the blank form to keep in your file. If the Obligor changes jobs in the future, you will need to fill out another request to have an IWO sent to the new employer.

Note 1. Fill in the caption just like you did for all your other forms. See chapter 3B

Note 2. Enter the date your IWO was signed by the judge.

Note 3. Enter the Employer's name and other requested contact information. If the Employer is a larger company, they may have a particular office, department, or person who handles wage withholding. It is the contact information for that person or department that you want to enter here. Call the company and ask about this. If they don't cooperate, just send it to their local address where Obligor works.

Note 4. Enter the date you signed this form, your signature, and add your own contact information on the lines below.

Privacy. In cases where you need to protect the location of a party, you can omit this information.

Then what?

Make three copies of the completed form. You do not have to present these at the hearing, but keep them in your file anyway, just in case. If for some reason you are not going to ask the clerk to serve the order(s) on the employer right now, just keep this form in your file until the time comes that you do want the Withholding Order issued and served.

Request to Issue Withholding Order

Cause Number _____

IN THE MATTER OF THE MARRIAGE OF

Petitioner: _____   In the

Note 1

_____ ☐ District Court ☐ County Court
And   at Law of

Respondent: _____   _____ County, Texas

☐ AND IN THE INTEREST OF:

1. _____ 2. _____ 3. _____
4. _____ 5. _____ 6. _____

Request to Issue
Income Withholding Order / Notice

To the Clerk of the Court:

Pursuant to Family Code § 158, please issue a certified copy of the following order in this cause:

Income Withholding Order/Notice for Support

Note 2

Signed by the Court on *Date your IWO was signed by the judge* _____

And deliver the order to Employer's current address at:

Obligor's Employer: *Name of Employer - If there's a particular person to send to, add "Attention: (their name)"*

Note 3

Employer's Address: *Address where payroll or billing or personnel matters are handled*

City, State, Zip: _____

Employer's Phone: _____ Fax: _____

Employer's Email _____

Note 4

Request Submitted on *Date you signed this form* _____

_____
Signed: Obligee / Requestor

Daytime phone: _____

_____
Address

_____
City   State   Zip

10. The Military Status Affidavit

What it is

In every default case—that is, where Respondent has not filed a Response or a Waiver of Service—the court needs to know for sure whether or not Respondent is on active military duty. So in default cases, you have to file a Military Status Affidavit with your Decree, stating under oath if you know whether or not Respondent is on active duty.

Why? If Respondent **is** on active duty, the Court *must* appoint a lawyer (that you pay for) to represent him/her.

Don't know? If you don't know for sure either way, you might be ordered to post a bond (money or guarantee of money) that would be used to help Respondent if it later turns out that he/she was on active duty when the judgment was ordered.

If the Court grants a judgment and it later turns out that Respondent was on active duty, Respondent has until 90 days after discharge to set the judgment aside.

If Respondent is on active duty and refuses to sign the Waiver, you will probably need to get an attorney to help you complete your case (see chapter A8).

How. You have to state **facts** in your Affidavit to show what you know about Respondent's military status. If you have Respondent's Social Security Number, you can request a report from the Department of Defense to establish if Respondent is on active duty. Go to www.dmdc.osd.mil/appj/scra/single_record.xhtml If your browser throws up a red warning that the site's security certificate is not trusted, it is okay to keep going. If you want to know why, it's the first item on the site's FAQ list.

If that doesn't work, contact a local military office and ask their help or hire an investigator who specializes in finding information about people, dig around. List on your Affidavit what steps you took to determine that Respondent is or is not on active duty.

Notarization. Statements on the Military Status Affidavit are made under penalty of perjury and must be signed in the presence of a notary or a court clerk who is authorized to take statements under oath. (The Waiver is easier: troops who are deployed can have the Waiver notarized by any field-grade officer, such as their commanding officer or executive officer.)

How to fill it out. Fill it out as shown in the illustrations on the next page.

Then what? Sign the form under oath before either a notary or clerk of the court. Make three copies and file it along with your Decree or bring it to your hearing.

Military Status Affidavit

Page 1. Fill out the caption as shown on page 81, just as you did for all the other forms. Then enter your name and Respondent's name.

Item 3. Check all boxes that apply, as shown below. Item 3 continues on page 2.

Page 1, item 3

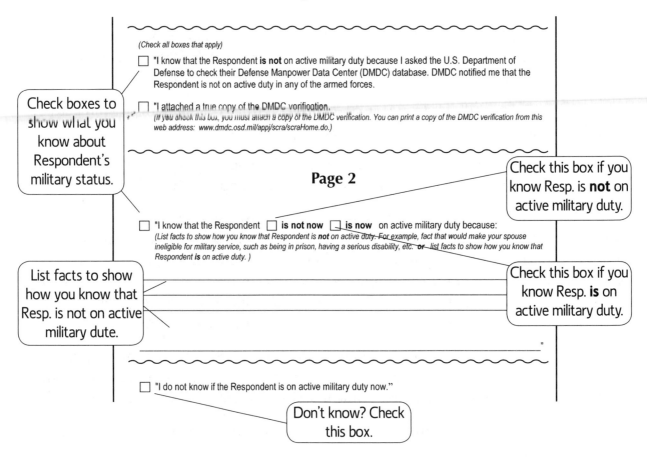

Signature. Don't date and sign until you are before a notary. This is a sworn statement.

11. The Hearing

In order to complete your divorce, and as the *last* (hooray!) item of business, you must attend a hearing and say a few words about your case. The hearing will be very brief, usually a mere formality. Most of your time will be spent waiting for it to start, and it will be over in a few minutes. So don't worry. In the next few pages, we show you how to set the date, what to do when you get there, and what to say. It is not likely that you will have any problems, but we have advice to cover even that remote event.

A. Are you ready? Prehearing checklist

1. All cases

Waiting periods. There is a 61 day waiting period that is required in all cases. It can sometimes be quite tricky to compute, so it is safer to allow two months plus two weeks to pass from the date you filed your Petition before the day of your hearing. Other shorter waiting periods (chapter A3) will likely fall within that 61 days, but if not, wait them out.

Before you go, make sure you have your Decree with needed attachments, the Withholding Order (if there's child or spousal support), and the Information on Suit Affecting Family Relationship form. If you plan to have your spouse's signature on the Decree or any other written agreements, this must be done before you go to the hearing.

2. Waiver cases

If your spouse signed the Waiver form, and it is properly signed, notarized, and on file at the District Clerk's Office, then you can set the hearing as soon as the 61 day waiting period is over.

3. Default cases

You can have your hearing no sooner than:
1) At least 61 days after the date you filed your Petition.
   • If a Waiver of Service was signed, this is the only waiting period.
   • This period can be waived if you have a protective order against your spouse for domestic violence, or deferred adjudication or conviction for family violence against you or a family member.
2) If your spouse was served by a process server, you must wait at least 21 days after the date of service, then go to the next Monday for your earliest

hearing date. *And* the Return of Service must have been filed at least 12 days before your hearing date. The long and the two short waiting periods are not consecutive: if a short period ends before the end of the 61 day period, it won't have any effect.

3) If you served by posting your Citation (chapter 6), wait at least 28 days after the date the Return of Citation was filed with the District Clerk.

4. Wife pregnant?

Not exactly a waiting period, but if the wife is pregnant, few judges would finalize a divorce until the baby is born and child related orders are included in the Decree.

B. Getting into court

The way uncontested divorces are scheduled varies. It is usually informal and always easy. When you are ready to set the date, call the court clerk and ask when uncontested divorce hearings are scheduled and how you go about getting a date. Then ask how the court's file for your case will get to the courtroom for your hearing. In some counties you go to clerk's office before the hearing, get your file and carry it to the courtroom yourself. In other counties, you notify the clerk ahead of time when you are coming in for your hearing and they get your file there for you. In that case, when you first arrive for your hearing, check with the bailiff or clerk to make sure your file is there.

We strongly recommend that you go into your courtroom as a spectator sometime before your hearing to watch other uncontested divorces. This will give you a very good idea of what will happen in your own case and how your judge runs his/her courtroom. It will help you get ready and feel confident.

C. The day of the hearing

Documents to bring (or file well before the hearing)

In every case

Statistics Form (chapter 8)
Final Decree of Divorce with attached exhibits as needed

Some cases

Certificate of Last Known Address — *If you have a default case (chapter A5)*
Military Status Affidavit — *If you have a default case*
Income Withholding Order — *If child or spousal support is ordered*

Cases with minor children

Family Information — *Information about parents and children*
Out of State Parent Affidavit — *If a parent lives outside TX*

Dress as you would for a business job interview: clean, neat, conventional. You don't want to stand out one way or the other. In the courtroom turn off all devices and put them away. Don't chew gum or bring food or drink with you. Be calm and polite to everyone and don't talk to your spouse if he/she shows up. If anyone comes with you, ask them to follow this advice, too.

Get to the courthouse a little before your case is scheduled. Unless your county is one where the clerk does it for you, you should get your file from the clerk's office, take it to your courtroom, and hand it to the bailiff (the guy with the uniform) or the clerk. Whether or not you are delivering a file, you should go up to the clerk or bailiff and let him/her know you are present and ready. Have a seat among the spectators and wait for your case to be called.

When your case is called, say "ready" and go up before the judge. The judge will administer the oath, then tell you to proceed. You'll stand before the judge's bench or take the witness stand—the judge will tell you which to do. Take time to arrange your papers and notes, relax, and give your testimony. Always refer to the judge as "Your Honor" and don't lean on the bench if you are standing before it.

In some counties an appointed family law "master" or "referee" will hear your case. They have the duties and authority of a judge but their decisions must be approved by an elected judge. This won't be a problem, especially if you have an agreed or default divorce. If the master asks if you object to having him/her hear the case, say no. A master is called "Your Honor" just like a judge. If the master makes a ruling you disagree with, you have 3 days to ask a judge to review the master's decision.

No court reporter needed. If you are asked, state that you waive the presence of the court reporter. There is no particular advantage to having a word-for-word record of an uncontested divorce, and it is very expensive to make.

Lead or follow? Very likely the judge will take over and ask questions. In that case, just answer exactly what is asked—don't wander or volunteer anything extra. But make sure that the questioning covers everything that you want to ask for. If it doesn't, politely say, "Excuse me, Your Honor, but there's more," and explain. However, if the judge just looks at you or tells you to proceed, that's when you take out your prepared testimony, taken from the Guide below, and go through each item in order, checking them off, until you've covered everything that applies to your case. Basically, you recite facts pretty much in the order and as they appear in your Decree.

The continuance. Almost certainly everything will go smoothly. But if things go very wrong or you get into a situation you can't handle, just do what lawyers do: say, "Your Honor, I respectfully request that this matter be continued to another date so I can have time to seek advice and further prepare for presentation." This way, you can come back another day, giving you time to try to find out what went wrong. Maybe ask to see the judge in chambers and see if the judge will tell you what the problem was. It's worth a try. At least go over this book carefully to see if you left anything out.

The outline below is by no means exactly what you must say, but rather it is a guide to help you order your testimony. It wouldn't be good to take this book to court and read from it, so we put the guide on the CD in the Forms Etc folder so you can print it out. Or you can type or write notes from these pages. Check off each item as you give it in court, and don't skip or forget to say any part that relates to your case. Take your time, relax. If the judge asks questions, it is only because s/he is trying to make sure that things are being done fairly and correctly. Don't worry, just answer *briefly* and *exactly* the question asked. Don't volunteer information the judge does not ask for.

A Guide for Your Testimony*

* This guide is also found on the companion CD in the Testimony folder, so you can easily print it and take it with you.

TESTIMONY GUIDE

I. In every case, give the following information

A. Your Honor, my name is _____, and I am the Petitioner in this case.

B. All of the facts stated in my Petition are true.

C. At the time I filed the Petition, I had been continually a resident of Texas for more than six months, and of this county for more than 90 days.

D. I am now married to _____, who is the Respondent in this case. We were married on *(date)* _____, and we separated on *(date)* _____, and have not lived together as husband and wife since that time.
(These dates must be the same as those given in the Petition. For common-law marriages, the language in the Petition is your guide for what to say about it.)

E. I am asking for a divorce because our marriage has become unworkable and there is no reasonable chance for a reconciliation.
(If the judge asks for it, give a brief statement as to why your marriage cannot continue. Do not emphasize fault or blame, but describe differences, arguing, conflict, personality clashes, and so on. Tell about efforts to save the marriage. If there was any, describe violence, cruelty, drug abuse, abandonment, failure to support, neglect by your spouse. Conclude by stating that there is no possibility for a reconciliation.)

F. ☐ I am ☐ My wife is not expecting a child at this time.

(Use 1 or 2 below)

1. ☐ I ☐ My wife did not have children with anyone else during the marriage.

2. ☐ I did ☐ She did have a child/children with someone else during our marriage. Paternity of that/those child/ren has been established legally and a copy of the document(s) that prove this is/are attached to my proposed Decree of Divorce.

II. Continue, using the parts that apply to your case

A. The Decree and Agreements *(check one or two boxes)*

☐ If your spouse signed the Decree, say "My proposed Decree has been approved and signed by my spouse on the last page. I am familiar with the signature of my spouse and can state that it is genuine."

☐ If you attached a written settlement agreement to your Decree, say "A written settlement agreement between my spouse and myself is attached to the proposed Decree. I am familiar with the signature of my spouse and can state that it is genuine.

B. Children

☐ **None.** My spouse and I have no children under the age of 18 or still in high school, and none are expected.

☐ **If You Have Children**
My spouse and I are the parents of _____ child/ren who is/are under 18 years *(if applicable, add)* or 18 or more and still in high school.

☐ If child custody and support are part of a written agreement, tell the judge, "Our written agreement contains provisions concerning the custody and support of the child/ren."

State one of the following:

☐ The Respondent is a resident of Texas, or

☐ The Respondent is not a resident of Texas, but: *(State the best reasons that apply to your case from the list under item 4 in the Petition).*

And say I ask that custody, visitation and support for our child/ren be ordered as set out in the Decree of Divorce that I have presented to the Court. I believe that these orders will be in the child/ren's best interest.

Child Support. *Be prepared to show the past 2 year's tax returns, current pay stubs and a financial statement. Use the Financial Information form in the back of this book. Be prepared to describe the income and earning ability of both spouses and the custodial parent's expenses.*

☐ **Personal information.** In my Petition I requested that personal family information ☐ not be shared with Respondent (and/or) ☐ be sealed and kept from public view. *(State your reasons for requesting this.)*

☐ **Parenting Class** *(If required in your county and if the judge asks)*:

☐ My spouse and I have completed the class required for parents ☐ and our certificates of completion have been filed.

or

☐ I have completed the class required for parents ☐ and my certificate of completion was filed with the court. I was unable to find my spouse to have him/her take the course. I request that you waive the requirement that my spouse take this class.

☐ *(if certificates are **not** already on file)* Here is/are the original certificate(s) of completion to be filed with the court.

☐ **Handicapped Child** *(if applicable in your case)*
Our child (Name of child) has a disability and requires continuous care and personal supervision and will not be capable of self-support. I request that payments for the support of this child be continued past the child's 18th birthday and extended for an indefinite period.

C. Property and Debts
(Choose one)

☐ **None.** There is no community property or debts of any significant value apart from our personal effects.

☐ **Approved Decree.** The Respondent and I have agreed to the division of property and debts as set forth in the Decree, we have both signed the last page of that Decree. *(If asked, use your Petition as a guide and recite your community property, debts, and any separate property, then indicate which property and debts you wish the court to award to you and which to your spouse.)*

☐ **Written Agreement.** The division of our community property and debts is covered by the written contract that is attached to the Decree. I request that you approve our agreement and incorporate it into the Decree.

☐ **Divided by the Court.** I ask that our property and debts be divided as set out in the proposed Decree. I believe that this division is fair to both parties. *(If this is a default case, you must also tell the judge the value of the property and why your proposed division is fair. A list of community property and debts is on page 6 of your Petition.)*

D. Spousal Maintenance

☐ Spousal maintenance is covered in our written agreement, which is attached to the proposed Decree.

☐ I ask that this court award spousal maintenance as set out in the proposed Decree. *(State the qualifying grounds as in item 9 of your Decree and the reason you need support. Offer to show the judge your Financial Form [on the CD] to show clearly your financial condition.)*

E. Change Of Name

☐ I request that my name be changed to a name that was used before we were married, which is *(state the desired name in full).*

☐ Respondent requests that his/her name be changed to a name that was used before we were married, which is *(state the desired name in full).*

"Your Honor, that concludes my testimony."

The judge may ask further questions, which you should answer briefly, sticking just to the point he asked about.

Usually the judge will announce the orders, sign your Decree, and you are finished. Divorced. It's over. Congratulations! Most courtroom clerks transport your file for you; if not, you take it straight to the Clerk's Office. Also take all copies of your Decree and get them certified. You may need them later.

If your Decree needs minor adjustments, the courtroom clerk may make them on the spot, but if the judge's orders were very different from your prepared Decree, you might have to make up a new Decree conforming exactly to the judge's orders, and present it for signing and stamping at a later time. To get the revised Decree just right, you might want to see the docket notes the courtroom clerk took when the judge made his/her orders. Do it as soon as possible.

D. Troubleshooting Guide

We said it before and say it again: 99 times out of 100 there will be no trouble with the hearing. However, it will make you feel better if you know what to do just in case you are that unfortunate one.

1. Before the hearing begins

If someone is obstructing your way, it is very possible that there's a reason. If so, you must find it out and correct the problem. Ask what is the matter; at least get them to indicate the general area of the problem, or give you some hints as to the reason for their action or conduct. If necessary, ask to speak to another clerk, or to the supervisor. Don't get upset—the only important thing is for you to figure out and correct any errors in your papers or procedures. Go over this book and double-check everything. You can always come back to the clerk's office or to court another day.

2. After your hearing begins

If the judge refuses to grant your divorce at the end of your testimony, this means he/she is not satisfied with some portion of it. Maybe it was incomplete, or something was left out. Ask the judge, politely, to please explain his/her reasons, as it may be that you can give additional testimony that will solve the problem. If the judge indicates which portion of your case is incomplete, go over it again, more carefully and fully. If the judge will not help or explain, ask to have your case continued to another day. During the recess, see if the clerk or bailiff will help you, or ask to see the judge in chambers. Go over this book and double-check everything.

Assuming you find out what went wrong, go in for another hearing, and try it again.

3. After the hearing

If the judge grants your divorce but refuses to sign your Decree, this probably means the judge thinks something is wrong with it. Probably it is different from the orders announced in court. The divorce is still valid and effective, but your case will not be over and complete until you can prepare a Decree that the judge will sign. Ask the judge what is wrong and make careful note of the explanation. Or ask the courtroom clerk. Look at the clerk's docket sheet (it's a public record) where notes are entered about the orders in your case. Make up a new Decree and bring it in at another time, but do it as soon as possible.

Appendix A

Affidavit of Inability to Pay

Rule 145 of the Texas Rules of Civil Procedure guarantees that no low-income Texan will be denied access to the courts simply because he or she cannot afford to pay the court costs. A party who is unable to afford costs is defined as "a person who is presently receiving a governmental entitlement based on indigence or any other person who has no ability to pay costs."

Anyone receiving public assistance automatically qualifies under this rule.

The law does not contain guidelines for exactly how much income people not receiving public assistance can have and still qualify for the pauper's oath, but you would have to show that you can't pay for the essentials of life and also pay court fees. If you think you might qualify, go ahead and try it. The worst thing that can happen is they will decide you don't qualify.

The two-page form, "Affidavit of Inability," is found at the back and on the CD that comes with this book. Fill it out as completely as possible, checking all relevant boxes. Sign it before a Notary Public and file it at the same time that you file your Petition.

Appendix B

Custody Rules for Military Personnel

When things change, it is always much better if parents can work things out for themselves, and a good idea to put their arrangements in a signed and witnessed written agreement, but if that's not possible, here's what you can get from a court.

If a military parent is deployed to duty so far from the child's residence that time with the child is greatly reduced, or if deployment means a significant reduction in pay, the military parent can ask the Court for an expedited (fast track) hearing to get temporary orders for support and care of the child during the deployment. If already deployed, it is possible to request that testimony and evidence be given by electronic means, including teleconferencing.

After you read this appendix, if you want help with understanding the rules or applying them, check to see if your military unit offers counseling and legal advice services for personnel and their families. If not, call a local family law attorney (see chapter A8).

A. When a military parent is deployed—temporary court orders

Designated stand-in. If a military parent is ordered away, he/she can ask the court to designate someone to have the same rights, duties (other than support) and care time as the parent. The court will give preference to naming the other parent, but if that's not in the child's best interest, then someone named by the military parent, and if *that's* not in the child's best interest, then someone appointed by the court.

Temporary order for child support. If being ordered away reduces the military parent's income, the military parent can request an expedited (faster than normal) hearing to ask for temporary orders to change the amount of support. This modification **can't** be accomplished by an agreement between the parents: it requires a court order.

B. When a military parent returns from deployment—back to normal

Termination of temporary orders. If a deployed military parent had temporary orders covering the term of deployment, those orders terminate on the return of the deployed parent to his/her usual residence or anywhere in the same general area. The parents and children then resume living under the same terms they had before deployment.

Additional care time. If the deployed parent did **not** have the exclusive right to designate the child's residence, and if that parent was deployed so far that access to the child was not reasonably possible, then on return from deployment that parent has up to 90 days to petition the court for additional care time to make up for contact with the child that was lost due to the deployment. The court has broad discretion to consider all circumstances and determine whether and how much additional care time is in the best interest of the child. If additional care time is ordered, when it has been exercised, all parties return to the orders as they were before the deployment.

Appendix C

The Special Warranty Deed

A special warranty deed is included with the forms on the companion CD. It transfers title from one party to the other, with **no guarantee** from the party who is transferring away the property that the chain of title is correct. If a title insurance policy was involved in the original purchase of the house and you and your spouse have not assigned away any part of your property to anyone during the marriage, you're probably okay. If you purchased your house without a title policy, you may want to contact a title company to verify that there are no "clouds" on the title, particularly if you are the person receiving the house. A title search generally costs about $100.

Do not use this deed form if you are not transferring property between spouses. It has specialized language regarding the transfer that is not applicable to a general sale of land. Consult an attorney if you have questions about other types of deeds. See chapter A8 for advice about finding the right attorney.

Either fill in the blanks with a typewriter or retype this special warranty deed on a letter-size piece of paper. It is okay if the deed runs over to a second page.

The "Grantor" is the person giving the property and the "Grantee" is the person receiving the property.

1. Type in Grantor's name and name of county where Grantor resides.

2. Copy the cause number and style (caption) of the case as it appears on your Original Petition or Divorce Decree. If you have children, you will have to add the "And in the Interest of _____ Child(ren)" block as on your other papers. That would definitely mean typing the whole warranty deed over.

    If you are filing the deed *before* you file the divorce petition, you don't need any of the court information on lines 5 to 7. Draw lines through all this, starting on line 4 with "namely the division of property in:" and ending with "Judicial District Court of _____County, Texas."

3. Type in Grantee's name and name of county where Grantee resides.

4. Type the property description *exactly* as it appears on the warranty deed you received when you bought the property. It is extremely important that you list it in the same way it is spelled out, otherwise the transfer of title might be defective and cause problems later on. If you have a very long description (like a surveyor's sheet that runs for a page or more), you may want to photocopy it, attach it to the back page of the deed, and call it "Exhibit A." If so, type "See Exhibit A" in this space.

5. Skip the rest of the blanks for the moment and type in Grantee's name and address on the bottom left side of the deed.

6. The Grantor must now take the warranty deed to a Notary Public, and sign and date it in the Notary's presence. The Notary Public fills in the rest of the blank lines.

After this is all done, the deed must be filed with the county clerk in the county where the property is located. There is a nominal filing fee, usually $5 for the first page and $3 for each successive page. *The deed must be filed with the county clerk in order to be valid.*

Forms in the Back of the Book* and on the CD

* You don't use all of these forms—just the ones you need for your case.

CD #	Title
01	Original Petition for Divorce
01A	Out of State Parent Affidavit
02	Waiver of Service
~~03~~	*(no longer in use)*
04	Information for Serving the Citation
05	Final Decree of Divorce
05-Ex1	Children's Property
05-Ex2	Conservatorship Order
05-Ex3	Standard Possession Order
05-Ex4	Child Support Order
05-Ex5a	Medical Support Order *(health care)*
05-Ex5b	Dental Support Order *(dental care)*
05-Ex6	Family Information
05-Ex7	Orders Re Property and Debts
05A	Certificate of Last Known Address
06	Statistics Form
07	Income Withholding Order
~~08~~	*(no longer in use)*
09	Request to Issue Withholding Order
10	Military Status Affidavit
11	Financial Information
12	Affidavit of Inability to Pay
13	Notice of Change of Address

More forms and info on the companion CD

14	Power of Attorney to Transfer Motor Vehicle
15	Special Warranty Deed (to Transfer Real Property)
16	Order to Keep Information Confidential
MSA	Marital Settlement Agreement
•	2015 Tax Charts for child support
•	Property Checklist
•	Testimony Guide
Kits	Citations by Publication or Posting
	Motion to Consolidate

And more . . . including demo version of Nolo's DealMaker software

Cause Number _____

IN THE MATTER OF THE MARRIAGE OF

Petitioner: _____

And

Respondent: _____

☐ **AND IN THE INTEREST OF:**

1. _____ 2. _____ 3. _____

4. _____ 5. _____ 6. _____

In the

_____ ☐ District Court ☐ County Court
at Law of

_____ County, Texas

Original Petition for Divorce

1. **Parties**

   Petitioner

   My name is: _____.
                                  First   *Middle*   *Last*

   The last three numbers of my driver's license number are: ____ ____ ____. My driver's license
   was issued in the State of _____.

   or ☐ I do not have a driver's license number.

   The last three numbers of my social security number are ____ ____ ____.

   or ☐ I do not have a social security number.

   Respondent
   My spouse's name is: _____.
                                      First   *Middle*   *Last*

2. **Discovery.** The discovery level in this case is Level 2.

3. **Jurisdiction**

   State and County of Residence (check all that apply)

   ☐ I have ☐ My spouse has lived in this county for the last 90 days and in Texas for the last six months.

   Out-of-State Respondent

   ☐ My spouse does not live in Texas, **and** (check all that apply)

       ☐ My spouse agrees that a Texas court can make orders dividing our property and orders for custody
   and support of our children.

       ☐ Texas is the last state where we lived together as a married couple. This petition is filed less than
   two years after we separated.

   (this item is continued on next page)

☐ The children live in Texas because of my spouse's actions.

☐ My spouse has lived in Texas with the children.

☐ My spouse has lived in Texas and provided prenatal expenses or support for the children.

☐ My spouse had sexual intercourse in Texas, and the children may have been conceived by that act of intercourse.

☐ Our child was born in Texas and my spouse registered with the paternity registry maintained by the bureau of vital statistics or signed an acknowledgment of paternity.

☐ My spouse will be personally served with citation within the State of Texas.

4. Protective Order Statement

☐ There is no protective order between the parties and no application for one is pending.

☐ A protective order is presently in effect **or** an application for protective order is pending at this time in _____ County, _____, Cause No. _____.
         Name of County   *State*   *Case number*

A true and correct copy of the protective order
    ☐ is attached to this Original Petition   ☐ will be filed before any hearing in this case.
    ☐ if issued, will be filed with the court before any hearings in this case.

5. Marriage and Grounds for Divorce

Petitioner and Respondent were married on or about _____, and ceased to live together as husband and wife on or about _____.

☐ Common-Law Marriage: Petitioner and Respondent agreed to be married on or about _____, and thereafter we lived together in Texas as husband and wife and we represented to others that we were married, thus creating a common-law marriage. We separated on or about _____.

The marriage has become insupportable due to discord or conflict of personalities that destroys the legitimate ends of the marriage relationship and prevents any reasonable expectation of reconciliation.

6. Children

☐ **No minor children.**

My spouse and I do **not** have any biological or adopted children together who are under the age of 18, or any who are 18 years old or older who are still in high school.

My spouse and I do **not** have any disabled children of any age.

The wife has **not** had a child by another man since the date of marriage.

The wife is **not** pregnant.

☐ **Children of the marriage**

The following children now under eighteen years old were born to or adopted by the parties:

	Name	Age	Sex	Birth date	Birthplace
1.					
2.					
3.					
4.					
5.					
6.					

☐ **Children born during marriage but husband is NOT the father**

  ☐ The wife did not have children with another man while married to the husband.

  ☐ All children born during the marriage that are NOT the husband's adopted or biological children are listed below.

	Name	Age	Sex	Birth date	Birthplace
1.					
2.					
3.					

  ☐ Paternity of children listed above **has not** been established. I understand that paternity must be established before I can finish my divorce.

  ☐ Paternity of children listed above **has** been established.

    ☐ A court order has determined the father of each child named above. I understand that I must attach a file-stamped copy of the order to my Final Decree of Divorce.

    ☐ An Acknowledgment of Paternity signed by the genetic father **and** a Denial of Paternity signed by Husband herein has been filed with the Bureau of Vital Statistics for each child listed above. I understand that I must attach a copy of these documents to my Final Decree of Divorce.

A. Disabled child

  ☐ My spouse and I do not have any disabled children.

  ☐ _____, a child of this marriage named above, requires continuous care and personal supervision because of a disability and will not be capable of self-support. The Court is requested to order that payments for the support of this child be continued after the child's eighteenth birthday and extended for an indefinite period.

B. Pregnancy. ☐ The wife in this marriage **is not** pregnant
             ☐ The wife in this marriage **is** pregnant **and**
               ☐ The husband **is** the father. ☐ The husband **is not** the father.

C. Court orders involving children (check one box)

☐ There are no court orders in effect now for any of the children listed above.

☐ There is a court order in effect for ☐ all of the above named children ☐ the following children

_____

County/State where order was made _____

Date of order _____ Cause number _____

Name of order _____

This order is ☐ temporary ☐ final

D. Custody, visitation, and child support

I will try to make an agreement with my spouse about custody, visitation, and support for our children. If we cannot make an agreement by the time of the hearing, I ask the court to make the following orders:

1. Custody

☐ Petitioner and Respondent should be appointed Joint Managing Conservators of the child/ren

and_____ will have the right to establish the child/ren's primary residence.

☐ _____ to be appointed the Sole Managing Conservator of the child/ren

and _____ to be appointed Possessory Conservator of the child/ren.

2. Support

☐ Petitioner ☐ Respondent should be ordered to make payments for the support of the children in the manner specified by the Court.

E. Children's health and dental insurance

1 ☐ Private health insurance IS in effect.

Name of insurance company _____

Policy number _____ Cost of premium $_____

Name of person who pays for the insurance _____

This insurance policy ☐ is ☐ is not available through the parent's work

2 ☐ Private health insurance is NOT in effect.

The children ☐ do ☐ do not receive medical insurance through CHIPS or Medicaid.

Cost of premium (if any) $_____

Health insurance ☐ is ☐ is not available at reasonable cost to the parent who pays child support.

(continued on next page)

3 ☐ **Private dental insurance IS in effect.**

Name of insurance company _____

Policy number _____ Cost of premium $_____

Name of person who pays for the insurance _____

This insurance policy ☐ is ☐ is not available through the parent's work

4 ☐ **Private dental insurance is NOT in effect.**

The children ☐ do ☐ do not receive dental insurance through CHIPS or Medicaid.

Cost of premium (if any) $_____

Health insurance ☐ is ☐ is not available at reasonable cost to the parent who pays child support.

F. Children's property

☐ The children do not own any property.

☐ The children own the following property:

_____

_____

_____

_____

G. Family information

☐ I will fill out and file the Family Information form when I file the Final Decree of Divorce, as required by section 105.006 of the Texas Family Code.

☐ **Potential harm.** I believe my children or I will be harassed, abused, seriously harmed, or injured if I am required to give my spouse the information checked below for myself and the children.

☐ home address ☐ mailing address ☐ employer ☐ work address,
☐ home phone # ☐ work phone # ☐ social security # ☐ driver's license #.

I ask the Court to Order that I not have to give this information or notice of changes in this information to my spouse.

☐ **Identity theft.** I ask the Court to seal and keep confidential this information, any attachment to the Final Decree, and any Orders to Withhold Earnings that the court might issue, that disclose the Social Security and driver's license numbers, current address, and telephone numbers of parties or children in order to protect parties and children from exposure to identity theft. Such information will be provided to parties and the court but should not be made part of files to which the public has access.

H. Out of state parent information

The information required by Texas Family Code § 152.209 (check one box)

☐ Is not required because both parents reside in Texas.

☐ Is submitted in an attached affidavit.

☐ Is not provided because the health, safety, or liberty of a party or child would be jeopardized by disclosure of identifying information.

7. Property and debts

☐ **No property.** To Petitioner's knowledge, other than personal effects there is no community property of any significant value which is subject to division by the Court at this time.

☐ **Agreement anticipated.** Petitioner believes the parties will reach an agreed property division and ask the Court to approve that agreement when presented to the Court or, absent agreement, divide the assets and debts of the parties according to Texas law.

☐ **Marital Settlement Agreement.** The parties have entered into a Marital Settlement Agreement, a copy of which is attached and incorporated by reference.

☐ **Community property and debts to be divided by the Court**
To Petitioner's knowledge and belief, community property owned by the parties consists of the following assets and debts that were acquired during the marriage.

Item #	Description	Value

Division: Petitioner requests the Court to order a division of the community property in a manner that the Court deems just and right, as provided by law.

☐ It would be fair to divide the property into approximately equal portions.

☐ There are many equities which the court should consider making it fair that

☐ Petitioner ☐ Respondent be awarded a substantial portion of the property.

☐ It will be fair and equitable for the Court to order Respondent to assume and to pay without any right to contribution or reimbursement from Petitioner the debts described in the above list, namely items numbered: _____.

Separate property to be confirmed by the Court

☐ I request that the following items be confirmed as Petitioner's separate property as they were owned before the marriage or acquired during marriage by inheritance, gift to Petitioner only, or represents the proceeds, other than lost wages, of a personal injury lawsuit:

<u>Item #</u>   <u>Description</u>   <u>Value</u>

_____

_____

_____

_____

_____

_____

_____

_____

_____

_____

_____

_____

☐ I request that the following items be confirmed as Respondent's separate property as they were owned before the marriage or acquired during marriage by inheritance, gift to Respondent only, or represents the proceeds, other than lost wages, of a personal injury lawsuit:

<u>Item #</u>   <u>Description</u>   <u>Value</u>

_____

_____

_____

_____

_____

_____

_____

_____

_____

8. Spousal Maintenance

☐ Spousal maintenance is not requested.

☐ The parties have entered into a Marital Settlement Agreement regarding maintenance, a copy of which is attached and incorporated by reference.

☐ Petitioner requests that this court award spousal maintenance according to Texas law.

9. Name Change

☐ No change of name is requested.

☐ I ask the Court to change my name back to a name I had before my marriage. I am not asking the court to change my name to avoid criminal prosecution or creditors.

_____.
      First   *Middle*   *Last*

10. Privacy – Identity Theft

☐ **Identity theft.** I ask the Court to seal and keep confidential the information in this cause, any pleadings or attachments, and any Orders that the court might issue, that disclose the Social Security and driver's license numbers, current address, and telephone numbers of parties in order to protect them from exposure to identity theft. All information will be provided to parties and the court but should not be made part of files to which the public has access.

11. Prayer

I ask the Court to grant me a divorce.

I also ask the Court to make the other orders I have asked for in this Original Petition for Divorce and any other orders to which I am entitled.

_____   _____
Petitioner's Name (Print)   *Date*

_____   _____
Petitioner's Signature   *Phone Number*

_____   _____
Petitioner's Mailing Address   *City*   *State*   *Zip*

I understand that I *must* let the Court and my spouse (or my spouse's attorney) know in writing if my mailing address or phone number changes during this case. If I don't, any notices about this case will be sent to me at the address on this form.

Attachment(s) to this Petition:

☐ Copy of Protective Order described in item 4 above

☐ Paternity documents

☐ Standing Orders for this county

☐ Out of State Parent Affidavit

☐ Settlement Agreement

Cause Number _____

EXHIBIT _____. OUT-OF-STATE PARENT AFFIDAVIT

Information Required By Texas Family Code § 152.209

BEFORE ME the person who signed this affidavit appeared in person and stated under oath:

I am above the age of 18 years and fully competent to make this affidavit. The facts stated herein are within my personal knowledge and are true and correct.

1. Personal Information

My name is: _____.
　　　　　　　　　First　　　　　　　　　　　　Middle　　　　　　　　　　　　Last

I am the ☐ Petitioner.　☐ Respondent.

I am representing myself in this case.

☐ I believe that the health safety or liberty of myself or my children will be jeopardized by disclosure of the information in this affidavit. I ask the Clerk's Office to seal this affidavit and not disclose this information to the other party or the public unless the court orders the information disclosed after a hearing, as required by Texas Family Code § 152.209 (e).

2. Children in this case (under 18)

First Child's Name: _____

Present address: _____

Now lives with ☐ Petitioner ☐ Respondent ☐ Other: _____

and has lived at this address since _____.

During the past 5 years, this child has lived at the following other addresses: *(month/day/year)*

From _____ to _____ resided at _____
with ☐ Petitioner ☐ Respondent ☐ Other: _____
whose current address is _____

From _____ to _____ resided at _____
with ☐ Petitioner ☐ Respondent ☐ Other: _____
whose current address is _____

From _____ to _____ resided at _____
with ☐ Petitioner ☐ Respondent ☐ Other: _____
whose current address is _____

From _____ to _____ resided at _____
with ☐ Petitioner ☐ Respondent ☐ Other: _____
whose current address is _____

Second Child's Name: _____
Present address: _____
Now lives with ☐ Petitioner ☐ Respondent ☐ Other: _____
and has lived at this address since _____.

During the past 5 years, this child has lived at the following addresses: *(month/day/year)*

From _____ to _____ resided at _____
with ☐ Petitioner ☐ Respondent ☐ Other: _____
whose current address is _____

From _____ to _____ resided at _____
with ☐ Petitioner ☐ Respondent ☐ Other: _____
whose current address is _____

From _____ to _____ resided at _____
with ☐ Petitioner ☐ Respondent ☐ Other: _____
whose current address is _____

From _____ to _____ resided at _____
with ☐ Petitioner ☐ Respondent ☐ Other: _____
whose current address is _____

Third Child's Name: _____
Present address: _____
Now lives with ☐ Petitioner ☐ Respondent ☐ Other: _____
and has lived at this address since _____.

During the past 5 years, this child has lived at the following addresses: *(month/day/year)*

From _____ to _____ resided at _____
with ☐ Petitioner ☐ Respondent ☐ Other: _____
whose current address is _____

From _____ to _____ resided at _____
with ☐ Petitioner ☐ Respondent ☐ Other: _____
whose current address is _____

From _____ to _____ resided at _____
with ☐ Petitioner ☐ Respondent ☐ Other: _____
whose current address is _____

From _____ to _____ resided at _____
with ☐ Petitioner ☐ Respondent ☐ Other: _____
whose current address is _____

☐ See attached page for additional children

3. Other Court Cases

I have not participated in any capacity in any other proceeding concerning the custody of or visitation with these children, in Texas or any other state or country.

A. I do not know of any proceeding that could affect the current proceeding, including proceedings for enforcement, domestic violence, protective orders, termination of parental rights, and adoption.

☐ except as follows: (identify court, case number, and nature of the proceeding)

_____

_____

_____

_____

_____

B. I do not know of any person not a party to the current proceeding who has physical custody of the child or claims rights of legal custody or physical custody of, or visitation with, the child.

☐ except as follows: (give names and addresses of those persons)

Name: _____ Relationship to Children _____
Address: _____

Name: _____ Relationship to Children _____
Address: _____

Name: _____ Relationship to Children _____
Address: _____

_____   _____
        Signed before a notary   Date

STATE OF TEXAS
County of _____

SUBSCRIBED AND SWORN to before me this _____day of_____, 20____.

_____
             Notary Public, State of Texas
             or Officer Authorized to Administer Oaths

Cause Number _____

IN THE MATTER OF THE MARRIAGE OF

Petitioner: _____   **In the**

                                       _____ ☐ District Court ☐ County Court

              And   **at Law of**

Respondent: _____   _____ **County, Texas**

☐ **AND IN THE INTEREST OF:**

1. _____ 2. _____ 3. _____

4. _____ 5. _____ 6. _____

Waiver of Service

The person who signed this affidavit appeared, in person, before me, the undersigned notary, and stated under oath:

"I am the Respondent in this case.

"My name is: _____.
                    First   *Middle*   *Last*

"My mailing address is: _____.
                     Address   *City*   *State*   *Zip*

"My phone number is: (_____) _____.

"The last three numbers of my driver's license number are: ___ ___ ___.

 My driver's license was issued in *(State)*: _____.

☐ " I do not have a driver's license number.

"The last three numbers of my social security number are: ___ ___ ___.

☐ " I do not have a social security number.

" I have been given a copy of the *Original Petition for Divorce* filed in this case. I have read it and understand what it says. I do not give up my right to review a different *Petition for Divorce* if it gets changed (*amended*).

" I understand that I have the right to be given a copy of the *Original Petition for Divorce* and official notice of this case by an official process server. I do not want to be given official notice. I give up my right to issuance and service of citation in this case and enter my appearance in this case for all purposes.

"I also give up my right to be notified of any and all hearings in this case.

"I agree that a Judge or Associate Judge in the county and state where this case is filed may make decisions about my divorce, even if the divorce should have been filed in another county. I do not want a court reporter to make a record of the testimony in this case.

"I understand that I must let the Court, my spouse and my spouse's attorney (if my spouse has an attorney) know in writing if my mailing address or phone number changes during this case.

"If I am in the military, I waive all rights, privileges, and exemptions I may have under the Servicemembers Civil Relief Act in this case, including having a lawyer appointed to represent me.

"I agree that the judge may make decisions about my divorce without further notice to me."

Military Status *(Check only one)*

☐ " I am not in the military.

☐ " I am in the military. I agree to the provisions stated above and I waive only the rights, privileges, and exemptions I have under the Servicemembers Civil Relief Act that are contrary to those provisions.

Name Change

☐ " I am NOT asking the court to change my name.

☐ " I ask the Court to change my name back to a name I had before my marriage. I am not asking the court to change my name to avoid criminal prosecution or creditors."

_____.
       First   *Middle*   *Last*

. _____   Date: _____
          Signed before a notary

Notary fills out below

State of Texas, County of _____

Sworn to and subscribed before me, the undersigned notary,

on this date: _____/_____/____ at _____ a.m./p.m.

by _____
      Print name of person who is signing this Affidavit. NOT the notary.

/s/ _____
                           Notary

INFORMATION FOR SERVICE OF PROCESS

FROM:_____

      Address: _____

      _____

      Phone(s): _____

TO: _____

      _____

      _____

     RE: In the Matter of the Marriage of:

           _____, Petitioner,

           and _____, Respondent.

           Cause No. _____

           In the _____ ☐ District Court ☐ County Court at Law

           of _____County, Texas

Dear Sir:

Enclosed are copies of a Petition and Citation, and a money order for $_____.

The enclosed papers **must** be served within 90 days of the date of issuance of the Citation in order to be valid. The Return portion of the Citation must, of course, be completely and accurately filled out and signed.

Note To Officers Outside The State Of Texas

The signature of the officer delivering the Citation and Petition MUST be sworn and Notarized in order to be effective in Texas.

Information For Service Of Process

Person to Be Served: _____

Residence Address: _____

_____

Work Address: _____

Other: _____

Physical Description: _____

_____

Comments:

Cause Number _____

IN THE MATTER OF THE MARRIAGE OF

Petitioner: _____   In the

                               _____ ☐ District Court ☐ County Court

            And   at Law of

Respondent: _____ _____ County, Texas

☐ **AND IN THE INTEREST OF:**

1. _____   2. _____   3. _____

4. _____   5. _____   6. _____

Final Decree of Divorce

A hearing took place on _____. There was no jury. Neither party asked for a jury.
                                         Date

1. Appearances

Petitioner
Petitioner's name is: _____.
                                 First   *Middle*   *Last*

The Petitioner is the ☐ Husband ☐ Wife

(check one box)

☐ The Petitioner **was present**, representing him/herself, and has agreed to the terms of this Final Decree of Divorce *(called "Decree" throughout this document)*.

☐ The Petitioner **was not present** but has signed below, agreeing to the terms of this Decree.

Respondent
Respondent's name is: _____.
                                  First   *Middle*   *Last*

(check one box)

☐ The Respondent **was present**, Pro Se, and announced ready for trial.

☐ The Respondent **was present**, Pro Se, and has signed below agreeing to the terms in this Decree.

☐ The Respondent was **not present** but filed an Answer or Waiver of Service and has signed below, agreeing to the terms in this Decree.

☐ The Respondent was **not present** but filed a Waiver of Service that waived Respondent's right to notice of this hearing and did not otherwise appear.

☐ The Respondent was **not present** but was served and has defaulted. The Petitioner has filed a Certificate of Last Known Address and a Military Status Affidavit.

2. Record

The Court fills out item 2

☐ A Court reporter did not record today's hearing because the parties and judge agreed not to make a record.

☐ A Court reporter recorded today's hearing.

3. Jurisdiction

The Court heard evidence and finds that it has jurisdiction over this case and the parties, that the residency and notice requirements have been met, and the *Petition for Divorce* meets all legal requirements.

The Court finds that: *(Check one.)*

☐ it has been at least 60 days since the *Petition for Divorce* was filed.

☐ the 60 day waiting period is not required because: *(Check one.)*

☐ Petitioner has an active Protective Order under Title 4 of the Texas Family Code, or an active magistrate's order for emergency protection under Article 17.292 of the Texas Code of Criminal Procedure against Respondent because Respondent committed family violence during the marriage.

☐ Respondent has a final conviction or has received deferred adjudication for a crime involving family violence against Petitioner or a member of Petitioner's household.

4. Divorce

IT IS ORDERED that the Petitioner and the Respondent are divorced.

5. Children

☐ **No children**

The parties do **not** have **any** biological or adopted children together who are under the age of 18.

The parties do **not** have **any** biological or adopted children together who are 18 years old or older and are still in high school.

The parties do **not** have any **disabled children** of any age.

The wife has **not** had a child by another man since the date of marriage.

The wife is **not** pregnant.

☐ **Children the Parties Have Together**

The Court finds that the parties are the parents of the children listed below and that there are no other children born to or adopted by Husband and Wife who are under 18 or still in high school.

Dates are mo / day / year

1. Name:_____ Sex:___ Age:_____ Birth date: _____

   Birthplace: _____ Home State: _____

2. Name:_____ Sex:___ Age:_____ Birth date: _____

   Birthplace: _____ Home State: _____

3. Name:_____ Sex:___ Age:_____ Birth date: _____

   Birthplace: _____ Home State: _____

4. Name:_____ Sex:___ Age:_____ Birth date: _____

   Birthplace: _____ Home State: _____

5. Name:_____ Sex:___ Age:_____ Birth date: _____

   Birthplace: _____ Home State: _____

6. Name:_____ Sex:___ Age:_____ Birth date: _____

   Birthplace: _____ Home State: _____

THE COURT FINDS that there are no other children of the marriage under age 18 or otherwise entitled to support and that none are expected.

THE COURT FINDS that there are **no other court orders** regarding any of the children listed above.

THE COURT FINDS that the children do not own or possess any property other than their personal effects ☐ except as stated in Exhibit _____.

5A. Children Born During the Marriage but Husband is NOT the Father *(check 1st or 2nd box)*

☐ The court finds that the Wife did **not** have children with another man while married to the Husband.

☐ The Court finds that the child/ren listed below was/were born to the Wife during the marriage, but the Husband is not the biological father. The Court further finds that:

(Check all that apply – continues on next page.)

☐ A court order has established that another man is the biological father of the child/ren listed below. A copy of the court order is attached to this Decree as Exhibit _____.

☐ A court order has established that the Husband is not the biological father of the child/ren listed below. A copy of the court order is attached to this Decree as Exhibit _____.

(continued on next page)

☐ A valid *Acknowledgement of Paternity* was signed by the biological father and a valid *Denial of Paternity* was signed by the Husband for the child/ren listed below. The *Acknowledgment of Paternity* and *Denial of Paternity* were filed with the Vital Statistics Unit. A copy of said documents is attached to this Decree as Exhibit _____.

*(List all children born during the marriage who are **not** the biological or adopted children of the husband)*

Dates are mo / day / year

1. Name:_____ Sex:___ Age:____ Birth date: _____
2. Name:_____ Sex:___ Age:____ Birth date: _____
3. Name:_____ Sex:___ Age:____ Birth date: _____
4. Name:_____ Sex:___ Age:____ Birth date: _____
5. Name:_____ Sex:___ Age:____ Birth date: _____
6. Name:_____ Sex:___ Age:____ Birth date: _____

5B. Parenting Plan

The Court finds that the following orders concerning the rights and duties of the Husband and Wife in relation to their child/ren, including orders for conservatorship (custody), possession and access (visitation), child support and medical support, are in the child/ren's best interest.

The Court further finds that these orders constitute the parenting plan of the Court for the child/ren listed by name in **5A** above.

5C. Conservatorship (custody)

THE COURT ORDERS that conservatorship, rights, duties, and responsibilities are awarded as provided in Exhibit ___, which is attached and incorporated into this Decree for all purposes.

5D. Possession and Access (visitation)

THE COURT ORDERS that the parties shall have possession of the child/ren as set forth in Exhibit ____, which is fully incorporated into this Decree for all purposes.

☐ For any child now under three years of age, the above schedule shall take effect on the child's third birthday. Until such time, the schedule shall be at times and places set forth in the attached Possession Order For Children Under Three Years, Exhibit ___, which is incorporated into this Decree for all purposes.

5E. Child Support

THE COURT ORDERS that child support shall be paid as set forth in Exhibit _____, which is attached and incorporated into this Decree for all purposes.

5F. Medical Support

THE COURT ORDERS that medical support shall be provided as set forth in Exhibit ____, which is attached and incorporated into this Decree for all purposes.

5G. Dental Support

THE COURT ORDERS that dental support shall be provided as set forth in Exhibit _____, which is attached and incorporated into this Decree for all purposes.

5H. Information Regarding Parties And Children
Required by Section 105.006 of the Texas Family Code

☐ The information required by § 105.006 of the Texas Family Code is attached in Exhibit _____, which is incorporated herein for all purposes.

☐ **Protection from identity theft.** The information required by § 105.006 of the Texas Family Code is attached in Exhibit _____, which is incorporated herein for all purposes. THE COURT FINDS that making personal information available to the public would expose the parties and their child/ren to unnecessary risk of identity theft. THEREFORE IT IS ORDERED that ☐ this Exhibit ☐ the Decree and all attachments be sealed and made unavailable to the public.

☐ **Protection from abuse.** THE COURT FINDS, pursuant to Texas Family Code 105.006(c) and 105.007(c), that disclosure of Petitioner's information to Respondent is likely to cause Petitioner or the children harassment, abuse, serious harm or injury. The Court ORDERS that Petitioner's address and other identifying information not be disclosed. The Court further ORDERS that Petitioner is not required to give his/her address or other identifying information to Respondent or notify Respondent or the Court of changes in that information. The Court ORDERS Petitioner to provide his/her mailing address and changes in his/her mailing address to the State Case Registry, Contract Services Section, MC046S, P.O. Box 12017, Austin, Texas 78711-2017.

5I. Required Notices

This section is not applicable to the extent it conflicts with the Court's Order regarding disclosure of information in section 5H above.

EACH PERSON WHO IS A PARTY TO THIS ORDER IS ORDERED TO NOTIFY EVERY OTHER PARTY, THE COURT, AND THE STATE CHILD SUPPORT REGISTRY OF ANY CHANGE IN THE PARTY'S: CURRENT RESIDENCE ADDRESS, MAILING ADDRESS, HOME TELEPHONE NUMBER, NAME OF EMPLOYER, ADDRESS OF EMPLOYMENT, DRIVER'S LICENSE NUMBER, AND WORK PHONE NUMBER.

THE PARTY IS ORDERED TO GIVE NOTICE OF AN INTENDED CHANGE IN ANY OF THE REQUIRED INFORMATION TO THE OTHER PARTY, THE COURT, AND THE STATE CASE REGISTRY ON OR BEFORE THE 60TH DAY BEFORE THE INTENDED CHANGE. IF THE PARTY DOES NOT KNOW OR COULD NOT HAVE KNOWN OF THE CHANGE IN SUFFICIENT TIME TO GIVE NOTICE OF THE CHANGE TO PROVIDE 60-DAYS NOTICE, THE PARTY IS ORDERED TO GIVE NOTICE OF THE CHANGE ON OR BEFORE THE 5TH DAY AFTER THE DATE THAT THE PARTY KNOWS OF THE CHANGE.

THE DUTY TO FURNISH THIS INFORMATION TO EVERY OTHER PARTY, THE COURT, AND THE STATE CASE REGISTRY CONTINUES AS LONG AS ANY PERSON, BY VIRTUE OF THIS ORDER, IS UNDER AN OBLIGATION TO PAY CHILD SUPPORT OR ENTITLED TO POSSESSION OF OR ACCESS TO A CHILD.

FAILURE BY A PARTY TO OBEY THE ORDER OF THIS COURT TO PROVIDE EVERY OTHER PARTY, THE COURT, AND THE STATE CASE REGISTRY WITH THE CHANGE IN THE REQUIRED INFORMATION MAY RESULT IN FURTHER LITIGATION TO ENFORCE THE ORDER, INCLUDING CONTEMPT OF COURT. A FINDING OF CONTEMPT MAY BE PUNISHABLE BY CONFINEMENT IN JAIL FOR UP TO SIX MONTHS,

A FINE OF UP TO $500 FOR EACH VIOLATION AND A MONEY JUDGMENT FOR PAYMENT OF ATTORNEY'S FEES AND COURT COSTS.

Notice shall be given to every other party by delivering a copy of the notice to each party by registered or certified mail, return receipt requested.

Notice shall be given to the Court by delivering a copy of the notice either in person to the clerk of the Court or by registered or certified mail addressed to the clerk.

Notice shall be given to the State Case Registry by mailing a copy of the notice to the State Case Registry, Contract Services Section, MC046S, P.O. Box 12017, Austin, Texas 78711-2017.

5J. WARNINGS TO PARTIES

FAILURE TO OBEY A COURT ORDER FOR CHILD SUPPORT OR FOR POSSESSION OF OR ACCESS TO A CHILD MAY RESULT IN FURTHER LITIGATION TO ENFORCE THE ORDER, INCLUDING CONTEMPT OF COURT. A FINDING OF CONTEMPT MAY BE PUNISHED BY CONFINEMENT IN JAIL FOR UP TO SIX MONTHS, A FINE OF UP TO $500 FOR EACH VIOLATION, AND A MONEY JUDGMENT FOR PAYMENT OF ATTORNEY'S FEES AND COURT COSTS.

FAILURE OF A PARTY TO MAKE A CHILD SUPPORT PAYMENT TO THE PLACE AND IN THE MANNER REQUIRED BY A COURT ORDER MAY RESULT IN THE PARTY'S NOT RECEIVING CREDIT FOR MAKING THE PAYMENT.

FAILURE OF A PARTY TO PAY CHILD SUPPORT DOES NOT JUSTIFY DENYING THAT PARTY COURT-ORDERED POSSESSION OF OR ACCESS TO A CHILD. REFUSAL BY A PARTY TO ALLOW POSSESSION OF OR ACCESS TO A CHILD DOES NOT JUSTIFY FAILURE TO PAY COURT-ORDERED CHILD SUPPORT TO THAT PARTY.

6. Property and Debts

☐ THE COURT FINDS THAT the parties do not own separate or community property of any significant value other than their personal effects. IT IS ORDERED that each party is awarded the personal effects presently in his/her possession as his/her separate property.

☐ THE COURT FINDS THAT the parties have entered into a written agreement for the division of their property and debts and that the agreement is just and right. IT IS ORDERED that the agreement of the parties, which is attached hereto and incorporated herein for all purposes, be and is approved.

☐ THE COURT FINDS THAT the parties possess separate and/or community property and debts which should be confirmed and/or divided. IT IS ORDERED that the estate of the parties is confirmed and divided as set forth in Exhibit ___, which is attached and incorporated into this Decree for all purposes.

7. Muniment of Title.
This Decree shall serve as a muniment of title to transfer ownership of all property awarded to any party in this Final Decree of Divorce.

8. Income Taxes

THE COURT ORDERS that Petitioner and Respondent shall each be responsible for all taxes attributable to their own income only and each entitled to their own refunds for the year of the divorce.

☐ IT IS FURTHER ORDERED that Petitioner shall pay ___ percent and Respondent shall pay ___ percent of any income tax liability accrued prior to the year of the divorce, and that Petitioner shall receive ___ percent and Respondent shall receive ___ percent of any income tax refund accrued prior to the year of the divorce.

9. Spousal Maintenance

☐ THE COURT FINDS that on dissolution, ☐ Petitioner ☐ Respondent will lack sufficient property, including that party's separate property, to provide for that party's minimum reasonable needs; and that maintenance should be awarded on the following grounds:

☐ Petitioner and Respondent were married for at least ten (10) years.

☐ Respondent ☐ Petitioner was convicted of or received deferred adjudication for a family violence act against the other party's child, and the offense occurred during the marriage and within two years before the filing of this suit or while suit was pending.

In addition to the above, ☐ Petitioner ☐ Respondent

☐ lacks the ability to earn sufficient income to provide for his/her minimum reasonable needs.

☐ is unable to earn sufficient income to provide for his/her minimum reasonable needs because of an incapacitating physical or mental disability.

☐ is the custodian of a child of this marriage who requires substantial care and personal supervision because of a physical or mental disability that prevents him/her from earning sufficient income to provide for his/her minimum reasonable needs.

THEREFORE, THE COURT ORDERS that ☐ Petitioner ☐ Respondent pay to
☐ Petitioner ☐ Respondent for spousal maintenance the sum of $_____ per month, due and payable beginning _____, 20____ and continuing on the same day of each month thereafter until either party dies; or the receiving party remarries. This order for maintenance shall continue for _____ months or further order of this court. All payments shall be made to any address designated in writing by the recipient.

10. Mediation
☐ THE COURT ORDERS, and the Parties agree, that in the event disputes arise between the parties, the parties will seek mediation to resolve the disputes before any judicial proceeding, unless the matter to be determined concerns a serious question regarding the health and safety of the child.

11. Name Change
☐ IT IS ORDERED THAT the name of

☐ Petitioner is changed back to a name used before marriage, as it appears below.

_____.

☐ Respondent is changed back to a name used before marriage, as it appears below.

_____.

12. Court Costs
The costs of court shall be paid by the party who incurred them to the extent the party is required to pay such costs. A party who filed an Affidavit of Indigency is not required to pay costs, unless a contest to the Affidavit of Indigency was sustained by the Court in a separate written order.

13. Other Orders
The court has the right to make other orders, if needed, to clarify or enforce the orders above.

14. Final Orders
Any orders requested that do not appear above are denied. This Decree is a final judgment that disposes of all claims and all parties and is appealable.

_____   _____
Judge's Name   *Judge's signature*

                                                                            _____
                                                                            Date of Judgment

Exhibits Attached:

☐ Exhibit ___ Property Owned by Children
☐ Exhibit ___ Standard Possession Order
☐ Exhibit ___ Possession Order for Children Under Three Years
☐ Exhibit ___ Child Support Order
☐ Exhibit ___ Medical Support Order for Children   ☐ Exhibit ___ Dental Support Order for Children
☐ Exhibit ___ Information Required by Texas Family Code §§ 105.006 and 105.007
☐ Exhibit ___ Orders re Property and Debts
☐ Exhibit ___ Settlement Agreement

By signing below, the Petitioner agrees to the form and substance of this Decree.

_____
Petitioner's Name (print)   Phone number

_____
Petitioner's Signature   Date

_____
Mailing Address

_____
City   State   Zip

By signing below, the Respondent agrees to the form and substance of this Decree.

_____
Respondent's Name (print)   Phone number

_____
Respondent's Signature   Date

_____
Mailing Address

_____
City   State   Zip

Cause Number _____

Exhibit _____. Property Owned by Children of the Parties

THE COURT FINDS that the parties' child/ren is/are possessed of the following property in addition to personal effects.

Name of child: _____

Item #	Description	Value

Name of child: _____

Item #	Description	Value

Name of child: _____

Item #	Description	Value

Name of child: _____

Item #	Description	Value

☐ See attached page for additional children

Exhibit _____. Conservatorship Order

The Court, having considered the circumstances of the parents and of the children, finds that the following orders are in the best interest of the children.

A. Rights and Duties of the Parents

Rights of both parents. THE COURT ORDERS that, at all times, both parents shall have the following rights:

1. The right to receive information from the other parent or conservator about the health, education, and welfare of the children;

2. The right to talk or confer with the other parent to the extent possible before making a decision concerning the health, education, and welfare of the children;

3. The right of access to medical, dental, psychological, and educational records of the children;

4. The right to consult with physicians, dentists, or psychologists of the children;

5. The right to consult with school officials, including teachers and school staff, concerning the children's welfare and educational status and school activities;

6. The right to attend the children's school activities;

7. The right to be designated as an emergency contact on the children's school records;

8. The right to consent to medical, dental, and surgical treatment if the children's health or safety is in immediate danger; and

9. The right to manage the estate(s) of the child/ren to the extent the estates have been created by the parent or the parent's family.

Duties of both parents. THE COURT ORDERS that, at all times, both parents shall have the following duties:

1. The duty to inform the other parent in a timely manner of significant information concerning the health, education, and welfare of the children;

2. The duty to inform the other parent if the parent resides with for at least thirty days, marries, or intends to marry a person who the parent knows is registered as a sex offender under chapter 62 of the Code of Criminal Procedure or is currently charged with an offense that would require the person to register as a sex offender under that chapter, if convicted. The parent IS ORDERED to give this notice as soon as practicable, but no later than the 40th day after the date the parent or conservator begins to reside with the person, or within 10 days of marrying the person. The notice must include a description of the offense that required the person to register as a sex offender or the offense that the person is charged with that may require the person to register as a sex offender. WARNING: A CONSERVATOR COMMITS AN OFFENSE PUNISHABLE AS A CLASS C MISDEMEANOR IF THE CONSERVATOR FAILS TO PROVIDE THIS NOTICE.

Rights and duties during periods of possession. THE COURT ORDERS that each parent, during his or her periods of possession, shall have the following rights and duties:

1. duty to care for, control, protect, and reasonably discipline the child/ren;

2. The duty to support the child/ren, including providing them with food, clothing, shelter, and medical, and dental care not involving an invasive procedure;

3. The right to consent to non-invasive medical and dental care for the child/ren; and

4. The right to direct the children's moral and religious training.

Passports for the child/ren.

THE COURD ORDERS that ☐ Petitioner ☐ Respondent ☐ Neither parent shall have the exclusive right to apply for and renew passports for the child/ren.

B. Parents Appointed Conservators

B1. ☐ **Joint Managing Conservators.** THE COURT ORDERS that the parents are appointed **Joint Managing Conservators and**

☐ **One parent has the exclusive right to decide where the child/ren live(s).**

THE COURT ORDERS that _____
Print full name of the parent

has the exclusive right to designate the primary residence of the child/ren and that he/she

☐ may designate the child/ren's residence without regard to geographic location.

☐ must designate the child/ren's residence within the following geographic area:

☐ the school attendance zone of _____

☐ this county ☐ this county or county adjacent to this county

☐ Texas ☐ other: _____

☐ **Neither parent has the exclusive right to decide where the child/ren live(s).**

THE COURT ORDERS that neither parent has the exclusive right to designate the primary residence of the child/ren. However, both parents are ORDERED not to move the primary residence of the child/ren from the following geographic area:

☐ the school attendance zone of _____

☐ this county ☐ this county or county adjacent to this county

☐ Texas ☐ other: _____

THE COURT ORDERS that the parents, as Joint Managing Conservators, also have the rights and duties as marked in the list below.

The right or duty listed in the first column shall be exercised by the parent or parents as marked in the second, third, fourth and fifth columns.

(check one box in each row)	Petitioner exclusively.	Respondent exclusively	Parents jointly.	Either parent independently
1. The right to consent to invasive medical, dental, and surgical treatment and to consent to psychiatric or psychological treatment of the children;	☐	☐	☐	☐
2. The right to consent to psychiatric or psychological treatment of the children;	☐	☐	☐	☐
3. The right to receive child support and save or spend these funds for the child/ren's benefit.	☐	☐	☐	☐
4. The right to represent the children in legal action and to make other decisions of substantial legal significance concerning the children;	☐	☐	☐	☐
5. The right to consent to marriage and to enlistment in the armed forces of the United States;	☐	☐	☐	☐
6. The right to make decisions concerning the children's education;	☐	☐	☐	☐
7. The right to services and earnings of the children;	☐	☐	☐	☐
8. The right to make decisions for the children about their estates if the decision is required by law -- **unless** the child/ren have guardian or attorney ad litem or a guardian of the estate; and	☐	☐	☐	☐
9. The duty to manage the child/ren's estates to the extent the estates have been created by the parent's community or joint property.	☐	☐	☐	☐

B2. ☐ **Sole Managing Conservator and Possessory Conservator.**

THE COURT ORDERS that _____
Print full name of the parent
is appointed **Sole Managing Conservator** of the child/ren.

THE COURT ORDERS that _____
Print full name of the parent
is appointed **Possessory Conservator** of the child/ren.

THE COURT ORDERS that the **Sole Managing Conservator** has the following **exclusive** rights and duty:

1. the right to designate the primary residence of the child/ren without geographic restriction;
2. the right to consent to medical, dental, and surgical treatment for the child/ren involving invasive procedures;
3. the right to consent to psychiatric and psychological treatment of the child/ren;
4. the right to receive child support and to save or spend these funds for the benefit of the child/ren;
5. the right to represent the child/ren in legal action and to make other decisions of substantial legal significance concerning the child/ren;
6. the right to consent to marriage and to enlistment in the United States Armed Forces;
7. the right to make decisions concerning the child/ren's education;
8. the right to the services and earnings of the child/ren;
9. except when a guardian of the child/ren's estates or a guardian or attorney ad litem has been appointed for the child/ren, the right to act as an agent of the child/ren in relation to the child/ren's estates if the child/ren's action is required by law;
10. the duty to manage the estates of the child/ren to the extent the estates have been created by community property or the joint property of the parents.

Cause Number _____

Exhibit ____. Standard Possession Order

In this Standard Possession Order

_____ is Home Parent (managing conservator) and

_____ is Co-Parent (possessory conservator).

THE COURT ORDERS that this order is effective immediately and that each parent shall comply with the terms herein.

IT IS ORDERED that the conservators (Home Parent and Co-Parent) shall have possession of the child at any times mutually agreed to in advance. In the absence of mutual agreement, the court ORDERS that Home Parent and Co-Parent shall have possession of the child as set out below in this Standard Possession Order.

Home Parent shall have the right of possession of the child at all times not specifically designated in this Order.

Definitions. "Child" includes each child, whether one or more, who is a subject of this suit while that child is under the age of eighteen years and not otherwise emancipated.

"School" means the elementary or secondary school in which the child is enrolled or, if the child is not enrolled in an elementary or secondary school, the public school district in which the child primarily resides.

"Written notice" includes notice provided by mail, email or fax and is deemed to have been timely if postmarked or received before or at time notice is due.

"After school" means the time the child is regularly dismissed from school before the visitation.

I. PARENTS WHO RESIDE 100 MILES OR LESS APART

If Co-Parent resides 100 miles or less from the primary residence of the child, Co-Parent shall have the right to possession of the child as follows:

1. **Weekends**. On the first, third, and fifth Friday of each month
   beginning on Friday ☐ at 6 p.m. ☐ after school
   and ending ☐ Sunday at 6 p.m. ☐ when school next resumes.

   Weekend Extended By Holiday. If Co-Parent's weekend period of possession coincides with a school holiday during the regular school term, or with a federal, state or local holiday during the summer months when school is not in session, the weekend possession shall begin at 6:00 o'clock p.m. Thursday for a Friday holiday or school holiday, and ending at 6:00 o'clock p.m. on a Monday holiday or school holiday, as applicable.

2. **Thursdays**. On Thursday of each week during the regular school term
   beginning on Thursday ☐ at 6 p.m. ☐ after school
   and ending ☐ at 8 p.m. on Thursday ☐ when school resumes on Friday.

The following provisions for spring and summer school holidays supersede conflicting weekend or Thursday periods of possession. The Co- Parent and Home Parent shall have rights of possession of the child as follows:

3. **Spring Break**. Co-Parent shall have possession in even-numbered years, beginning ☐ at 6 p.m. ☐ after school on the day the child is dismissed from school for the school's spring vacation and ending at 6 p.m. on the day before school resumes after that vacation.

   Home Parent shall have possession for the same period in odd-numbered years;

4. **Summer Possession by Co-Parent**

   A. **With Written Notice by April 1**. If Co-Parent gives Home Parent written notice by April 1 of each year specifying an extended period or periods of summer possession for that year, Co-Parent shall have possession of the child for 30 days beginning not earlier than the day after the child's school is dismissed for the summer vacation and ending not later than seven days before school resumes at the end of the summer vacation, to be exercised in not more than two separate periods of at least seven consecutive days each.

   B. **Without Written Notice by April 1.** If Co-Parent does not give Home Parent written notice by April 1 of each year specifying an extended period or periods of summer possession, Co-Parent shall have possession of the child for 30 consecutive days beginning at 6 p.m. on July 1 and ending at 6 p.m. on July 31.

5. **Summer Possession by Home Parent**

   A. **With Written Notice by April 15**. If Home Parent gives Co-Parent written notice by April 15 of each year, the Home Parent shall have possession of the child on any one weekend beginning Friday at 6 p.m. and ending at 6 p.m. on the following Sunday during one period of summer possession by the Co-Parent, provided that if a period of possession by the Co-Parent exceeds 30 days, the Home Parent may have possession of the child on two non-consecutive weekends during that time period, and further provided that the Home Parent picks up the child from the Co-Parent and returns the child to that same place; and

   B. If Home Parent gives Co-Parent written notice by April 15 of each year or gives Co-Parent 14 days' written notice on or after April 16 of each year, the Home Parent may designate one weekend beginning not earlier than the day after the child's school is dismissed for the summer vacation and ending not later than seven days before school resumes at the end of the summer vacation, during which an otherwise scheduled weekend period of possession by the Co-Parent will not take place, provided that the weekend designated does not interfere with the Co-Parent's period or periods of extended summer possession or with Father's Day if Co-Parent is the father.

6. **Holidays.** Terms for Christmas, Thanksgiving, Mother's and Father's Day, and the child's birthday are defined in Section III below.

II. PARENTS WHO RESIDE MORE THAN 100 MILES APART

If Co-Parent resides more than 100 miles from the residence of the child, Co-Parent shall have the right to possession of the child as follows:

1. **Weekends.** On the first, third, and fifth Friday of each month
beginning on Friday ☐ at 6 p.m. ☐ after school
and ending ☐ Sunday at 6 p.m. ☐ when school next resumes.

   Weekend Extended By Holiday. If Co-Parent's weekend period of possession coincides with a school holiday during the regular school term, or with a federal, state or local holiday during the summer months when school is not in session, the weekend possession shall begin at 6:00 o'clock p.m. Thursday for a Friday holiday or school holiday, and ending at 6:00 o'clock p.m. on a Monday holiday or school holiday, as applicable.

2. **Alternate Weekend Possession.** Instead of the foregoing, Co-Parent shall have the right to possession of the child for not more than one weekend per month of Co-Parent's choice beginning at 6 p.m. on the day school recesses for the weekend and ending at 6 p.m. on the day before school resumes after the weekend.
To choose the alternative period of weekend possession, Co-Parent must give written notice to Home Parent of this choice within 90 days after the parties begin to reside more than 100 miles apart, and Co-Parent must also give Home Parent 14 days' written or telephonic notice preceding a designated weekend.

3. **Spring Break.** Co-parent shall have possession of the child every year, beginning on the day the child is dismissed from school for the school's spring vacation and ending at 6 p.m. on the day before school resumes after that vacation.

4. **Extended Summer Possession by Co-Parent**

   A. **With Written Notice by April 1**. If Co-Parent gives Home Parent written notice by April 1 of each year specifying an extended period or periods of summer possession, Co-Parent shall have possession of the child for 42 days beginning not earlier than the day after the child's school is dismissed for the summer vacation and ending no later than seven days before school resumes at the end of the summer vacation in that year, to be exercised in no more than two separate periods of at least seven consecutive days each,

   B. **Without Written Notice by April 1**. If Co-Parent does not give Home Parent written notice by April 1 of a year specifying an extended period or periods of summer possession for that year, Co-Parent shall have possession of the child for forty-two consecutive days beginning at 6 p.m. on June 15 and ending at 6 p.m. on July 27.

5. **Summer Possession by Home Parent**

   A. **With Written Notice by April 15**. If Home Parent gives Co-Parent written notice by April 15 of each year, the Home Parent shall have possession of the child on any one weekend beginning Friday at 6 p.m. and ending at 6 p.m. on the following Sunday during one period of summer possession by the Co-Parent, provided that if a period of possession by the Co-Parent exceeds 30 days, the Home Parent may have possession of the child on two non-consecutive weekends during that time period, and further provided that the Home Parent picks up the child from the Co-Parent and returns the child to that same place; and

B. If Home Parent gives Co-Parent written notice by April 15 of each year, the Home Parent may designate 21 days beginning not earlier than the day after the child's school is dismissed for the summer vacation and ending not later than seven days before school resumes at the end of the summer vacation, to be exercised in not more than two separate periods of at least seven consecutive days each, during which the Co-Parent may not have possession of the child, provided that the period or periods so designated do not interfere with the Co-Parent's period or periods of extended summer possession or with Father's Day if the possessory conservator is the father.

III. HOLIDAY POSSESSION

The following provisions for specific holidays supersede conflicting weekend or Thursday periods of possession without regard to the distance the parents reside apart.

1. **Christmas Holidays**

   A. Co-Parent shall have possession of the child in **even**-numbered years beginning ☐ at 6 p.m. ☐ after school on the day the child is dismissed from school for the Christmas school vacation and ending at noon on December 26, and Home Parent shall have possession for the same period in **odd**-numbered years.

   B. Co-Parent shall have possession of the child in **odd**-numbered years beginning at noon on December 26 and ending at 6 p.m. on the day before school resumes after that vacation, and Home Parent shall have possession for the same period in **even**-numbered years.

2. **Thanksgiving.** Co-Parent shall have possession of the child in odd-numbered years, beginning at 6 p.m. on the day the child is dismissed from school before Thanksgiving, and ending at 6 p.m. on the following Sunday. The Home Parent shall have possession for the same period in even-numbered years.

3. **Child's Birthday** [Check box if appropriate]
   The parent not otherwise entitled under this Order to possession of the child on the child's birthday shall have possession of the child beginning at 6 p.m. and ending at 8 p.m. on that day, provided that the parent picks up the child from the residence of the parent entitled to possession and returns the child to that same place. ☐ This visit shall include the child's minor siblings.

4. **Parent's Day Weekend**

   a. Father's Day. The Father shall have possession of the child beginning ☐ at 6 p.m. ☐ after school on the Friday before Father's Day and and ending ☐ Sunday at 6 p.m. ☐ when school next resumes after Father's Day, provided that if he is not otherwise entitled under this Order to possession of the child, he shall pick up and return the child at the residence of the parent entitled to possession.

   b. Mother's Day. The Mother shall have possession of the child beginning ☐ at 6 p.m. ☐ after school on the Friday before Mother's Day and and ending ☐ Sunday at 6 p.m. ☐ when school next resumes after Mother's Day, provided that if she is not otherwise entitled under this Order to possession of the child, she shall pick up and return the child at the residence of the parent entitled to possession

IV. GENERAL TERMS AND CONDITIONS

THE COURT ORDERS the following terms and conditions without regard to the distance between the residence of a parent and the child.

1. **Exchange of Children at Start of Co-Parent's Possession.** The Home Parent shall surrender the child to Co-Parent at the beginning of Co-Parent's possession at:

    ☐ Home Parent's residence.
    ☐ Co-Parent's residence.
    ☐ The following location: _____.

    If a period of possession begins at the time the child's school is regularly dismissed, Home Parent shall surrender the child to Co-Parent at the beginning of each such period of possession at the school in which the child is enrolled. If the child is not in school, Co-Parent shall pick up the child at the location designated above and Home Parent shall surrender the child to Co-Parent at that location at 6 pm. If the child will not be in school, Home-Parent shall immediately notify Co-Parent.

2. **Exchange of Children at end of Co-Parent's Possession.** Co-Parent shall surrender the child to Home Parent at the end of Co-Parent's possession at:

    ☐ Home Parent's residence.
    ☐ Co-Parent's residence.
    ☐ The following location: _____.

    However, if both parents live in the same county when the order is signed and Co-Parent remains in the county, but Home Parent moves out of the county, then beginning on the date Home Parent moves, Co-Parent shall return the child to Home parent at:

    ☐ Co-Parent's residence.
    ☐ the location designated above.

    If a period of possession ends at the time the child's school resumes, Co-Parent shall surrender the child to Home Parent at the end of each such period at the school in which the child is enrolled or, if the child is not in school, at the residence of Home Parent at 7 a.m.

    If the child will not be delivered to school on that day, Co-Parent shall immediately notify the school and Home Parent that the child will not or has not been returned to school.

3. **Personal Effects of Child.** Each parent shall return with the child whatever personal effects the child brought at the beginning of the period of possession.

4. **Designation of Competent Adult.** Each parent may designate any competent adult to pick up and return the child, as applicable. The court ORDERS that a parent or designated competent adult be present when the child is picked up or returned.

5. **Notice if Unable to Exercise Possession.** Each party is ORDERED to give notice to the person in possession of the child on each occasion that the party will be unable to exercise that party's right of possession for any specified period.

6. Notice to School and Home Parent. If Co-Parent's time of possession of the child ends at the time school resumes and for any reason the child is not or will not be returned to school, Co-Parent shall immediately notify the school and Home Parent that the child will not be or has not been returned to school.

7. Notice to Any Peace Officer of the State of Texas

YOU MAY USE REASONABLE EFFORTS TO ENFORCE THE TERMS OF CHILD CUSTODY SPECIFIED IN THIS ORDER.

A PEACE OFFICER WHO RELIES ON THE TERMS OF A COURT ORDER, AND HIS AGENCY, ARE ENTITLED TO THE APPLICABLE IMMUNITY AGAINST ANY CLAIM, CIVIL OR OTHERWISE, REGARDING THE OFFICER'S GOOD FAITH ACTS PERFORMED IN THE SCOPE OF THE OFFICER'S DUTIES IN ENFORCING THE TERMS OF THE ORDER THAT RELATE TO CHILD CUSTODY.

ANY PERSON WHO KNOWINGLY PRESENTS FOR ENFORCEMENT AN ORDER THAT IS INVALID OR IS NO LONGER IN EFFECT COMMITS AN OFFENSE THAT MAY BE PUNISHABLE BY CONFINEMENT IN JAIL FOR AS LONG AS TWO YEARS AND A FINE OF AS MUCH AS $10,000.

Cause Number _____

Exhibit ____. Child Support Order

THE COURT ORDERS _____, **(Obligor)**
*Print full name of the parent who will **pay** child support*

to pay child support to _____, **(Obligee)**
*Print full name of the parent who will **receive** child support*

in the amount and manner described below until any one of the following events that terminate child support occurs for **each** child.

- The child reaches the age of eighteen years, unless when the child turns 18 he/she is enrolled and complying with attendance requirements in a secondary school program leading toward a high school diploma, or enrolled in courses for joint high school and junior college credit, or on a full-time basis in a private secondary school program leading toward a high school diploma; *or*

- The child marries, dies, or is emancipated by court order, **or**

- The child commences active duty in the United States Armed forces; **or**

- A court terminates the parent-child relationship between the Obligor and the child based on genetic testing that determines the Obligor is not the genetic parent of the child; **or**

- The marriage or re-marriage of Obligor and Obligee to each other, unless a non-parent or agency has been appointed conservator of the child.

1. **Obligor and Obligee.** In this order and in this Exhibit: *([Check one box on each line)*

   ☐ Petitioner   ☐ Respondent is the **Obligor**, the person who must pay child support.

   ☐ Petitioner   ☐ Respondent is the **Obligee**, the person who has a right to receive child support.

2. **Child Support Amount(s)**

☐ **For a Single Child**

Obligor is ORDERED to pay $_____ as and for child support per month. The first payment is due on _____ *(month / day / year)* and the same amount is due on the first day of the first month after that until child support is terminated for the child.

☐ **For Multiple Children** *(Enter the total amount for **all** children with the date the first payment is due. On each additional line, enter the amount due for **one less** child.)*

Obligor is ORDERED to pay $_____ child support per month. The first payment is due on _____ *(month / day / year)* and the same amount is due on the first day of the first month after that until child support is terminated for **one** child.

Obligor is ORDERED to pay $_____child support per month. The first payment is due on _____ *(month / day / year)* and the same amount is due on the first day of the first month after that until child support is terminated for **a second** child.

Obligor is ORDERED to pay $_____ child support per month. The first payment is due on _____ *(month / day / year)* and the same amount is due on the first day of the first month after that until child support is terminated for **a third** child.

Obligor is ORDERED to pay $_____ child support per month. The first payment is due on _____ *(month / day / year)* and the same amount is due on the first day of the first month after that until child support is terminated for **a fourth** child.

Obligor is ORDERED to pay $_____ child support per month. The first payment is due on _____ *(month / day / year)* and the same amount is due on the first day of the first month after that until child support is terminated for **a fifth** child.

Obligor is ORDERED to pay $_____ child support per month. The first payment is due on _____ *(month / day / year)* and the same amount is due on the first day of the first month after that until child support is terminated for **a sixth** child.

3. **Place of Payment**
THE COURT ORDERS Obligor to send all child support payments to the **Texas Child Support Disbursement Unit, PO Box 659791, San Antonio, TX 78265** for distribution according to law.

Payments shall be made out to the Texas State Disbursement Unit or TXSDU.

THE COURT ORDERS Obligor to include the following information with each payment:
   - The name of the parent ordered to pay child support, **and**
   - The name of the parent ordered to receive child support, **and**
   - The Cause Number and County of the Decree or Order, **and**
   - The Attorney General Case Number, if available.

4. **No Credit for Informal Payments**
THE COURT ORDERS that money paid by Obligor directly to Obligee or spent while in possession of the child/ren does **not** count as child support and shall be deemed in addition to, not instead of, the support ordered herein.

5. **Child Support Account and Fees**
Each parent is ORDERED to:
   - . Fill out any forms necessary to set up a child support account, **and**
   - Take the forms to the local Domestic Relations Office or county child support liaison within 5 days after the judge orders child support, **and**
   - Pay when due all fees charged to that parent by the state disbursement unit and any other agency authorized by law to a charge a fee for the collection and distribution of child support.

6. Child Support Guideline *(See Texas Family Code, Chapter 154, Subchapter C.)*

☐ **Guideline Support.** The amount of child support herein is approximately the amount recommended in the Texas Family Code Child Support Guidelines.

☐ **Non-Guideline Support.** The amount of child support differs significantly from the amount recommended by the Texas Family Code Child Support Guidelines.

The net monthly income/resources of the Obligor is $_____.

The net monthly income/resources of the Obligee is $_____.

Guideline support would be ___% of Obligor's **net** monthly resources, which is $_____ per month.

The actual monthly child support amount ordered is $_____, which is _____ % of Obligor's **net** monthly resources..

Guideline support would be unjust or inappropriate under the circumstances because:

_____

_____

_____

_____

7. Disabled Child

☐ THE COURT FINDS THAT _____ is a child in need of support as defined in section 154.302 of the Texas Family Code, and therefore THE COURT ORDERS that of the above amount ordered for child support, and notwithstanding any other language above, the amount of $_____ per month for the support of said child shall be a continuing obligation until further order of the Court.

8. Income Withholding

IT IS ORDERED that any employer of Obligor shall withhold child support from Obligor's disposable earnings.

If an income withholding for support order is served on Obligor's employer, the employer shall withhold child support payments from Obligor's pay, and send it to the **Texas Child Support Disbursement Unit, PO Box 659791, San Antonio, TX 78265**, where the payments shall be recorded, and forwarded to Obligee.

All child support withheld and paid in accordance with this order shall be credited against Obligor's child support obligation.

If the employer withholds less than 100% of the child support ordered, Obligor is ORDERED to send the balance owed to the **Texas Child Support Disbursement Unit, PO Box 659791, San Antonio, TX 78265**.

If an income withholding for support order is not served on the employer, or if Obligor is self-employed or unemployed, Obligor is ORDERED to send all child support payments to the **Texas Child Support Disbursement Unit, PO Box 659791, San Antonio, TX 78265**.

IT IS ORDERED that the Clerk of this Court shall cause a certified copy of the income withholding for support order to be delivered to any employer of Obligor, if asked to do so by Obligor, Obligee, a prosecuting attorney, the title IV-D agency, a friend of the Court, or a domestic relations office.

9. **Suspension of Income Withholding** *(Check this if parties agree not to have income withholding at this time)*
☐ The parties agree, and the Court ORDERS that an income withholding for support order shall not be served on the employer unless: 1) child support payments are more than 30 days late, 2) the past due amount is the same or more than the monthly child support amount, 3) another violation of this child support order occurs or 4) the Office of the Attorney General Child Support Division is providing services to Obligee. Obligor is ORDERED to send all child support payments to the **Texas Child Support Disbursement Unit, PO Box 659791, San Antonio, TX 78265**, where the payment will be recorded, and forwarded to Obligee.

10. **Change of Address or Employment.** Obligor is ORDERED to notify this Court and Obligee by US certified mail, return receipt requested, of any changes of address and of any termination of employment. This notice shall be given no later than seven days after the change of address or the termination of employment. This notice or a subsequent notice shall also provide the current address of Obligor and the name and address of Obligor's current employer, as soon as that information becomes available.

11. **Child Support After Death.** IT IS ORDERED that the provisions for child support in this decree shall be an obligation of the estate of Obligor and shall not terminate on the death of Obligor. Payments received for the benefit of the children, including payments from the Social Security Administration, Department of Veterans Affairs, other government agency, life insurance proceeds, annuity payments, trust distributions, or retirement survivor benefits, shall be a credit against this obligation. Any remaining balance of child support is an obligation of Obligor's estate.

12. **Life Insurance Policy**
(Check if Obligor should be ordered to have life insurance for as long as child support is ordered)
☐ As additional child support, the person paying child support under this order is ORDERED to obtain and maintain a life insurance policy on his or her life for as long as child support is ordered. The value of the policy shall be at least as much as the total child support obligation. The person receiving child support under this order must be named as the primary beneficiary for the benefit of the children.

"The court may modify this order that provides for the support of a child, if: (1) the circumstances of the child or a person affected by the order have materially and substantially changed; or (2) it has been three years since the order was rendered or last modified and the monthly amount of the child support award under the order differs by either 20 percent or $100 from the amount that would be awarded in accordance with the child support guidelines."

Cause Number _____

Exhibit ____. Medical Support Order

THE COURT ORDERS, **as additional child support**, that so long as the obligation to support the child/ren continues, the parents are ORDERED to provide medical support as set forth below:

A. Availability of Health Insurance

The Court makes the following findings regarding the availability of health insurance:

(Check box A1 or A2 and enter the requested information.)

A1. ☐ Health insurance for the children **is** available at **reasonable cost** to **Obligor** through:

(Note: Cost is reasonable if it is not more than 9% of Obligor's monthly resources for all of Obligor's children.)

☐ **Obligor's** work or membership in a union, trade association, or other organization.
The actual cost of the health insurance is $ _____ per month.

☐ **Obligee's** work or membership in a union, trade association, or other organization.
The actual cost of the health insurance is $ _____ per month.

☐ another source available to **Obligor**.
The actual cost of the health insurance is $ _____ per month.

☐ another source available to **Obligee**.
The actual cost of the health insurance is $ _____ per month.

(Note: If health insurance for children is available to Obligee, and Obligee has other children covered by the same plan, then to determine the actual cost of insuring children in this case, divide the total cost of insuring all children covered by by the number of children insured, then multiply that amount by the number of children in this case.)

A2. ☐ Private health insurance for the children **is not** available to either parent at reasonable cost.

The child/ren ☐ **is/are** ☐ Is **not/are not** currently covered by **Medicaid**.

The child/ren ☐ **is/are** ☐ Is **not/are not** currently currently covered by **C.H.I.P.**

The cost, if any, is $ _____ ☐ per month ☐ per year.

(Check only if applicable.)

☐ Good cause exists to make an order that does not follow the priorities set out in Texas Family Code Section 154.182 for the following reasons: (See note about the law above.)

_____

_____

B. Orders Regarding Health Care Coverage

(Check one, either B1, B2 or B3 and enter the requested information)

B1. ☐ Obligor to Provide and Pay for Health Insurance

THE COURT ORDERS Obligor, _____, as additional child support, to get health insurance for the child/ren within **15 days** of the date of this order through: (check one)

☐ **Obligor's** work or membership in a union, trade association, or other organization.

☐ another source available to **Obligor**.

Obligor is ORDERED to pay, as additional child support, all costs of such health insurance, including but not limited to enrollment fees and premiums.

The health insurance ordered must cover basic healthcare services, including usual physician services, office visits, hospitalization, and laboratory, X-ray, and emergency services.

Obligor is ORDERED to keep such health insurance in full force and effect on each child, who is the subject of this suit, so long as the obligation to support each child continues.

Obligor is ORDERED to give Obligee the following **within 30 days** of the date of this order:
- Obligor's social security number and the name and address of Obligor's employer, **and**
- the name of the insurance carrier, the policy number, and proof the child/ren are covered, **and**
- a copy of the insurance policy and list of benefits covered, **and**
- insurance membership cards for the child/ren, **and**
- any forms needed to use the health insurance, **and**
- any forms needed to submit a claim.

Obligor is ORDERED to give Obligee the following within **3 days** of receipt:
- any insurance checks or other payments for medical expenses paid by Obligee **and**
- any explanations of benefits relating to medical expenses paid or incurred by Obligee.

If health insurance benefits for the child/ren are **changed** in any way, Obligor is ORDERED to give Obligee information about the change and any new forms needed to use the insurance **within 15 days** of the change.

If health insurance benefits are **cancelled**, Obligor is ORDERED to get new health insurance for the children **within 15 days** of the date of cancellation. The new insurance must equal or exceed the prior level of coverage.

If Obligor is eligible for dependent health coverage but fails to apply to obtain coverage for the child/ren, the insurer is ORDERED to enroll the child/ren on application of Obligee or others as authorized by law. *(See Texas Insurance Code, Section 1504.051)*

B2. ☐ Obligee to Provide Health Insurance / Obligor to Reimburse Cost

THE COURT ORDERS Obligee, _____, as additional child support, to get health insurance for the child/ren within **15 days** of the date of this order through: (check one)

☐ **Obligee's** work or membership in a union, trade association, or other organization.

☐ another source available to **Obligee**.

The health insurance ordered must cover basic healthcare services, including usual physician services, office visits, hospitalization, and laboratory, X-ray, and emergency services.

Obligee is ORDERED to keep such health insurance in full force and effect on each child, who is the subject of this suit, so long as the obligation to support each child continues.

Obligee is ORDERED to give Obligor the following **within 30 days** of the date of this order:
- Obligee's social security number and the name and address of Obligee's employer, **and**
- the name of the insurance carrier, the policy number, and proof the child/ren are covered, **and**
- a copy of the insurance policy and list of benefits covered, **and**
- insurance membership cards for the child/ren, **and**

- any forms needed to use the health insurance, **and**
- any forms needed to submit a claim.

Obligee is ORDERED to give Obligor the following within **3 days** of receipt:
- any insurance checks or other payments for medical expenses paid by Obligor **and**
- any explanations of benefits relating to medical expenses paid or incurred by Obligor.

If health insurance benefits for the child/ren are **changed** in any way, Obligee is ORDERED to give Obligor information about the change and any new forms needed to use the insurance **within 15 days** of the change.

If health insurance benefits are **cancelled**, Obligee is ORDERED to get new health insurance for the children **within 15 days** of the date of cancellation. The new insurance must equal or exceed the prior level of coverage.

If Obligee is eligible for dependent health coverage but fails to apply to obtain coverage for the child/ren, the insurer is ORDERED to enroll the child/ren on application of Obligor or others as authorized by law. *(See Texas Insurance Code, Section 1504.051)*

As **additional child support**, the Court ORDERS Obligor, _____,
to pay Obligee **cash medical support** of $ _____ per month for **reimbursement** of health insurance premiums. The 1st payment is due on _____ *(month / day / year)*. A like payment is due on the 1st day of each month after that until child support is terminated for **each** child.

Obligor is ORDERED to send all cash medical support payments to the **Texas Child Support Disbursement Unit, PO Box 659791, San Antonio, TX 78265**, for distribution according to law.

The Court ORDERS that money paid by Obligor directly to Obligee or spent while in possession of the children does **NOT** count as cash medical support.

The Court ORDERS that the cash medical support provisions of this order shall be an obligation of the estate of Obligor and shall not terminate on his/her death.

B3. ☐ **Obligee to Apply for Coverage Under a Government Medical Assistance Program or Health Plan / Obligor to Reimburse Cost**

THE COURT ORDERS Obligee, _____, to apply on behalf of each child for coverage under a governmental medical assistance program or health plan (i.e. Medicaid or C.H.I.P) **within 15 days** of the date this decree or order is signed by the Court. If the children are already covered under such a program or plan, the Court ORDERS Obligee to continue such coverage.

When such health coverage is obtained, Obligee is ORDERED to maintain the coverage in full force and effect on each child by paying all applicable fees required for the coverage, including but not limited to enrollment fees and premiums for as long as the children are eligible for such coverage.

Obligee is ORDERED to give the Office of the Attorney General Child Support Division a copy of the insurance policy and list of benefits covered **within 30 days** of the date of this order.

Obligee is ORDERED to give Obligor the following **within 30 days** of the date of this order:
- the name of the insurance company and the policy number, **and**
- a copy of the insurance policy and list of benefits covered, **and**
- insurance membership cards for the child/ren, **and**

- any forms needed to use the health insurance, **and**
- any forms needed to submit a claim.

Obligee is ORDERED to give Obligor the following within **3 days** of receipt:
- any insurance checks or other payments for medical expenses paid by Obligor **and**
- any explanations of benefits relating to medical expenses paid or incurred by Obligor.

If Obligee is eligible for dependent health coverage but fails to apply to obtain coverage for the child/ren, the insurer is ORDERED to enroll the child/ren on application of Obligor or others as authorized by law. *(See Texas Insurance Code, Section 1504.051)*

As **additional child support**, the Court ORDERS Obligor, _____, to pay Obligee **cash medical support** of $ _____ per month for **reimbursement** of health insurance premiums. The 1st payment is due on _____ *(month / day / year)*. A like payment is due on the 1st day of each month after that until child support is terminated for **each** child.

Obligor is ORDERED to send all cash medical support payments to the **Texas Child Support Disbursement Unit, PO Box 659791, San Antonio, TX 78265**, for distribution according to law.

The Court ORDERS that money paid by Obligor directly to Obligee or spent while in possession of the children does **NOT** count as cash medical support.

IT IS ORDERED that Obligor is allowed to **stop paying of cash medical support**, for the time Obligor is providing health insurance coverage for the children, **if**:

1. health insurance for the children becomes available to Obligor at a reasonable cost; **and**

2. Obligor enrolls the child/ren in the insurance plan and pays all costs of the insurance; **and**

3. Obligor provides Obligee and the Texas Office of the Attorney General, Child Support Division the following information:

    (a) proof that health insurance has been provided for the child/ren, and

    (b) Obligor's social security number, and

    (c) name and address of the Obligor's employer, and

    (d) whether the employer is self-insured or has health insurance available, and

    (i) if the employer is self-insured, a copy of the schedule of benefits, a membership card, claim forms, and any other information necessary to submit a claim, or

    (ii) if the employer has health insurance available, the name of the health insurance carrier, the policy number, a copy of the policy and schedule of benefits, a health insurance membership card, claim forms, and any other information necessary to submit a claim.

C. Uninsured Health-Care Expenses

The Court ORDERS that the reasonable and necessary health-care expenses for the child/ren that are not covered by health insurance shall be paid by the parents as follows:

If B1 above is checked, Obligor and Obligee are each ORDERED to pay **50 percent** of all reasonable and necessary health-care expenses for the child/ren that are not covered by health insurance **if**, at the time the expenses are incurred, Obligor is providing health insurance as ordered. If, at the time the expenses are incurred, Obligor is **not** providing health insurance as ordered Obligor is liable for **100 percent** of all necessary medical expenses of the child/ren.

If B2 above is checked, Obligor and Obligee are each ORDERED to pay **50 percent** of all reasonable and necessary health-care expenses for the child/ren that are not reimbursed by health insurance **if**, at the time the expenses are incurred, Obligee is providing health insurance as ordered. If, at the time the expenses are incurred, Obligee is **not** providing health insurance as ordered Obligee is liable for 100 **percent** of all necessary medical expenses of the child/ren.

If B3 above is checked, Obligee is ORDERED to pay **50 percent** of all reasonable and necessary health-care expenses for the child/ren that are not reimbursed by health insurance or covered by the cash medical support paid by Obligor and Obligor is ORDERED to pay **50 percent** of the total unreimbursed health-care expenses that exceed the amount of cash medical support paid by Obligor. Obligor is liable for **100 percent** of all necessary medical expenses incurred for the child/ren in any month that Obligor neither pays cash medical support nor provides health insurance for the child/ren.

Reasonable and necessary health care expenses that must be paid by the parents if not covered by insurance include:

- copayments for office visits and prescription drugs, **and**
- the yearly deductible, if any, **and**
- medical, surgical, and prescription drug expenses, **and**
- mental health-care services, **and**
- dental and orthodontic expenses, **and**
- eye care and ophthalmological expenses.

These reasonable and necessary health-care expenses do not include expenses for travel to and from the health-care provider or for nonprescription medication.

The parent who incurs a health-care expense on behalf of a child (called the "incurring parent") is ORDERED to give the other parent (called the "nonincurring parent") a copy of all forms, receipts, bills, statements, and explanations of benefits that show the portion of the expense not covered by insurance **within 30 days** of receipt.

The nonincurring parent is ORDERED to pay his or her percentage of any uninsured expense **within 30 days** of receiving documentation of the expense by:

- paying the health-care provider directly, **or**
- reimbursing the incurring parent, if the nonincurring parent's portion of the expense has already been paid.

D. Claims

Either parent may file claims and receive payments directly from the insurance carrier. Further, for the sole purpose of Texas Insurance Code Sections 1204.251 and 1204.252, the party who is not carrying the insurance policy is designated the managing conservator or possessory conservator of the children.

Any reimbursement payments received from the health insurance carrier belongs to the parent who paid the expense. If the insurance carrier sends reimbursement to the parent who did not pay the expense, he or she is ORDERED to endorse the check and deliver it to the parent who paid the expense within 3 days.

E. Health Insurance Policy Requirements

Each parent is ORDERED to follow all requirements of any health insurance policy covering the child/ren to get maximum reimbursement and direct payment from the insurance company, including requirements for:

- giving advance notice to the insurance company, **and**
- getting second opinions, **and**
- using "preferred providers."

If a parent incurs health-care expenses for the child/ren using "out-of-network" health-care providers or services, or fails to follow the health insurance company procedures or requirements, that parent shall pay all such health-care expenses incurred unless:

- the expenses are emergency health-care expenses, **or**
- the parents have a written agreement regarding such health-care expenses, **or**
- the Court makes a different order.

Denial of a bill by an insurance carrier does not excuse the obligation of the parents to pay the expense.

Cause Number _____

Exhibit _____. Dental Support Order

THE COURT ORDERS, **as additional child support**, that so long as the obligation to support the child/ren continues, the parents are ORDERED to provide dental support as set forth below:

A. Availability of Dental Insurance

The Court makes the following findings regarding the availability of insurance:

(Check box A1 or A2 and enter the requested information.)

A1. ☐ Dental insurance for the children **is** available at **reasonable cost** to **Obligor** through:

> *(Note: Cost is reasonable if it is not more than 9% of Obligor's monthly resources for all of Obligor's children.)*

☐ **Obligor's** work or membership in a union, trade association, or other organization.
The actual cost of the dental insurance is $ _____ per month.

☐ **Obligee's** work or membership in a union, trade association, or other organization.
The actual cost of the dental insurance is $ _____ per month.

☐ another source available to **Obligor**.
The actual cost of the dental insurance is $ _____ per month.

☐ another source available to **Obligee**.
The actual cost of the dental insurance is $ _____ per month.

> *(Note: If dental insurance for children is available to Obligee, and Obligee has other children covered by the same plan, then to determine the actual cost of insuring children in this case, divide the total cost of insuring all children covered by the number of children insured, then multiply that amount by the number of children in this case.)*

A2. ☐ Private dental insurance for the children **is not** available to either parent at reasonable cost.

The child/ren ☐ **is/are** ☐ Is **not/are not** currently covered by **Medicaid**.

The child/ren ☐ **is/are** ☐ Is **not/are not** currently currently covered by **C.H.I.P.**

The cost, if any, is $ _____ ☐ per month ☐ per year.

(Check only if applicable.)

☐ Good cause exists to make an order that does not follow the priorities set out in Texas Family Code Section 154.182 for the following reasons:

_____

_____

B. Orders Regarding dental Care Coverage

(Check one, either B1, B2 or B3 and enter the requested information)

B1. ☐ Obligor to Provide and Pay for dental Insurance

THE COURT ORDERS Obligor, _____, as additional child support, to get dental insurance for the child/ren within **15 days** of the date of this order through: (check one)

☐ **Obligor's** work or membership in a union, trade association, or other organization.

☐ another source available to **Obligor**.

Obligor is ORDERED to pay, as additional child support, all costs of such dental insurance, including but not limited to enrollment fees and premiums.

The dental insurance ordered must cover basic healthcare services, including usual physician services, office visits, hospitalization, and laboratory, X-ray, and emergency services.

Obligor is ORDERED to keep such dental insurance in full force and effect on each child, who is the subject of this suit, so long as the obligation to support each child continues.

Obligor is ORDERED to give Obligee the following **within 30 days** of the date of this order:
- Obligor's social security number and the name and address of Obligor's employer, **and**
- the name of the insurance carrier, the policy number, and proof the child/ren are covered, **and**
- a copy of the insurance policy and list of benefits covered, **and**
- insurance membership cards for the child/ren, **and**
- any forms needed to use the dental insurance, **and**
- any forms needed to submit a claim.

Obligor is ORDERED to give Obligee the following within **3 days** of receipt:
- any insurance checks or other payments for dental expenses paid by Obligee **and**
- any explanations of benefits relating to dental expenses paid or incurred by Obligee.

If dental insurance benefits for the child/ren are **changed** in any way, Obligor is ORDERED to give Obligee information about the change and any new forms needed to use the insurance **within 15 days** of the change.

If dental insurance benefits are **cancelled**, Obligor is ORDERED to get new dental insurance for the children **within 15 days** of the date of cancellation. The new insurance must equal or exceed the prior level of coverage.

If Obligor is eligible for dependent dental coverage but fails to apply to obtain coverage for the child/ren, the insurer is ORDERED to enroll the child/ren on application of Obligee or others as authorized by law. *(See Texas Insurance Code, Section 1504.051)*

B2. ☐ Obligee to Provide dental Insurance / Obligor to Reimburse Cost

THE COURT ORDERS Obligee, _____, as additional child support, to get dental insurance for the child/ren within **15 days** of the date of this order through: (check one)

☐ **Obligee's** work or membership in a union, trade association, or other organization.

☐ another source available to **Obligee**.

The dental insurance ordered must cover basic healthcare services, including usual physician services, office visits, hospitalization, and laboratory, X-ray, and emergency services.

Obligee is ORDERED to keep such dental insurance in full force and effect on each child, who is the subject of this suit, so long as the obligation to support each child continues.

Obligee is ORDERED to give Obligor the following **within 30 days** of the date of this order:
- Obligee's social security number and the name and address of Obligee's employer, **and**
- the name of the insurance carrier, the policy number, and proof the child/ren are covered, **and**
- a copy of the insurance policy and list of benefits covered, **and**
- insurance membership cards for the child/ren, **and**

- any forms needed to use the dental insurance, **and**
- any forms needed to submit a claim.

Obligee is ORDERED to give Obligor the following within **3 days** of receipt:
- any insurance checks or other payments for dental expenses paid by Obligor **and**
- any explanations of benefits relating to dental expenses paid or incurred by Obligor.

If dental insurance benefits for the child/ren are **changed** in any way, Obligee is ORDERED to give Obligor information about the change and any new forms needed to use the insurance **within 15 days** of the change.

If dental insurance benefits are **cancelled**, Obligee is ORDERED to get new dental insurance for the children **within 15 days** of the date of cancellation. The new insurance must equal or exceed the prior level of coverage.

If Obligee is eligible for dependent dental coverage but fails to apply to obtain coverage for the child/ren, the insurer is ORDERED to enroll the child/ren on application of Obligor or others as authorized by law.
(See Texas Insurance Code, Section 1504.051)

As **additional child support**, the Court ORDERS Obligor, _____,
to pay Obligee **cash dental support** of $ _____ per month for **reimbursement** of dental insurance premiums. The 1st payment is due on _____ *(month / day / year)*. A like payment is due on the 1st day of each month after that until child support is terminated for **each** child.

Obligor is ORDERED to send all cash dental support payments to the **Texas Child Support Disbursement Unit, PO Box 659791, San Antonio, TX 78265**, for distribution according to law.

The Court ORDERS that money paid by Obligor directly to Obligee or spent while in possession of the children does **NOT** count as cash dental support.

The Court ORDERS that the cash dental support provisions of this order shall be an obligation of the estate of Obligor and shall not terminate on his/her death.

B3. ☐ **Obligee to Apply for Coverage Under a Government Assistance Program or Dental Plan / Obligor to Reimburse Cost**

THE COURT ORDERS Obligee, _____, to apply on behalf of each child for coverage under a governmental dental assistance program or dental plan (i.e. Medicaid or C.H.I.P) **within 15 days** of the date this decree or order is signed by the Court. If the children are already covered under such a program or plan, the Court ORDERS Obligee to continue such coverage.

When such dental coverage is obtained, Obligee is ORDERED to maintain the coverage in full force and effect on each child by paying all applicable fees required for the coverage, including but not limited to enrollment fees and premiums for as long as the children are eligible for such coverage.

Obligee is ORDERED to give the Office of the Attorney General Child Support Division a copy of the insurance policy and list of benefits covered **within 30 days** of the date of this order.

Obligee is ORDERED to give Obligor the following **within 30 days** of the date of this order:
- the name of the insurance company and the policy number, **and**
- a copy of the insurance policy and list of benefits covered, **and**
- insurance membership cards for the child/ren, **and**

- any forms needed to use the dental insurance, **and**
- any forms needed to submit a claim.

Obligee is ORDERED to give Obligor the following within **3 days** of receipt:
- any insurance checks or other payments for dental expenses paid by Obligor **and**
- any explanations of benefits relating to dental expenses paid or incurred by Obligor.

If Obligee is eligible for dependent dental coverage but fails to apply to obtain coverage for the child/ren, the insurer is ORDERED to enroll the child/ren on application of Obligor or others as authorized by law. *(See Texas Insurance Code, Section 1504.051)*

As **additional child support**, the Court ORDERS Obligor, _____, to pay Obligee **cash dental support** of $ _____ per month for **reimbursement** of dental insurance premiums. The 1st payment is due on _____ *(month / day / year)*. A like payment is due on the 1st day of each month after that until child support is terminated for **each** child.

Obligor is ORDERED to send all cash dental support payments to the **Texas Child Support Disbursement Unit, PO Box 659791, San Antonio, TX 78265**, for distribution according to law.

The Court ORDERS that money paid by Obligor directly to Obligee or spent while in possession of the children does **NOT** count as cash dental support.

IT IS ORDERED that Obligor is allowed to **stop paying cash dental support**, for the time Obligor is providing dental insurance coverage for the children, **if**:

1. dental insurance for the children becomes available to Obligor at a reasonable cost; **and**

2. Obligor enrolls the child/ren in the insurance plan and pays all costs of the insurance; **and**

3. Obligor provides Obligee and the Texas Office of the Attorney General, Child Support Division the following information:

    (a) proof that dental insurance has been provided for the child/ren, and

    (b) Obligor's social security number, and

    (c) name and address of the Obligor's employer, and

    (d) whether the employer is self-insured or has dental insurance available, and

    　　(i) if the employer is self-insured, a copy of the schedule of benefits, a membership card, claim forms, and any other information necessary to submit a claim, or

    　　(ii) if the employer has dental insurance available, the name of the dental insurance carrier, the policy number, a copy of the policy and schedule of benefits, a dental insurance membership card, claim forms, and any other information necessary to submit a claim.

C. Uninsured Dental Care Expenses

The Court ORDERS that the reasonable and necessary dental care expenses for the child/ren that are not covered by dental insurance shall be paid by the parents as follows:

If B1 above is checked, Obligor and Obligee are each ORDERED to pay **50 percent** of all reasonable and necessary dental care expenses for the child/ren that are not covered by dental insurance **if**, at the time the expenses are incurred, Obligor is providing dental insurance as ordered. If, at the time the expenses are incurred, Obligor is **not** providing dental insurance as ordered Obligor is liable for **100 percent** of all necessary dental expenses of the child/ren.

If B2 above is checked, Obligor and Obligee are each ORDERED to pay **50 percent** of all reasonable and necessary dental care expenses for the child/ren that are not reimbursed by dental insurance **if**, at the time the expenses are incurred, Obligee is providing dental insurance as ordered. If, at the time the expenses are incurred, Obligee is **not** providing dental insurance as ordered Obligee is liable for 100 **percent** of all necessary dental expenses of the child/ren.

If B3 above is checked, Obligee is ORDERED to pay **50 percent** of all reasonable and necessary dental care expenses for the child/ren that are not reimbursed by dental insurance or covered by the cash dental support paid by Obligor and Obligor is ORDERED to pay **50 percent** of the total unreimbursed dental care expenses that exceed the amount of cash dental support paid by Obligor. Obligor is liable for **100 percent** of all necessary dental expenses incurred for the child/ren in any month that Obligor neither pays cash dental support nor provides dental insurance for the child/ren.

Reasonable and necessary dental and dental care expenses that must be paid by the parents if not covered by insurance include:

- copayments for office visits and prescription drugs, **and**
- the yearly deductible, if any, **and**
- dental, oral surgery, and prescription drug expenses, **and**
- dental care services, **and**
- orthodontic expenses, **and**
- eye care and ophthalmological expenses.

These reasonable and necessary dental-care expenses do not include expenses for travel to and from the dental care provider or for nonprescription medication.

The parent who incurs a dental care expense on behalf of a child (called the "incurring parent") is ORDERED to give the other parent (called the "nonincurring parent") a copy of all forms, receipts, bills, statements, and explanations of benefits that show the portion of the expense not covered by insurance **within 30 days** of receipt.

The nonincurring parent is ORDERED to pay his or her percentage of any uninsured expense **within 30 days** of receiving documentation of the expense by:

- paying the dental care provider directly, **or**
- reimbursing the incurring parent, if the nonincurring parent's portion of the expense has already been paid.

D. Claims

Either parent may file claims and receive payments directly from the insurance carrier. Further, for the sole purpose of Texas Insurance Code Sections 1204.251 and 1204.252, the party who is not carrying the insurance policy is designated the managing conservator or possessory conservator of the children.

Any reimbursement payments received from the dental insurance carrier belongs to the parent who paid the expense. If the insurance carrier sends reimbursement to the parent who did not pay the expense, he or she is ORDERED to endorse the check and deliver it to the parent who paid the expense within 3 days.

E. Dental Insurance Policy Requirements

Each parent is ORDERED to follow all requirements of any dental insurance policy covering the child/ren to get maximum reimbursement and direct payment from the insurance company, including requirements for:

- giving advance notice to the insurance company, **and**
- getting second opinions, **and**
- using "preferred providers."

If a parent incurs dental care expenses for the child/ren using "out-of-network" dental-care providers or services, or fails to follow the dental insurance company procedures or requirements, that parent shall pay all such dental-care expenses incurred unless:

- the expenses are emergency dental care expenses, **or**
- the parents have a written agreement regarding such dental-care expenses, **or**
- the Court makes a different order.

Denial of a bill by an insurance carrier does not excuse the obligation of the parents to pay the expense.

Exhibit ____. FAMILY INFORMATION
Required by Texas Family Code sections 105.006 and 105.007

Petitioner's Name: _____
    Social Security number: _____
    Driver's license number: _____ Issuing state: _____
    Current residence address: _____
    Mailing address: _____
    Home telephone number: _____ Work phone: _____
    Name of employer: _____
    Address of employment: _____

Respondent's Name: _____
    Social Security number: _____
    Driver's license number: _____ Issuing state: _____
    Current residence address: _____
    Mailing address: _____
    Home telephone number: _____ Work phone: _____
    Name of employer: _____
    Address of employment: _____

Other Person Named as a Party in this Case (if applicable)
    Name: _____ Relationship to Children: _____
    Social Security number: _____
    Driver's license number: _____ Issuing state: _____
    Current residence address: _____
    Mailing address: _____
    Home telephone number: _____ Work phone: _____
    Name of employer: _____
    Address of employment: _____

Name of first child (under 18): _____
    Social Security number: _____
    Driver's license number: _____ Issuing state: _____
    Current residence address: _____
    Mailing address: _____
    Home telephone number: _____ Work phone: _____
    Name of employer: _____
    Address of employment: _____

Name of second child: _____
    Social Security number: _____
    Driver's license number: _____ Issuing state: _____
    Current residence address: _____
    Mailing address: _____
    Home telephone number: _____ Work phone: _____
    Name of employer: _____
    Address of employment: _____

Name of third child: _____
    Social Security number: _____
    Driver's license number: _____ Issuing state: _____
    Current residence address: _____
    Mailing address: _____
    Home telephone number: _____ Work phone: _____
    Name of employer: _____
    Address of employment: _____

Name of fourth child: _____
    Social Security number: _____
    Driver's license number: _____ Issuing state: _____
    Current residence address: _____
    Mailing address: _____
    Home telephone number: _____ Work phone: _____
    Name of employer: _____
    Address of employment: _____

Name of fifth child: _____
    Social Security number: _____
    Driver's license number: _____ Issuing state: _____
    Current residence address: _____
    Mailing address: _____
    Home telephone number: _____ Work phone: _____
    Name of employer: _____
    Address of employment: _____

☐ See attached page for additional children

Each person who is a party to this order is ordered to notify every other party, the court, and the state child support registry of any change in the party's current residence address, mailing address, home telephone number, name of employer, address of employment, driver's license number, and work telephone number.

The party is ordered to give notice of an intended change in any of the required information to the other party, the court, and the state case registry on or before the 60th day before the intended change. If the party does not know or could not have known of the change in sufficient time to give notice of the change to provide 60-days notice, the party is ordered to give notice of the change on or before the 5th day after the date that the party knows of the change.

The duty to furnish this information to every other party, the court, and the state case registry continues as long as any person, by virtue of this order, is under an obligation to pay child support or entitled to possession of or access to a child.

Failure by a party to obey the order of this court to provide every other party, the court, and the state case registry with the change in the required information may result in further litigation to enforce the order, including contempt of court. A finding of contempt may be punishable by confinement in jail for up to six months, a fine of up to $500 for each violation, and a money judgment for attorney's fees and court costs.

Notice shall be given to every other party by delivering a copy of the notice to each party by registered or certified mail, return receipt requested.

Notice shall be given to the court and the state case registry by delivering a copy of the notice either in person to the clerk of the court or by registered or certified mail addressed to the clerk.

Exhibit _____. Orders Re Property and Debts

A. SEPARATE PROPERTY CONFIRMED.

THE COURT FINDS that property listed in items A1 or A2 below was owned by one party before marriage, or received by that party as a gift or inheritance, or acquired with separate assets and is therefore the property of that party. The court therefore ORDERS as follows:

☐ **1. Separate Property Confirmed to Petitioner**

THE COURT ORDERS that the following is confirmed as Petitioner's sole and separate property:

_____

_____

_____

_____

_____

_____

☐ **2. Separate Property Confirmed to Respondent**

THE COURT ORDERS that the following is confirmed as Respondent's sole and separate property:

_____

_____

_____

_____

_____

_____

B. DIVISION OF COMMUNITY PROPERTY AND DEBTS

THE COURT ORDERS that the community property of the parties is divided as follows:

☐ **1. Court to Retain Jurisdiction Over Employee Retirement Benefits**

THE COURT FINDS that _____ is a participant in a retirement program known as

_____

_____,

as to which the Court reserves jurisdiction to adjudicate the respective rights of the parties at a future date upon application of either party. THE COURT ORDERS that _____ shall not apply for or accept benefits under said program without prior written notice to the other party and application to this Court for determination and division of community rights in said plan. IT IS FURTHER ORDERED that any party requesting a division or clarification of retirement shall do so within two (2) years of the date this decree is signed by the court, or the party shall lose that right.

☐ **2. Petitioner's Community Property**

The Court ORDERS that Petitioner is awarded the following as his/her sole and separate property, and Respondent conveys to him/her all interest in it and has no right, title, interest, or claim to such property. Respondent is ORDERED to sign any documents needed to transfer property listed below to Petitioner. Petitioner is responsible for preparing such documents.

2a. All property in Petitioner's care, custody or control or in Petitioner's name, and not otherwise specifically awarded to Respondent.

2b. ☐ The following specific property:

_____

_____

_____

_____

2c. ☐ A house or other real estate:
THE COURT ORDERS that Petitioner is awarded the following property as Petitioner's sole and separate property, and Respondent conveys to Petitioner all of Respondent's interest in it, and Respondent is divested of all right, title, interest and claim and in and to that property:
[Street address and legal description of real property, including name of county and state.]

_____

_____

_____

2d. ☐ The following employment benefits, retirement accounts, pension plans, military retirement benefits, profit-sharing, or stock option plans that are in Petitioner's name alone:

_____

_____

_____

2e. ☐ All cash and money in any in bank or other financial institution in Petitioner's sole name.
[This means you must separate your accounts **before** the judge signs the Decree]

2f. ☐ The following cars, trucks, or motorcycles: [List year, make, model and Vehicle Identification No. VIN.]

_____

_____

_____

2g. ☐ Any and all policies of life insurance (including cash values) insuring the life of Petitioner.

2h. ☐ Additional property that Petitioner will keep:

_____

_____

☐ **3. Petitioner's Debts**

THE COURT ORDERS that Petitioner pay the following community debts:

3a. ☐ All encumbrances, taxes, liens, assessments, or other charges due or to become due on real and personal property awarded to Petitioner in this decree unless express provision is made herein to the contrary.

3b. ☐ Balances due on any loan or mortgage for property awarded to Petitioner alone in this decree.

3c. ☐ Any debt Petitioner incurred after separation on _____, 20____.

3d. ☐ Balances due on loans secured by vehicles awarded to Petitioner.

3e. Any debts solely in Petitioner's name, except as otherwise provided for herein.

3f. ☐ The following debts and obligations that are not in Petitioner's name alone:
[credit cards, student loans, medical bills, income taxes, etc.]

_____

_____

_____

_____

☐ **4. Respondent's Community Property**

The Court ORDERS that Respondent is awarded the following as his/her sole and separate property, and Petitioner conveys to him/her all interest in it and has no right, title, interest, or claim to such property. Petitioner is ORDERED to sign any documents needed to transfer property listed below to Respondent. Respondent is responsible for preparing such documents.

4a. All property in Respondent's care, custody or control or in Respondent's name, and not otherwise specifically awarded to Petitioner.

4b. ☐ The following specific property:

_____

_____

_____

4c. ☐ A house or other real estate:
THE COURT ORDERS that Respondent is awarded the following property as Respondent's sole and separate property, and Petitioner conveys to Respondent all of Petitioner's interest in such property, and Petitioner is divested of all right, title, interest and claim and in and to that property:
[Street address and legal description of real property, including name of county and state.]

_____

_____

_____

4d. ☐ The following employment benefits, retirement accounts, pension plans, military retirement benefits, profit-sharing, or stock option plans that are in Respondent's name alone:

_____

_____

_____

4e. ☐ All cash and money in any in bank or other financial institution in Respondent's sole name.
[This means you must separate your accounts **before** the judge signs the Decree]

4f. ☐ The following cars, trucks, or motorcycles: [List year, make, model and Vehicle Identification No. VIN.]

_____

_____

_____

4g. ☐ Any and all policies of life insurance (including cash values) insuring the life of Respondent.

4h. ☐ Additional property that Respondent will keep:

_____

_____

_____

☐ **5. Respondent's Debts**

THE COURT ORDERS that Respondent pay the following community debts:

5a. ☐ All encumbrances, taxes, liens, assessments, or other charges due or to become due on real and personal property awarded to Respondent in this decree unless express provision is made herein to the contrary.

5b. ☐ Balances due on any loan or mortgage for property awarded to Respondent in this decree.

5c. ☐ Any debt incurred by Respondent after separation on _____, 20____.

5d. ☐ Balances due on loans secured by vehicles awarded to Respondent.

5e. Any debts solely in Respondent's name, except as otherwise provided for herein.

5f. ☐ The following debts and obligations that are not in Respondent's name alone:
[credit cards, student loans, medical bills, income taxes, etc.]

_____

_____

_____

Cause Number _____

IN THE MATTER OF THE MARRIAGE OF

Petitioner: _____   **In the**

_____ ☐ District Court ☐ County Court
at Law of

And

Respondent: _____   _____ County, Texas

☐ **AND IN THE INTEREST OF:**

1. _____   2. _____   3. _____
4. _____   5. _____   6. _____

Certificate of Last Known Mailing Address

I, _____, am Petitioner.
       First   *Middle*   *Last*

Respondent is: _____.
                    First   *Middle*   *Last*

I hereby certify that the last known mailing address that I have for Respondent is:

_____.
Address

_____.
          City   *State*   *Zip*

_____
Telephone with Area Code

_____
Fax with Area Code

_____   Date: _____
Petitioner's Signature

INFORMATION ON SUIT AFFECTING THE FAMILY RELATIONSHIP
(EXCLUDING ADOPTIONS)

SECTION I GENERAL INFORMATION (REQUIRED)	STATE FILE NUMBER

1a. COUNTY _____   1b. COURT NO. _____

1c. CAUSE NO. _____   1d. DATE OF ORDER (mm/dd/yyyy) _____

2. HAS THERE BEEN A FINDING BY THE COURT OF: ☐ DOMESTIC VIOLENCE?   ☐ CHILD ABUSE?

3. TYPE OF ORDER (CHECK ALL THAT APPLY):

☐ DIVORCE/ANNULMENT <u>WITH</u> CHILDREN(Sec. 1,2,3,4)   ☐ DIVORCE/ANNULMENT WITHOUT CHILDREN(Sec 1,2)

☐ PATERNITY <u>WITH</u> CHILD SUPPORT(Sec 1,3,4,5)   ☐ PATERNITY <u>WITHOUT</u> CHILD SUPPORT(SEC 1,3,5)

☐ CHILD SUPPORT OBLIGATION/MODIFICATION(Sec 1,3,4)   ☐ TERMINATION OF RIGHTS (Sec 1,3,6)

☐ CONSERVATORSHIP (SEC 1, 3)   ☐ OTHER (SPECIFY) _____

☐ TRANSFER TO (SEC 1, 3) COUNTY _____ COURT NO. _____ STATE COURT ID# _____

4a. NAME OF ATTORNEY FOR PETITIONER	4b. ATTORNEY GENERAL ACCT/CASE #
4c. CURRENT MAILING ADDRESS STREET & NO. CITY STATE ZIP	4d. TELEPHONE NUMBER (including area code) ( )

SECTION 2 (IF APPLICABLE) REPORT OF DIVORCE OR ANNULMENT OF MARRIAGE			

	5. FIRST NAME MIDDLE LAST SUFFIX		6. DATE OF BIRTH (mm/dd/yyyy)
HUSBAND	7. PLACE OF BIRTH CITY STATE OR FOREIGN COUNTRY	8. RACE	9. SOCIAL SECURITY NUMBER
	10. USUAL RESIDENCE STREET NAME & NUMBER CITY STATE ZIP		
WIFE	11. FIRST NAME MIDDLE LAST MAIDEN		12. DATE OF BIRTH (mm/dd/yyyy)
	13. PLACE OF BIRTH CITY STATE OR FOREIGN COUNTRY	14. RACE	15. SOCIAL SECURITY NUMBER
	16. USUAL RESIDENCE STREET NAME & NUMBER CITY STATE ZIP		

17. NUMBER OF MINOR CHILDREN	18. DATE OF MARRIAGE (mm/dd/yyyy)	19. PLACE OF MARRIAGE City State	20. PETITIONER IS ☐ HUSBAND ☐ WIFE

SECTION 3 (IF APPLICABLE) CHILDREN AFFECTED BY THIS SUIT			

	21a. FIRST NAME MIDDLE LAST SUFFIX		21b. DATE OF BIRTH (mm/dd/yyyy)
CHILD 1	21c. SOCIAL SECURITY NUMBER	21d. SEX	21e. BIRTHPLACE CITY COUNTY STATE
	21f. PRIOR NAME OF CHILD: FIRST MIDDLE LAST SUFFIX	21g. NEW NAME OF CHILD FIRST MIDDLE LAST SUFFIX	
	22a. FIRST NAME MIDDLE LAST SUFFIX		22b. DATE OF BIRTH (mm/dd/yyyy)
CHILD 2	22c. SOCIAL SECURITY NUMBER	22d. SEX	22e. BIRTHPLACE CITY COUNTY STATE
	22f. PRIOR NAME OF CHILD: FIRST MIDDLE LAST SUFFIX	22g. NEW NAME OF CHILD FIRST MIDDLE LAST SUFFIX	
	23a. FIRST NAME MIDDLE LAST SUFFIX		23b. DATE OF BIRTH (mm/dd/yyyy)
CHILD 3	23c. SOCIAL SECURITY NUMBER	23d. SEX	23e. BIRTHPLACE CITY COUNTY STATE
	23f. PRIOR NAME OF CHILD FIRST MIDDLE LAST SUFFIX	23g. NEW NAME OF CHILD FIRST MIDDLE LAST SUFFIX	
	24a. FIRST NAME MIDDLE LAST SUFFIX		24b. DATE OF BIRTH (mm/dd/yyyy)
CHILD 4	24c. SOCIAL SECURITY NUMBER	24d. SEX	24e BIRTH CITY COUNTY STATE
	24f. PRIOR NAME OF CHILD FIRST MIDDLE LAST SUFFIX	24g. NEW NAME OF CHILD FIRST MIDDLE LAST SUFFIX	

1

SECTION 4 (IF APPLICABLE) OBLIGEE/OBLIGOR INFORMATION

OBLIGEE

THIS PARTY TO THE SUIT IS (CHECK ONE) ☐ 25a. TDPRS ☐ 25b. NON-PARENT CONSERVATOR – COMPLETE 26 – 32

☐ 25c. HUSBAND AS SHOWN ON FRONT OF THIS FORM – COMPLETE 31 – 32 ONLY ☐ 25d. WIFE AS SHOWN ON FRONT OF THIS FORM – COMPLETE 31 – 32 ONLY

☐ 25e. BIOLOGICAL FATHER – COMPLETE 26 – 32 ☐ 25f. BIOLOGICAL MOTHER – COMPLETE 26 – 32

26. FIRST NAME	MIDDLE	LAST	SUFFIX	MAIDEN

27. DATE OF BIRTH (mm/dd/yyyy)	28. PLACE OF BIRTH	CITY	STATE OR FOREIGN COUNTRY	

29. USUAL RESIDENCE	STREET NAME & NUMBER	CITY	COUNTY	STATE	ZIP

30. SOCIAL SECURITY NUMBER	31. DRIVER LICENSE NO & STATE	32. TELEPHONE NUMBER ( )

OBLIGOR #1

THIS PARTY TO THE SUIT IS (CHECK ONE) ☐ 33a. NON-PARENT CONSERVATOR – COMPLETE 34 – 43

☐ 33b. HUSBAND AS SHOWN ON FRONT OF THIS FORM – COMPLETE 39 – 43 ONLY ☐ 33c. WIFE AS SHOWN ON FRONT OF THIS FORM – COMPLETE 39 – 43 ONLY

☐ 33d. BIOLOGICAL FATHER – COMPLETE 34 – 43 ☐ 33e. BIOLOGICAL MOTHER – COMPLETE 34 – 43

34. FIRST NAME	MIDDLE	LAST	SUFFIX	MAIDEN

35. DATE OF BIRTH (mm/dd/yyyy)	36. PLACE OF BIRTH	CITY	STATE OR FOREIGN COUNTRY	

37. USUAL RESIDENCE	STREET NAME & NUMBER	CITY	COUNTY	STATE	ZIP

38. SOCIAL SECURITY NUMBER	39 DRIVER LICENSE NO. & STATE	40. TELEPHONE NUMBER ( )

41. EMPLOYER NAME	42. EMPLOYER TELEPHONE NUMBER

43. EMPLOYER PAYROLL ADDRESS	STREET NAME & NUMBER	CITY	STATE	ZIP

OBLIGOR #2

THIS PARTY TO THE SUIT IS (CHECK ONE) ☐ 44a. NON-PARENT CONSERVATOR – COMPLETE 45 – 54

☐ 44b. HUSBAND AS SHOWN ON FRONT OF THIS FORM – COMPLETE 50 – 54 ONLY ☐ 44c. WIFE AS SHOWN ON FRONT OF THIS FORM – COMPLETE 45 – 54 ONLY

☐ 44d. BIOLOGICAL FATHER – COMPLETE 45 – 54 ☐ 44e. BIOLOGICAL MOTHER – COMPLETE 45 – 54

45. FIRST NAME	MIDDLE	LAST	SUFFIX	MAIDEN

46. DATE OF BIRTH (mm/dd/yyyy)	47. PLACE OF BIRTH	CITY	STATE OR FOREIGN COUNTRY	

48. USUAL RESIDENCE	STREET NAME & NUMBER	CITY	COUNTY	STATE	ZIP

49. SOCIAL SECURITY NUMBER	50. DRIVER LICENSE NO & STATE	51. TELEPHONE NUMBER

52. EMPLOYER NAME	53. EMPLOYER TELEPHONE NUMBER

54. EMPLOYER PAYROLL ADDRESS	STREET NAME & NUMBER	CITY	STATE	ZIP

SECTION 5 (IF APPLICABLE) FOR ORDERS CONCERNING PATERNITY ESTABLISHMENT OF BIOLOGICAL FATHER

55. BIOLOGICAL FATHER'S NAME	FIRST	MIDDLE	LAST	56. DATE OF BIRTH (mm/dd/yyyy)

57. SOCIAL SECURITY NUMBER	58. CURRENT MAILING ADDRESS	STREET NAME & NUMBER	CITY	STATE	ZIP

59. DOES THIS ORDER REMOVE INFORMATION PERTAINING TO A FATHER FROM A CHILD'S CERTIFICATE OF BIRTH? ☐ NO ☐ YES

SECTION 6 TERMINATION OF RIGHTS – INFORMATION RELATED TO THE INDIVIDUAL(S) WHOSE RIGHTS ARE BEING TERMINATED IN THIS SUIT.

60a. FIRST NAME	MIDDLE NAME	LAST NAME	SUFFIX	60b. RELATIONSHIP
61a. FIRST NAME	MIDDLE NAME	LAST NAME	SUUFIX	61b. RELATIONSHIP
62a. FIRST NAME	MIDDLE NAME	LAST NAME	SUFFIX	62b. RELATIONSHIP

COMMENTS: _____

_____

I CERTIFY THAT THE ABOVE ORDER WAS GRANTED ON THE
DATE AND PLACE AS STATED.

_____
SIGNATURE OF THE CLERK OF THE COURT

INCOME WITHHOLDING FOR SUPPORT

☐ **ORIGINAL INCOME WITHHOLDING ORDER/NOTICE FOR SUPPORT (IWO)**
☐ **AMENDED IWO**
☐ **ONE-TIME ORDER/NOTICE FOR LUMP SUM PAYMENT**
☐ **TERMINATION of IWO**   Date: _____

☐ Child Support Enforcement (CSE) Agency ☒ Court ☐ Attorney ☐ Private Individual/Entity (Check One)
NOTE: This IWO must be regular on its face. Under certain circumstances you must reject this IWO and return it to the sender (see IWO instructions http://www.acf.hhs.gov/programs/cse/forms/OMB-0970-0154_instructions.pdf). If you receive this document from someone other than a State or Tribal CSE agency or a Court, a copy of the underlying order must be attached.

State/Tribe/Territory Texas_____   Remittance Identifier (include w/payment) _____
City/County/Dist./Tribe_____   Order Identifier_____
Private Individual/Entity_____   CSE Agency Case Identifier _____

_____   RE:_____
Employer/Income Withholder's Name   Employee/Obligor's Name (Last, First, Middle)

_____   _____
Employer/Income Withholder's Address   Employee/Obligor's Social Security Number

_____   _____
                                                         Custodial Party/Obligee's Name (Last, First, Middle)
Employer/Income Withholder's FEIN _____

Child(ren)'s Name(s) (Last, First, Middle)   Child(ren)'s Birth Date(s)

_____   _____
_____   _____
_____   _____
_____   _____
_____   _____

ORDER INFORMATION: This document is based on the support or withholding order from Texas___(State/Tribe). You are required by law to deduct these amounts from the employee/obligor's income until further notice.
$_____ Per month_____ current child support
$_____ Per month_____ past-due child support - **Arrears greater than 12 weeks?** ☐ **Yes** ☐ **No**
$_____ Per month_____ current cash medical support
$_____ Per month_____ past-due cash medical support
$_____ Per month_____ current spousal support
$_____ Per month_____ past-due spousal support
$_____ Per_____ other (must specify) _____.
or a **Total Amount to Withhold** of $ _____per month_____.

AMOUNTS TO WITHHOLD: You do not have to vary your pay cycle to be in compliance with the *Order Information*. If your pay cycle does not match the ordered payment cycle, withhold one of the following amounts:
$_____ per weekly pay period $_____ per semimonthly pay period (twice a month)
$_____ per biweekly pay period (every two weeks) $_____ per monthly pay period
$_____ **Lump Sum Payment:** Do not stop any existing IWO unless you receive a termination order.

REMITTANCE INFORMATION: If the employee/obligor's principal place of employment is Texas, you must begin withholding no later than the first pay period following the date this Order/Notice was delivered to the employer. Send payment on the same day as the pay date/date of withholding. If you cannot withhold the full amount of support for any or all orders for this employee/obligor, withhold up to 50% of disposable income for all orders. If the employee/obligor's principal place of employment is not Texas, obtain withholding limitations, time requirements, and any allowable employer fees at http://www.acf.hhs.gov/programs/cse/newhire/employer/contacts/contact_map.htm for the employee/obligor's principal place of employment.

Document Tracking Identifier _____   OMB 0970-0154

or electronic payment requirements and centralized payment collection and disbursement facility information (State Disbursement Unit [SDU]), see http://www.acf.hhs.gov/programs/cse/newhire/employer/contacts/contact_map.htm.

Include with payment: Pay date, Remittance Identifier (if known), Order Identifier, CSE Agency Case Identifier (if known), County identified on page 1, Employee/Obligor's name and social security number, Custodial Party/Obligee's name and social security number (if known), and this FIPS code: 48000.

Make payments payable in the name of the Custodial Party/Obligee identified on page 1.

Remit payment to <u>Texas Child Support State Disbursement Unit (SDU)</u>   (SDU/Tribal Order Payee)
t <u>PO BOX 659791 San Antonio, TX, 78265-9791</u>   (SDU/Tribal Payee Address)

] **Return to Sender [Completed by Employer/Income Withholder].** Payment must be directed to an SDU in accordance with 42 USC §666(b)(5) and (b)(6) or Tribal Payee (see Payments to SDU below). If payment is not directed o an SDU/Tribal Payee or this IWO is not regular on its face, you *must* check this box and return the IWO to the sender.

Signature of Judge/Issuing Official (if required by State or Tribal law): _____
Print Name of Judge/Issuing Official: _____
Title of Judge/Issuing Official: _____
Date of Signature: _____

the employee/obligor works in a State or for a Tribe that is different from the State or Tribe that issued this order, a copy f this IWO must be provided to the employee/obligor.

] If checked, the employer/income withholder must provide a copy of this form to the employee/obligor.

ADDITIONAL INFORMATION FOR EMPLOYERS/INCOME WITHHOLDERS

State-specific contact and withholding information can be found on the Federal Employer Services website located at:
http://www.acf.hhs.gov/programs/cse/newhire/employer/contacts/contact_map.htm

Priority: Withholding for support has priority over any other legal process under State law against the same income (USC 2 §666(b)(7)). If a Federal tax levy is in effect, please notify the sender.

Combining Payments: When remitting payments to an SDU or Tribal CSE agency, you may combine withheld amounts rom more than one employee/obligor's income in a single payment. You must, however, separately identify each mployee/obligor's portion of the payment.

Payments To SDU: You must send child support payments payable by income withholding to the appropriate SDU or to a Tribal CSE agency. If this IWO instructs you to send a payment to an entity other than an SDU (e.g., payable to the custodial party, court, or attorney), you must check the box above and return this notice to the sender. Exception: If this WO was sent by a Court, Attorney, or Private Individual/Entity and the initial order was entered before January 1, 1994 or ne order was issued by a Tribal CSE agency, you must follow the "Remit payment to" instructions on this form.

Reporting the Pay Date: You must report the pay date when sending the payment. The pay date is the date on which the mount was withheld from the employee/obligor's wages. You must comply with the law of the State (or Tribal law if pplicable) of the employee/obligor's principal place of employment regarding time periods within which you must mplement the withholding and forward the support payments.

Multiple IWOs: If there is more than one IWO against this employee/obligor and you are unable to fully honor all IWOs ue to Federal, State, or Tribal withholding limits, you must honor all IWOs to the greatest extent possible, giving priority o current support before payment of any past-due support. Follow the State or Tribal law/procedure of the mployee/obligor's principal place of employment to determine the appropriate allocation method.

Lump Sum Payments: You may be required to notify a State or Tribal CSE agency of upcoming lump sum payments to his employee/obligor such as bonuses, commissions, or severance pay. Contact the sender to determine if you are equired to report and/or withhold lump sum payments.

Liability: If you have any doubts about the validity of this IWO, contact the sender. If you fail to withhold income from the mployee/obligor's income as the IWO directs, you are liable for both the accumulated amount you should have withheld nd any penalties set by State or Tribal law/procedure.

Anti-discrimination: You are subject to a fine determined under State or Tribal law for discharging an employee/obligor rom employment, refusing to employ, or taking disciplinary action against an employee/obligor because of this IWO.

Employer's Name:_____ Employer FEIN: _____

Employee/Obligor's Name: _____

CSE Agency Case Identifier: _____Order Identifier: _____

Withholding Limits: You may not withhold more than the lesser of: 1) the amounts allowed by the Federal Consumer Credit Protection Act (CCPA) (15 U.S.C. 1673(b)); or 2) the amounts allowed by the State or Tribe of the employee/obligor's principal place of employment (see *REMITTANCE INFORMATION*). Disposable income is the net income left after making mandatory deductions such as: State, Federal, local taxes; Social Security taxes; statutory pension contributions; and Medicare taxes. The Federal limit is 50% of the disposable income if the obligor is supporting another family and 60% of the disposable income if the obligor is not supporting another family. However, those limits increase 5% - to 55% and 65% - if the arrears are greater than 12 weeks. If permitted by the State or Tribe, you may deduct a fee for administrative costs. The combined support amount and fee may not exceed the limit indicated in this section.

For Tribal orders, you may not withhold more than the amounts allowed under the law of the issuing Tribe. For Tribal employers/income withholders who receive a State IWO, you may not withhold more than the lesser of the limit set by the law of the jurisdiction in which the employer/income withholder is located or the maximum amount permitted under section 303(d) of the CCPA (15 U.S.C. 1673 (b)).

Depending upon applicable State or Tribal law, you may need to also consider the amounts paid for health care premiums in determining disposable income and applying appropriate withholding limits.

Arrears greater than 12 weeks? If the *Order Information* does not indicate that the arrears are greater than 12 weeks, then the Employer should calculate the CCPA limit using the lower percentage.

Additional Information:

_____

NOTIFICATION OF EMPLOYMENT TERMINATION OR INCOME STATUS: If this employee/obligor never worked for you or you are no longer withholding income for this employee/obligor, an employer must promptly notify the CSE agency and/or the sender by returning this form to the address listed in the Contact Information below:

☐ This person has never worked for this employer nor received periodic income.

☐ This person no longer works for this employer nor receives periodic income.

Please provide the following information for the employee/obligor:

Termination date: _____ Last known phone number: _____

Last known address: _____

_____

Final payment date to SDU/ Tribal Payee: _____ Final payment amount: _____

New employer's name: _____

New employer's address: _____

_____

CONTACT INFORMATION:

To Employer/Income Withholder: If you have any questions, contact _____ (Issuer name)

by phone at _____, by fax at _____, by email or website at: _____.

Send termination/income status notice and other correspondence to:

_____(Issuer address).

To Employee/Obligor: If the employee/obligor has questions, contact _____ (Issuer name)

by phone at _____, by fax at_____, by email or website at:_____.

IMPORTANT: The person completing this form is advised that the information may be shared with the employee/obligor.

Cause Number _____

IN THE MATTER OF THE MARRIAGE OF

Petitioner: _____   In the

_____ ☐ District Court ☐ County Court
                                                        at Law of

And

Respondent: _____   _____ County, Texas

☐ AND IN THE INTEREST OF:

1. _____   2. _____   3. _____

4. _____   5. _____   6. _____

Request to Issue
Income Withholding Order / Notice

To the Clerk of the Court:

Pursuant to Family Code § 158, please issue a certified copy of the following order in this cause:

Income Withholding Order/Notice for Support

Signed by the Court on _____

And deliver the order to Employer's current address at:

Obligor's Employer: _____

Employer's Address: _____

City, State, Zip: _____

Employer's Phone: _____   Fax: _____

Employer's Email _____

Request Submitted on _____

_____
Signed: Obligee / Requestor

Daytime phone: _____

_____
Address

_____
City   *State*   *Zip*

Cause Number _____

IN THE MATTER OF THE MARRIAGE OF

Petitioner: _____   In the

                                      _____ ☐ District Court   ☐ County Court
                 And   at Law of

Respondent: _____   _____ County, Texas

☐ **AND IN THE INTEREST OF:**

1. _____   2. _____   3. _____

4. _____   5. _____   6. _____

Military Status Affidavit

BEFORE ME the person who signed this affidavit appeared in person and stated under oath:

1. "My name is: _____ .
                    First   *Middle*   *Last*

2. "Respondent's name is: : _____ .
                          First   *Middle*   *Last*

3. "I am the Petitioner in this case. I am an adult and of sound mind.
   "I have personal knowledge of the facts stated in this affidavit.
   "The facts stated in this affidavit are true and correct.

(Check all boxes that apply)

☐ "I know that the Respondent **is not** on active military duty because I asked the U.S. Department of Defense to check their Defense Manpower Data Center (DMDC) database. DMDC notified me that the Respondent is not on active duty in any of the armed forces.

☐ "I attached a true copy of the DMDC verification.
   (If you check this box, you must attach a copy of the DMDC verification. You can print a copy of the DMDC verification from this web address: www.dmdc.osd.mil/appj/scra/scraHome.do.)

☐ "I know that the Respondent ☐ **is not now** ☐ **is now** on active military duty because:

*(List facts to show how you know that Respondent is **not** on active duty. For example, fact that would make your spouse ineligible for military service, such as being in prison, having a serious disability, etc. **or** list facts to show how you know that Respondent **is** on active duty.)*

_____

_____

_____

_____

_____

_____

_____

_____

_____

_____ "

_____

☐ "I do not know if the Respondent is on active military duty now."

. _____   Date: _____

     Signed before a notary

Notary fills out below

State of Texas, County of _____

Sworn to and subscribed before me, the undersigned notary,

on this date: _____ 20____ at _____ a.m./p.m.

by_____

    (Print name of person who signed this Affidavit)

_____

     Notary's Signature

Cause Number _____

IN THE MATTER OF THE MARRIAGE OF

Petitioner: _____   In the

                                                 _____ ☐ District Court ☐ County Court
                    And   at Law of

Respondent: _____   _____ County, Texas

☐ **AND IN THE INTEREST OF:**

1. _____ 2. _____ 3. _____

4. _____ 5. _____ 6. _____

Financial Information

I, _____, am the Petitioner. I would testify under oath in open Court that the following information is true and correct. I understand that in a Court hearing I may be required to prove these amounts by testimony and by records such as pay vouchers, canceled checks, receipts and bills.

A. **Petitioner's monthly resources** (Describe each source)	**Gross Amount**	**Allowed deductions** (Soc..Sec., union dues, w/holding tax, health insurance for child)
1. _____	$_____	$_____
2. _____	$_____	$_____
3. _____	$_____	$_____
4. _____	$_____	$_____
Total Resources Each Month	$_____	$_____

B. **Respondent's monthly resources** (Describe each source)	**Gross Amount**	**Allowed deductions** (Soc. Sec., union dues, w/holding tax, health insurance for child)
1. _____	$_____	$_____
2. _____	$_____	$_____
3. _____	$_____	$_____
4. _____	$_____	$_____
Total Resources Each Month	$_____	$_____

C. Total money needed per month by ☐ **Petitioner** ☐ **Respondent** ☐ **and minor child/ren**
(amounts not paid monthly are averages)

1. Rent or house payment	$_____	16. Clothing & shoes	$_____
2. Property tax not included in item 1	$_____	17. Insurance - auto	$_____
		18. Insurance - life	$_____
3. Residence maintenance	$_____	19. Insurance - health	$_____
4. Home insurance	$_____	20. Child care	$_____
5. Utilities	$_____	21. Child activities	$_____
6. Telephone (avg./mo.)	$_____	22. Cable TV, newspaper	$_____
7. Groceries & supplies	$_____	23. Other:_____	$_____
8. Meals away from home	$_____	_____	$_____
9. School lunches	$_____	_____	$_____
10. Dental	$_____	_____	$_____
11. Medical & medicine	$_____	_____	$_____
12. Laundry, dry clean	$_____	24. Support or alimony payments to others	$_____
13. Gas & car maintenance	$_____		
14. Entertainment	$_____	25. Monthly debt payments	
15. Haircuts	$_____	(total of item D)	$_____

Total Needed Per Month (Total of items C 1-25) $_____

Difference Between Money Received & Money Needed $_____

D. Monthly Payments On Indebtedness

Description Of Debt	Balance Owed	Amount Of Monthly Pmt.	Date Of Final Pmt.
1._____	$_____	$_____	_____
2._____	$_____	$_____	_____
3._____	$_____	$_____	_____
4._____	$_____	$_____	_____
5._____	$_____	$_____	_____
6._____	$_____	$_____	_____

Total Monthly Payments $_____
(enter on line C25 above)

I ask the Court to set support according to Texas law.

Signed this_____ day of _____, 20____

_____
Petitioner, Pro Se

(Print your answers in blue ink)

Cause Number: _____

(The Clerk's office will fill in the Cause Number when you file this form)

IN THE MATTER OF THE MARRIAGE OF

Petitioner: _____

(Print first, middle, and last name of the spouse filing for divorce)

And

Respondent: _____

(Print first, middle, and last name of other spouse)

In the *(check one):*

_____ ☐ District Court
(Court Number)

☐ County Court at Law of:

_____ County, Texas
(County)

Affidavit of Indigency
(Divorce Set 1 - Uncontested, No Minor Children, No Real Property)

WARNING: Read all of the Instructions for Divorce Set 1 before filling out this form.

The person who signed this affidavit appeared, in person, before me, the undersigned notary, and stated under oath:

"My name is _____ My phone number is: ( ) _____

"My mailing address is: _____

"I am above the age of eighteen (18) years, and I am fully competent to make this affidavit. I am unable to pay court costs. The nature and amount of my income, resources, debts, and expenses are described in this form.

Check ALL boxes that apply and fill in the blanks describing the amounts and sources of your income.

"I receive these **public benefits/government entitlements** that are based on indigency: ☐ SSI ☐ WIC
☐ Food stamps/SNAP ☐ TANF ☐ Medicaid ☐ CHIP ☐ Needs-based VA Pension
☐ County Assistance, County Health Care, or General Assistance (GA) ☐ Community Care via DADS
☐ AABD ☐ Public Housing ☐ Low-Income Energy Assistance ☐ LIS in Medicare ("Extra Help")
☐ Emergency Assistance ☐ Child Care Assistance under Child Care and Development Block Grant
☐ Other : _____

If you receive any of the above public benefits, you may attach proof to this form and label it "Exhibit: Proof of Public Benefits."

"My **income sources** are stated below *(check all that apply)*.

☐ Unemployed since: _____
                              Date
-or-
☐ Wages: I work as a _____ for _____
                          Your job title   *Your employer*

☐ Child/spousal support ☐ My spouse's income or income from another member of my household *(if available)*
☐ Tips, bonuses ☐ Military Housing ☐ Worker's Comp ☐ Disability ☐ Unemployment ☐ Social Security
☐ Retirement/Pension ☐ Dividends, interest, royalties ☐ 2nd job or other income: _____
                                                                                                              Describe

"My **income amounts** are stated below.

(A) My **monthly take-home wages**:	*Total amount received →*	$
(B) The amount I receive each month in **public benefits** is:	*Total amount received →*	$
(C) The amount of income from **other people in my household**: *(list this income only if other members contribute to your household income)*	*Total amount received →*	$
(D) The amount I receive each month from **other sources** is:	*Total amount received →*	$
(E) My **TOTAL monthly income**	*Add all sources of income above →*	= $

About my **dependents**:

The people who depend on me financially are listed below:

	Name	Age	Relationship to Me
1			
2			
3			
4			
5			
6			

My **property** includes:	Value*	"My **monthly expenses** are:	Amount
Cash	$	Rent/house payments/maintenance	$
Bank accounts, other financial assets (List)		Food and household supplies	$
	$	Utilities and telephone	$
	$	Clothing and laundry	$
	$	Medical and dental expenses	$
Vehicles (cars, boats) (List make and year)		Insurance (life, health, auto, etc.)	$
	$	School and child care	$
	$	Transportation, auto repair, gas	$
	$	Child / spousal support	$
Other property (like jewelry, stocks, etc.) (Describe)		Wages withheld by court order	$
	$	Debt payments paid to: (List)	$
	$		$
	$		$

Total value of property → =$ **Total Monthly Expenses →** =$

*The value is the amount the item would sell for less the amount you still owe on it, if anything.

My **debts** include: (List debt and amount owed)

_____

_____

I am unable to pay court costs. I verify that the statements made in this affidavit are true and correct."

To list any other facts you want the court to know, such as unusual medical expenses, family emergencies, etc., attach another page to this form and label it "Exhibit: Additional Supporting Facts." *Check here if you attach another page.* ☐

Do not sign until you are in front of a notary.

▶ _____   _____

    Signature of Person Signing Affidavit   Date

Notary fills out below.

State of Texas, County of _____

                (Print the name of county where this Affidavit is notarized)

Sworn to and subscribed before me, the undersigned notary, on this date: _____/____/20_____ at _____ a.m./p.m.

                                                       month day   year   time   (circle one)

by _____

    (Print name of person who is signing this Affidavit. NOT the notary's name.)

▶ _____

                      Notary's Signature

Form Approved by the Supreme Court of Texas by order in Misc. Docket No. 13-9085 (June 17, 2013)

Affidavit of Indigency (Divorce Set 1 - Uncontested, No Minor Children, No Real Property)   Page 2 of 2

Cause Number _____

IN THE MATTER OF THE MARRIAGE OF

Petitioner: _____   In the

              And   _____ ☐ District Court ☐ County Court at Law of

Respondent: _____   _____ County, Texas

☐ **AND IN THE INTEREST OF:**

1. _____ 2. _____ 3. _____
4. _____ 5. _____ 6. _____

Notice of Change of Address

I, _____, am a party in the
     First   *Middle*   *Last*

above-styled cause. My address or other contact information has changed. I request that the Court's records be updated accordingly.

My new contact information is as follows:

_____
Mailing Address

_____
City   *State*   *Zip*

_____
Telephone with Area Code

_____
Fax with Area Code

_____
Party's Signature

Certificate of Service
I gave a true copy of this *Notice of Change of Address* to my spouse (or my spouse's attorney, if applicable) in person, by fax, or by certified mail, return receipt requested.

_____   Date: _____
Party's Signature

TEXAS BOOKS, FORMS and SOFTWARE

Order online at www.nolodivorce.com/TX

or use form below, or call (800) 464-5502
M–F, 9–5 Pacific Time

Please send me

_____ Copies of *How to Do Your Own Divorce in Texas* at $29.95 ea. _____ _____

_____ Copies of *How to Make Any Divorce Better* at $24.95 ea. _____ _____

DealMaker™ Settlement Agreement Software. $64.95
Download for free from site and register via the software.

FORMS below are included in the Texas divorce book and are available separately on paper, or as PDF computer files sent via e-mail, or you can download them at **www.nolodivorce.com/TX**

	Send paper set	E-mail to me
_____ Complete sets of forms as in this book...................... $15 ea.	☐	☐
_____ Forms sets for Citation by Publication or by Posting where you have a missing/unlocatable spouse .... $15 ea.	☐	☐
_____ Both of the above sets of forms for..............................$25	☐	☐

Shipping and handling for paper sets add .... $ 5   for each order

TOTAL ENCLOSED $ _____

Name _____

Street address _____

City, State, Zip _____

Phone _____ Fax _____ E-mail _____

Charge my ☐ Visa ☐ MasterCard   ☐ Check or money order is enclosed

Card number _____ Expires _____ Signed _____

Mail form to

Nolo Press Occidental
2604 El Camino Real, Suite 353B
Carlsbad, CA 92008

Or call (800) 464-5502 to order by phone
M–F, 9–5 Pacific Time
Or fax to (831) 466-9927 with credit card information